Tough Choices

Tough Choices:

Living and Dying in the Twenty-First Century

Maureen A. McTeer

Tough Choices: Living and Dying in the Twenty-First Century
© Irwin Law

Published in 1999 by
Irwin Law
Suite 930, Box 235
One First Canadian Place
Toronto, Ontario
M5P 3K4

ISBN: 1-55221-040-5

Canadian Cataloguing in Publication Data

McTeer, Maureen, 1952–
    Tough choices: living and dying in the 21st Century

Includes bibliographical references and index.
ISBN 1-55221-040-5

1. Medical ethics.   2. Bioethics.   3. Medical laws and legislation.
I. Title.

R724.M235 1999   174'.2   C99-932676-7

Printed and bound in Canada

1   2   3   4   5   02   01   00   99

Contents

Foreword

*Concern for man himself and his fate must always be the chief
interest of all technical endeavors . . . in order that the creations
of our mind shall be a blessing and not a curse to mankind.*

Albert Einstein, 1931

Our technological capability today outpaces the science fiction
of only a few years ago. Present-day advances in science and
technology now touch every stage of our lives and penetrate
to the very origins of human beings. These advances raise complex
issues that form the core of this timely new work by Maureen McTeer.

Ms. McTeer emphasizes that every one of us will inevitably be affected
by science and technology's reach and promise. But she warns that we
also need to be prepared to make the tough choices that new developments force upon us. This message lies at the heart of this far-seeing book.

The reader is challenged to ponder a host of thorny questions.
Should embryos be sold? To what moral and social status should we
entitle them? Under what conditions should they be used in research? Is

it ethical to create a human being whose biological and genetic background cannot be traced? Should restrictions be placed on the cloning of human embryos? If patients have the right to refuse medical treatment, do they also have the right to demand treatment in all situations, even when further treatment is futile? Should Canadians begin to market organs and tissue? Should euthanasia be legal?

The huge, complex, and diverse industry made possible by our technological and scientific advances, coupled with the expanding holes in our national boundaries and social safety net caused by globalization, raise many issues. Increasingly, these issues will dominate newspaper headlines and political agendas. They are, as McTeer suggests, issues that together will shape our living and dying in the twenty-first century and beyond.

This compact and provocative book is the work of an extraordinary lawyer and political activist. *Tough Choices* is unique in providing a comprehensive and compelling overview of the complex issues that are inextricably part of the practice of medicine today. McTeer brings three key themes to light: the power of science and technology to enhance our future; the imperative to be informed about the possibilities and potential dangers opened up by science and technology; and the public's collective responsibility to participate in an informed way to ensure that humane rules and restrictions are created to govern the use of these technologies.

There is little doubt that these issues may well be among the most serious ever confronted by the human race. Knowledge that can help prevent and cure diseases also gives rise to difficult ethical dilemmas, such as medical privacy and the patenting of human genes. The question is not whether we should abandon our research because of these difficulties. It is rather how we can collectively control and manage new knowledge to maximize its benefits while addressing the ethical concerns and known risks.

The book has particular appeal to lawyers and to students interested in a career in law, to health care providers who want to learn more about how these issues affect their work and their place of work, and to politicians and other decision-makers who will increasingly be drawn into debate about these issues. But this work by McTeer may have a more important outcome. The book is a helpful tool for stimulating a heightened level of interest and concern in the larger public over issues that will profoundly affect the future of humanity as a whole.

McTeer has done us a favour in both sensitizing our awareness and inspiring us to move forward with an agenda that will, ideally, lead to a better understanding of the application of these technologies, ourselves, and our future. This new book deserves a wide audience.

Senator Wilbert J. Keon, OC, MD, FRCSC

Acknowledgments

I spent a great deal longer writing this book than I had originally planned. What started as a narrow legal text kept growing and changing into a book for laypeople and lawyers alike.

I was particularly fortunate in the expert advisers who helped me in my research and answered my questions. For Part One, Conception, I am grateful to three professionals at the Canadian Fertility and Andrology Society: Dr. Arthur Leader, professor of medicine at the University of Ottawa, and, in 1999, president of the society; Susan Orr-Mongeau, executive director; and Dr. Paul Claman, national director and an infertility specialist at the fertility clinic at the Ottawa Civic Hospital. For Part Two, Commercialization, Dr. Daniel Drell in the Life Sciences Division of the Office of Biological and Environmental Research at the U.S. Department of Energy provided me with American materials relating to the Human Genome Project and genetic testing. Charles Black, the senior adviser of the Canadian Life and Health Insurance Association, gave careful and complete answers to my questions about that industry and genetic testing. For Part Three, Consent, André LaPrairie, the expert in the area of xenotransplantation at Health Canada, supplied me with extensive reading lists on organ transplants and explained the many legal and public policy challenges in this area. Several parliamentarians offered me guidance on the issues of assisted suicide and euthanasia. Despite this generous assistance, any mistakes I make here are my own.

During the writing process I also incurred many debts. I owe thanks to friends who helped me with computer and clerical work along the way, especially Stacey Gray. Once again Donald Curtin at the Library of Parliament was outstanding in the assistance he gave me. Doug Dorward, a student at the UBC Law School, acted as my researcher in 1998 and found much useful material for me. Rosemary Shipton and Jane McWhinney edited the book and successfully brought the various subjects together. Kathy Martin checked the legal citations and Maraya Raduha did the proofreading.

I would also like to acknowledge the many people who shared their personal experiences of infertility, loss of a pregnancy, or the death of a beloved spouse or friend with me. To all of you, I offer my gratitude for your kindness and friendship. Finally, I thank Catherine, for volunteering to campaign in my place so I could write in the summer of 1998, and Joe, for pushing me along when my resolve to finish the book weakened. Both of you know I could not have done it without your love and support.

Introduction

Medical science fascinates and frightens us. It promises to cure disease and improve the quality and length of our lives. It allows us to imagine a society where all children are born healthy and where the diseases of old age no longer ravage us. Reproductive technology already helps the infertile to bear children, and genetic testing is available for an ever-growing number of serious diseases. Human tissue, organs, and even limbs can now be successfully transplanted. Genetically engineered animals are used as living laboratories to produce life-saving drugs, and huge advances in agricultural biotechnology predict an end to world hunger. In a remarkable few years, science has brought us to the threshold of a new era, with its promise of a better life — and its concomitant maelstrom of legal and ethical dilemmas.

From research on human embryos to the commercialization of life, from genetic testing to genetically engineered foods, from organ transplants to assisted suicide and euthanasia, medical technology now touches us intimately at every stage of our lives. It gives us unprecedented powers — to create, manipulate, and alter human life in the laboratory; to keep people alive in a state of living death; to use one person's organs and tissue so that another can live; to create clones of ourselves. All these possibilities and more are within our reach as we enter the new millennium. Our very definitions of who we are and what it means to be human are challenged as we struggle to make sense of the flood of information and points of view on these topics. The essential question has become: "How do we balance the ability of science and medicine to enhance our lives with our obligations to protect individual and collective interests?" In weighing this question, we need to reflect on what values and principles matter most to us and how we can have an impact on the choices and decisions medical-scientific advances are forcing us to make.

This book developed out of a course I offered to law students at the University of Calgary to encourage their interest in law, science, and public policy. It started as a legal text and grew into a hybrid that I hope will be useful to both lawyer and concerned layperson. It is intended as a resource to help Canadians better understand what is at stake in the debate surrounding us on these varied and fascinating questions. These are not the only issues we will have to meet in the new century, but they are some of the key ones on the horizon. Legislation is expected or pending on several of them. By starting here, I hope to encourage Canadians to reflect and respond to these issues — to take a stand on what they want their policies and laws to be. Many Canadians are already involved with one or more of these issues — professionally, as health care workers or physicians, or personally, as children of aging parents, or as parents of sick or disabled children. Every one of us will be affected by science and technology's scope and promise, and we all need to prepare ourselves to make the tough choices they will demand of us. Modern governments will say: "Tell us what you think." But if we are really going to participate, we need the tools to do so. I have written this book as a tool, a resource for Canadians as they ponder these issues and prepare to offer their views on how we might proceed. Having the necessary information readily at hand and in one place will help us participate as equals in the exciting and crucial discussions now under way.

Education, public debate, and consensus building are essential in this effort, but we must also establish ways in which our voices can be heard. We need a mechanism for debate and decision. Why is this key?

Because science waits for no one. It pushes back frontiers and challenges the status quo. Until recent years progress happened more slowly and the processes of public and parliamentary scrutiny could keep up with it. But now new technologies and practices are being developed and integrated into our health care and research systems — and our daily lives — with increasing speed. We must step up our response times too.

I am an enthusiast for these developments and the research that makes them possible. As many of them are essential to our long-term interests and health I believe they should be encouraged and publicly funded; and I want to ensure that Canadians have a real and meaningful role in deciding if and how they will be used and integrated. I want Canadians to see how intermeshed these technologies and practices are, even when they seem to be so different one from another. I want to illustrate how issues they raise move back and forth across interdisciplinary lines. In this climate our attitudes towards individual and human rights are being subtly coloured, and our notions of "goodness" and "benefit" are being redefined. Economic forces and financial considerations have shaped and controlled the development of many of the new technologies and practices, from the sale of human embryos to patents on human life forms. Is this a trend we want to continue?

I hope to give Canadians a glimpse at the kinds of questions we must ask and answer as we move into the twenty-first century. We all want medicine and science to find ways to cure disease and enhance human life. But we also want to ensure that their potential benefit to humankind is not achieved at any cost. How can we work towards what is valuable to us individually while safeguarding what is vital to our society's integrity? How will we legislate a balance between scientific progress, and the protection of our individual choices and human rights? Collective challenges require collective responses. The laws we propose must be crafted to maintain the centrality of human values such as relationship, integrity, dignity, diversity, and equality. Our legislation must keep medicine and science in their social context.

Law is society's tool of public policy, the way we give substance and sanction to our most important choices. Law will provide both a context and a process for protecting our interests and preventing harm. But the future shape of these laws will depend on us. We must decide what interests are most important and valuable and then look to law to articulate them. In many ways, our laws already provide the structure for action. The laws governing human rights, consent to treatment and the right to refuse it, contract, and family and criminal law, to name a few, are already capable of handling most of these issues, but some of them will need to be fine-tuned.

In essence, we have an opportunity to draw a new map for a society where these technologies can flourish. We need to inform ourselves about medicine, science, and technology to be sure that the agendas for the new century are not set without our input. We must fight to be included, because much is at stake and the decisions made now will determine who will have power and exercise control over the future. One expert has reminded us that we can neither put the genie back into the bottle nor let it go around granting any old wish. We must give the genie some rules.[1] Our challenge is to formulate the rules for the dynamic, exciting, and sometimes terrifying technological genies that will shape our living and dying in the twenty-first century. This book is my response to that challenge.

Part One

Conception

Nowhere will technology and modern medicine touch us more intimately than in human reproduction. Our power to create human life in the laboratory will revolutionize how we view and treat life, cure disease, and define our most intimate personal and family relationships. In this part, reproductive technologies and practices are identified and their impact is assessed. Management, professional training, and accountability are explored along with the conflicts that are created for our traditional family relationships when strangers join the reproductive relationship as donors and surrogates, when grandmothers carry their grandchildren, and sisters become both mother and aunt to each other's children.

Finally, embryos created in the laboratory are not always used only for reproduction. They also become available for research. Where will that research lead? What are the values we want to protect in human embryo research? How can we protect the embryo from abuse as a limitless tool of modern research? Should some kinds of research, such as human reproductive cloning, for instance, never be tried? Who decides these questions and how will Canadians have a real role in setting the rules? Part One looks for some of these answers.

Chapter One

Reproductive Technologies: Challenges for Regulation

W hile reproductive technologies have long been used in animals,[1] their practice in humans is more recent, and their personal and social impact will be enormous. The human sexual relationship and the embryo have traditionally been private matters, but the advent of new reproductive technologies has made them both public. The traditional bond of a couple's reproductive privacy has been broken with the introduction of one or more strangers into the reproductive relationship, as donors of sperm, ova, embryos, or reproductive capacity. The categories of people who can have children have been broadened to include single women and men without sexual partners, those involved in same-sex relationships, and heterosexual couples with one or two infertile or sterile partners. Commercial concerns such as surrogacy for hire and the purchase of ova[2] and sperm have arisen, and sex selection and pre-implantation diagnosis have involved eugenics. Finally, reproductive technologies are often twinned with genetic technologies to create an even more powerful dynamic. Referred to collectively as *reprogenetics,* they interact seamlessly with one another and raise troubling ethical concerns.

Our new-found power to create, manipulate, and alter human life in the laboratory is more exciting — and more ominous — than anything we have ever known. As we will see in chapter 4, this new power raises even more serious issues involving the research on embryos, including cloning and genetic alteration, that is made possible through in vitro fertilization (IVF). By making human embryonic life public and available through IVF, we have raised again the thorny question of the legal status of human life before birth — even before implantation. Of all the public policy debates we will have about genetics, the use of embryos for various forms of research will be among the most controversial.

The Canadian Fertility and Andrology Society[3] estimates that 15 percent of couples seek medical advice for infertility-related problems[4] and that fully two-thirds of them need specialist interventions.[5] One in six is the most frequent estimate for couples unable to conceive after one year of unprotected sexual intercourse.[6] These people have turned to artificial insemination, IVF, gamete intrafallopian embryo transfer (GIFT), intracytoplasmic sperm injection (ICSI), and other assisted-reproductive technologies and practices to help them have the family they want.[7] Meanwhile, failure to focus on the prevention, diagnosis, and treatment of sexually transmitted diseases,[8] and the impact of various chemical and environmental pollutants on fertility, will result in a new generation of infertile women and men who will continue the demand for intervention when they in turn want to start a family and learn they cannot.

IVF is the core reproductive technology. It was designed to allow a pregnancy in otherwise fertile women whose fallopian tubes were blocked, damaged, or absent. It became a public sensation with the birth of Louise Brown in Great Britain in 1978, and thousands of children have been born worldwide since then, through the use of IVF or one of its variants.[9] In IVF, one or more ova are retrieved from a woman and fertilized in a glass petri dish at a fertility clinic.[10] The sperm can be provided by the woman's partner or by a (usually anonymous) donor. Once fertilization has taken place in vitro, the early embryo (the zygote) is checked for known genetic diseases and other anomalies, so that only healthy and disease-free embryos are transferred (or frozen for later use by the couple). After the results of this pre-implantation diagnosis are known, one or more of the healthy embryos are inserted in the woman's womb. If all goes well, one will implant, develop, and result in the birth of a healthy child.

Management, Accreditation, and Public Safety

The regulation of reproductive technologies and practices raises two principal kinds of challenges for the law: one of management, accreditation, and training; and another of legitimacy and inheritance for the children who will be created. The first issue is discussed here, and the second in chapter 2.

Clinical management, accreditation and professional training, and public health and safety[11] are the three main areas that the regulation of reproductive technologies and practices will need to cover.[12] Most management matters are now handled in Canada by clinics themselves, using existing professional standards for treatment and accountability. The Canadian Fertility and Andrology Society offers professional and scientific advice to the doctors who practise reproductive medicine. Practice codes that offer us models already exist in countries like Great Britain,[13] which has had legislation in place since 1990.[14] Future Canadian legislation will also need to provide a context for the accreditation and regulation of fertility clinics to protect public health and ensure access for all infertile couples wanting to use these technologies to have a family. There are many urgent issues to address.

Standardization of Procedures and Data Administration

While practices and procedures have been simplified and generally standardized in the Canadian fertility clinics that offer IVF and related technologies,[15] current practices are not governed by specific legislation. In this, Canada lags behind. More than half of the countries that offer reproductive technologies already have some form of legislation in place,[16] and there is some international cooperation on the practice of reproductive medicine.[17] But while there is a voluntary moratorium on certain reproductive practices[18] in Canada, we still have no legislative framework[19] at either the federal or the provincial levels to regulate existing practices, ensure their safety, and protect against their abuse. We have no uniform definitions for terms like *success* and *failure* rate and no established and enforceable legal procedures for the collection and recording of data and statistics relating to the use of IVF and other assisted reproductive technologies.

Recent newspaper articles[20] have highlighted the lack of data and other record-keeping, reporting that most Canadian clinics do not provide relevant statistics about their "take home baby rates," the one figure of significance to infertile couples. The licensing and accreditation authority that has been promised by the federal health minister will need a mandate to collect and make publicly available such information as how IVF and other assisted reproductive technologies are being used; the number and percentage of full-term pregnancies that have resulted from each type of intervention; the health outcomes experienced by women who have undergone these procedures; the number and health status of the children they have given birth to as a result; the proportion of multiple to single births; and the long-term health status of both mother and child.

Access to Reproductive Technologies and Practices[21]

One of the main current concerns about reproductive technologies is their increasing use for all kinds of infertility. IVF is indicated, for example, for tubal-factor infertility, unexplained infertility, male factor infertility or sterility, and even in situations when other more routine fertility therapies have failed. There is also a strong demand for IVF and other assisted reproductive technologies (alone, or in concert with practices like surrogacy) by single women and men who want children but do not have a partner, or by couples in same-sex relationships. These factors have together created a growing and articulate constituency with a clear interest in the broad application and further medical development of IVF and other assisted reproduction techniques and practices.

Countries with publicly funded universal health care systems similar to ours have already felt the financial impact of general public access to new reproductive technologies and practices.[22] We cannot underestimate the effect on other health care priorities that a change towards universal access would have in Canada, and we must evaluate the potential costs directly as we proceed to fund more and more of these technologies as medically necessary procedures for infertility.

Concerns about the financial impact on the system must, however, be balanced by our compassion for the infertile. No province currently provides full funding for reproductive technologies,[23] and, as a result, infertile Canadians who cannot pay do not have access to them. This means that they will not be able to have genetically linked children, even though reproductive technologies exist that could help them. As a priority, we must address the issue of access[24] to both IVF and more recent reproductive technologies such as intracytoplasmic sperm injection (ICSI),[25] which infertile men will increasingly demand in the new century.[26]

Evaluating priorities for access may require each province to redefine "medically necessary" services as they relate to medical infertility and reproductive technologies under its health insurance scheme. I believe that our future legislative framework should guarantee that those suffering from medical infertility be provided access to these technologies through the public health care system. This key issue of access must be addressed and resolved.

Women's and Children's Health and Well-Being

IVF and other assisted reproductive techniques can involve a number of risks for the woman undergoing the procedure and for any children she might later bear. The drugs used to superovulate women are powerful and could have unintended consequences.[27] Multiple births create real health risks for the pregnant woman and the developing fetus.[28] Multiple embryo transferrals can also result in the implantation of more embryos than a woman's womb can safely carry to term. In such a situation, some of the implanted embryos normally have to be aborted. Yet, aborting some of the embryos disrupts the delicate uterine wall and jeopardizes the entire pregnancy.

Multiple births can also cause severe economic hardship for couples, especially if they already have other children at home. The physical demands of twins, triplets, or quadruplets usually mean the mother has to leave her job, with a resultant loss of income for the family at a time when it is most needed. Finally, premature multiple births place tremendous strains on the health care system and on the personnel and space of neonatal hospital units.[29] This problem is particularly acute for hospitals in areas where IVF and other assisted reproductive technologies are widely used.

Gender Equality

Many reproductive technologies and practices permit the identification of the sex of the embryo and the fetus, using either pre-implantation diagnosis or prenatal diagnosis techniques such as ultrasound, amniocentesis, chorionic villus sampling, or the analysis of maternal blood for the presence of fetal cells. This information can then be used to identify and abort fetuses suffering from identifiable genetic anomalies or conditions (or, if IVF is used, to support the decision not to implant them in a woman's womb). It can also allow sex selection for cultural or social reasons, including the universal preference for male children.

Sex selection challenges our notions of equality and undermines equality guarantees enshrined in the *Canadian Charter of Rights and Freedoms* and in our human rights laws. It also denies our international commitment to eliminate discrimination against women. The only possible justification for use of sex selection to date would be the compassionate one — to assist couples suffering from inheritable genetic conditions that could be passed on to offspring of a particular sex. There are many who would even challenge such practices. This issue will be hotly debated when new legislation is finally introduced.

The Requirement for Independent Counselling

Few decisions that a woman and her partner will make in their reproductive lives are more important than whether they will use IVF, alone or in concert with other assisted reproductive techniques and practices, to try to achieve a pregnancy. For that decision to be truly informed, both the partners need to evaluate all the relevant information. At present, counselling and information sessions relating to IVF practice in Canada are voluntary, vary from clinic to clinic, and are usually offered as part of a fertility clinic's package of services rather than as an independent initiative separate from the clinic. They focus primarily on issues of consent and are as much about protecting the clinic from lawsuits as they are about protecting the patient. Effective counselling is essential to the process of an IVF-assisted pregnancy and must be provided by professionally trained personnel whose services are covered under provincial health insurance schemes.

Experimental Techniques or Medical Therapy?

One of the most serious issues surrounding the use and development of assisted reproductive practices is whether and under what circumstances they can legitimately be described as routine medical therapy rather than experimental procedures. The answer to these questions is important for at least two reasons. First, modern medicine and science already conduct extensive research on human subjects, and rules have been established to govern that research. If certain reproductive and genetic technologies are considered experimental, then the stricter legal rules regulating research on human subjects must apply. Second, as long as these practices in fact remain experimental, merely relabelling them as therapy will not legitimize moving them into the category of interventions eligible for public funding under public health care insurance schemes.

There are other ways in which patients can legally be protected in these situations. New and existing rules to ensure that sperm and ova are safe and disease-free can be enforced; and actions for negligence can be maintained under existing medical malpractice law for cases where doctors, nurses, or reproductive technicians fail in their duty to use reasonable care and skill, and cause the patient to suffer damages. Legal rules of consent must be respected; otherwise actions for assault and battery can be brought.

In structuring new legislation, a key question will be: Who sets the rules for accreditation, and on what basis? I suggest that in setting medical standards, professional associations with such expertise as the Canadian Fertility and Andrology Society play a lead role. Once we have decided that we will offer reproductive technologies as medical tools to help the infertile, the practice of this kind of specialized reproductive medicine should fall within the general overview of the medical profession, and associations such as the CFAS, for the setting of standards, and the training, policing, and disciplining of doctors. In Canada, this kind of self-policing is accepted, and extensive rules already exist — for example, for the processing and distribution of semen for assisted reproduction by donor.[30] The anticipated new accreditation and licensing authority should make these regulations its first priority.

Chapter Two

Issues of Legitimacy and Inheritance

W e have seen that new assisted reproductive technologies and practices raise technical and regulatory issues in regard to management, training, accreditation, and public health and safety. But they also raise substantive issues, as they change the very nature of reproduction, introduce strangers into our reproductive relationships, and often make us genetic strangers to our own children. Practices such as surrogacy, for instance, allow a woman to become both the biological mother of, and aunt to, her sister's children, or to be both the grandmother and mother of her daughter's children. They allow an unknown donor to be biologically related to unlimited numbers of children across the country and around the world. What happens in families when the biological and social ties that bind us as spouses, parents, and siblings are severed by strangers? Can the human relationships that are at the heart of families withstand the pressures of these new reproductive options? And what about the children born through the use of these technologies and practices? Will they fare better than children who have been through the traditional adoption process? How can the law help us deal with the relationships and the legal issues, such as legitimacy and inheritance, that our use of reproductive technologies and practices raises?

We tend to think of all assisted reproductive procreation as different from normal procreation. But in some cases all that is done is to use the technology to help an otherwise fertile couple achieve their own pregnancy. This happens in situations where a fertile woman can produce ova, but her blocked, absent, or diseased fallopian tubes make conceiving in the regular way following sexual intercourse impossible.[1] IVF was originally proposed for just such a situation. The use of new reproductive technologies and related practices to help a married couple achieve a pregnancy using their own gametes, or reproductive cells, is widely accepted. They are merely tools to circumvent infertility and allow them to have children.

When the infertile couple use their own gametes, then the only legal issues are those of consent, professional training, and public health. As both parents are biological parents, no issues of legitimacy and inheritance will arise. But what happens when one or both partners are biological and genetic strangers to their child? How does the law treat the strangers that are often a necessary part of the process of reproduction through these technologies?

Donor Anonymity

The requirement for donor anonymity is a controversial issue in these reproductive practices because it denies children conceived through donated ova, sperm, or embryos the opportunity to know the identity of their biological "parents." Hundreds of thousands of children have been born since artificial insemination by donor became popular in the 1960s and, because donor anonymity remains the norm,[2] most of them will never know or be able to trace their biological roots. That situation is changing a bit. The 1996 document *Guidelines for Therapeutic Donor Insemination*,[3] prepared by the Canadian Fertility and Andrology Society for fertility clinics and doctors that use donor sperm in Canada, represents an effort to establish a fair balance among the interests of all concerned. Now, as long as consent is given by both the donor and the mature offspring, the identity of each can be divulged.[4] Otherwise, this information remains confidential and neither the donor, the recipient, or the child created have any right to disclosure.[5]

Why is the practice of donor anonymity so entrenched? There are several reasons. First, until recently, male infertility and sterility were taboo social subjects, treated as purely private matters. Fertility was the societal norm, and the sterile or infertile were often treated with pity and sometimes socially ostracized. Many couples maintained a veil of secrecy about their infertility to protect their privacy. Second, in almost all societies virility and manhood are equated. The popularity of Viagra since its introduction should remind us of this fact. This often-destructive equation of maleness and virility has added to the secrecy about a couple's infertility. Only now are such attitudes beginning to change.

A third reason for insistence on donor anonymity has been our perception of adultery. Adultery historically has been grounds for divorce, and has carried with it legal as well as societal sanctions. IVF and other assisted reproductive techniques and practices use donor sperm, in some cases perhaps even that of a family member. Even now, such arrangements carry with them a taint of adultery. As a result, the charade of legitimacy encouraged until recently through procedures such as sperm mixing, now banned,[6] became part of the practice of medically assisted procreation.

Finally, to the extent that infertility was treated as a medical condition, the intervention of a physician known to the couple to perform the insemination procedure helped ensure that secrecy would be maintained. Sometimes the sperm used would be his own or that of medical students. In this way, the medical profession played an integral part in instituting and maintaining the secrecy that marks the present practice of donor anonymity. Records were not kept and the child's biological past was extinguished to allow the family to pretend that they all shared a common family background. This annihilation of birthright mirrored the practice followed in adoptions. As we work to resolve the legal issue of donor anonymity, we have many lessons to learn from the adoption experience.

Challenges to Donor Anonymity

Should we challenge donor anonymity?[7] I argue that we should. As we map the human genome and learn what makes us tick, we know that a person's genetic and biological heritage offers important indicators of future health. We are acutely aware that genetic factors will predict or predispose us to certain hereditary conditions or diseases. Knowing this, can we justify denying a child access to that knowledge? Is it ethical to deliberately create a human being whose biological and genetic background cannot be traced? When it can be traced, under what circumstances would we allow it and how would we ensure discretion? I prefer a system that gives the child the option at maturity to meet with a donor or biological father or mother, accompanied by a professional social worker or religious adviser. Some young adults may not consider it important to know their genetic roots; but the experience of adoptees has taught us that many children need this "event" to complete their sense of self and move on to become full adults.

Protection from Consanguineous or Incestuous Relationships

Protection of an individual's right to know his or her genetic history in the event of genetic disease is one good reason for opening up the practice of donor anonymity. But there are other equally important considerations. As assisted reproductive technologies and practices become more widespread and socially acceptable, greater numbers of children risk being related to each other by blood. Society has traditionally guarded against the practice of incest, in part because it can lead to inbreeding and genetic defects. In Canada, the practice is a criminal offence,[8] punishable by imprisonment for as long as fourteen years. Everyone who knowingly has sexual intercourse with a blood relative (defined as a parent, child, brother, sister, grandparent, or grandchild) is guilty of the crime of incest. The law defines brother and sister to include half-brother and half-sister. No person can legally marry another to whom he or she is related by blood or by adoption. Marriage between related persons, including brothers, sisters, half-brothers, and half-sisters, is prohibited and void. Under provincial law today, children are deemed legitimate from birth, but no law can legalize a marriage that has been declared invalid or dissolved by the court.

Any policy that allows for the deliberate creation of human beings, while legally denying them the possibility of ever knowing the identity of their blood relatives, especially that of their half-brothers and half-sisters, also denies them the benefit and protection of the *Criminal Code* and other laws. The length of imprisonment for incest speaks to the seriousness with which our society treats this particular crime. Is this rule against incest worth keeping? Most Canadians would say it is. Incest is child abuse; children born of incestuous relationships can have detrimental health and social outcomes. As the use of assisted reproductive technologies and practices increases, so does the risk of "reproductive incest." The risks are heightened by the fact that there is no limit on the number of live births each sperm (or ovum) donor can create. The maximum number of live births allowed for one donor must be established and legally enforced to protect children from potentially devastating health and human situations.

Protecting Children's Rights

Attitudes towards children and their right to know their biological heritage are changing, most notably in the area of adoption. In certain jurisdictions in Canada, adopted children can now trace their biological mother and, should she agree, even meet with her in a supervised setting. This new openness is consistent with an overall increase in respect for the rights of children, and should be extended in any law we adopt to include children conceived through gamete donation. The once-popular view that revealing a child's adoptive status would put the dynamics of the adoptive family at risk and confuse the adopted child has lost much support. The various provincial adoption laws recognize the needs of children to have a permanent home and to develop family relationships, and their interests are to be paramount. Among the factors that will be considered to determine a child's best interests in new legislation are safety, emotional and developmental needs, continuity of care, and assurance of a positive and secure relationship within a family. Where children are old enough (usually twelve and over), their views on a proposed adoption will be sought and respected.

Other factors relating to adoption need to be considered as well. At the moment, all interprovincial and international adoptions require the approval of the provincial director of adoptions. Given the extent of donor sperm sales across borders and the likelihood that such sales will include ova and even embryos on a routine basis in the future, all the rules applicable to intraprovincial adoptions should be applied for situations where children are to be deliberately created for preconception or prenatal adoption. The Hague Convention on Intercountry Adoptions[9] applies in most Canadian provinces, and children adopted where this convention applies have the right to know all the information on file about them. This trend towards openness and honesty is also essential to the success of any new laws governing the future rights of children created using the range of assisted reproductive technologies and practices. Openness and disclosure agreements between an adoptive parent and the biological parent are encouraged in current adoption laws, and should be considered in these new forms of pre-natal adoption as well. All payments, except those to cover reasonable expenses that will be determined by the court on a case-by-case basis, must be prohibited; and human embryos should be subject to the exist-ing adoption laws, which prohibit the payment to, or acceptance of money by, a biological parent or a third party for the legal transfer of the child for adoption.[10] Human embryos must come under existing legal bans on the purchase and sale of human life.

Surrogacy

Some couples who can produce ova and sperm choose to seek out sur-rogacy arrangements because the condition of the woman's uterus, or its absence, makes it impossible for her to actually carry a pregnancy. But surrogacy arrangements have no legal status in Canada, and a court will consider such a contract for services as unenforceable against the surrogate. Under Canadian law the woman who is delivered of a child is deemed to be its legal mother. This presumption has become rebutta-ble for the first time in history with the advent of ova donation, where one woman donates an egg but another gestates and gives birth.

The controversial issue of commercial surrogacy is now covered by the federal voluntary moratorium introduced in 1995. All commercial dealing in children is prohibited in Canada; and while an argument could be made in equity that the intent of the parties to the preconcep-tion or surrogacy contract should be honoured and enforced, there are no Canadian cases on this point. It is unlikely that the courts will assume responsibility for setting this kind of controversial public policy. Until this issue is resolved, the infertile in these situations are on their own. Should a court refuse to recognize a surrogacy contract, family law would be hard pressed to intervene. Right now, a surrogate is con-sidered the legal "mother" of the child she delivers even when she is a genetic stranger to the future child and is acting only as a gestational surrogate, carrying an embryo conceived with both the sperm and the ovum of the couple who intend to raise it.

Most clinics in Canada do not use surrogates, in part to avoid the possibility of lawsuits like the one in the *Baby M* case[11] in the United States, where Mary Beth Whitehead bore a child as a surrogate for a couple and then decided she could not give up the baby. Clinic con-sent forms require the couple to decide before the process begins what they will do with their embryos should their marriage end in divorce or the female partner undergo a hysterectomy. Either one or both parties retain control over the frozen embryos, which will be kept for a year, or their control passes to the clinic for use either in reproduction for others or in research.[12] All of us want to avoid the legal nightmares associated with failed surrogacy arrangements; yet there are women for whom surrogacy is the only available option if they are to have a family.

The Human Factor

The Royal Commission on New Reproductive Technologies recommended against all surrogacy arrangements in its final report. I believe that all commercial surrogacy should be banned, but urge the judicial recognition of surrogacy arrangements for situations where sisters or close family members act as surrogates. This practice would fill the legal void by legitimizing the child and ensuring that the couple's intent to parent is recognized. As we see later in this chapter, the law gives parents rights and responsibilities both towards their biological and adopted children and towards those children to whom they choose to act as parents through legal guardianship.

I saw throughout the Royal Commission's public hearings that people will do just about anything to have a child, and it is not realistic to pretend that the law and the courts can wipe their hands of these complex cases. Our public policy should discourage surrogacy and our laws prohibit its commercialization, along with other commercial practices such as the sale of gametes and embryos, just as we ban the sale of children. But policy will not stop practice; the law will need to give guidance on which forms of surrogacy will be allowed and which will not. Both types of surrogacy now in practice — between strangers for money, and between sisters or mothers and daughters who volunteer to help — have drawbacks and detractors; but both raise serious questions. How can we control situations where strangers or our closest relatives join the reproductive relationship along with us to give our children as many as six possible "parents"? What do we call all these people? What are their roles and responsibilities?[13] What should they be?

In dealing with children conceived through IVF and other assisted reproductive technologies in the future, professional counselling should be mandatory for all players at all stages, and the intent of the parties should always be respected, except where there are mitigating factors such as duress or undue influence over the surrogate. No one wants legal battles over innocent children. We need to work out solutions right now to these very human dilemmas.

Openness and Confidentiality

Donor anonymity allows us to create a child whose genetic heritage intentionally cannot be traced or known. I believe that we need a different system, one that will require accurate and complete birth records, medical files, and family records to be kept. Any decision to introduce a more open policy in this area will lead naturally to other legal concerns, such as how to protect individual privacy and medical records. These are neither new nor insurmountable problems. As in cases of surrogacy, we have a lot to learn from current developments in adoption processes. By promoting honesty and openness, we can sensitize Canadians to the serious issue of infertility. At present, in the adoption context, some provinces require that the director of the adoption agency obtain and keep information about the medical and social history of an adopted child's biological family. The precedent is already in place in adoption, which can be seen as a form of "social" assisted reproduction, just as artificial insemination by donor is a technical one. At the very least, the same safeguards that are required for children conceived in the traditional way should be required for IVF-created children.

Legitimacy and Inheritance

In Canadian law, terms like *mother, father, parent, child of a marriage, brother, sister,* and *grandparent* have legal definitions. These definitions also create legal entitlements and responsibilities. Under the *Criminal Code*[14] a *child* includes an adopted and/or illegitimate child under sixteen of either a legal or a common law relationship for whom a parent, foster parent, legal guardian, or head of family responsible for that child's custody and control must provide necessities. According to case law, these necessities are such items "as tend to preserve life, and not in their ordinary legal sense and may include medical aid."[15] The Canadian *Divorce Act* [16] provides for corollary relief for all children of a marriage under sixteen, or older if they are unable to care for themselves.[17] Provincial child welfare laws define a *mother* or a *father* as being a biological or legal parent of a minor child, including a person with court-ordered custody, or the person with whom the child resides and who stands in the place of that child's parents.

Under most of these Acts, recognized child welfare agencies have the power to intervene where parents fail to provide basic protections and necessaries for the children in their charge. Their failure to do so triggers statutory protection from others, including the courts, who maintain a large *parens patriae*[18] jurisdiction whenever children are involved. We have deliberately acted to make courts a last resort for family issues such as access and custody, in large part because the decisions involve children, but also because we believe that issues of this nature are best resolved in a less formal and adversarial context. Wherever possible, a similar approach should govern uncertainty in legal relationships among parties creating children through assisted reproductive technologies. The relevant family law legislation can easily be amended to be more inclusive in its scope.

In the Interests of the Children

In matters of inheritance, a person shares in her or his legal parents' estate, and a body of law has developed respecting this claim.[19] But what happens in situations where birth is the result of assisted reproductive technologies and practices for which donor sperm, ova, or even embryos have been used? What happens when the woman delivering the child is a biological stranger to it, acting merely as a gestational surrogate? Does the law that defines the woman who gives birth to a child as a "mother" in all cases become just another refutable evidentiary assumption? We must accept that definition at the moment because our existing laws assume a traditional means of procreation.

The legal framework respecting assisted reproductive technologies and practices must consider the whole gamut of new questions raised by our dramatic departure from these traditions. Is a donor of sperm or of an ovum a "father" or a "mother" within existing definitions of family law and related statutes? Similarly, are embryo donors "parents"? Can such gamete or embryo donors demand custody of, or access to, the children born as a result of their sperm or ovum donation? Are these same children entitled to support from those whose gametes resulted in their creation? Can they demand a share in a gamete donor's property or become entitled to his or her estate?

As our laws now stand, the answers to such questions vary and are unclear. Up until now we have cloaked the process of technological reproduction in secrecy, blurring the biological ties that link us to one another. This practice should change. Laws that give rights and assign responsibility require a clarity and consistency that is lacking at present. We need to review all existing laws to ensure that they respond to the new reproductive realities that fracture traditional biological links and impose new types of legal responsibilities.

As reproductive technologies become more sophisticated, more legal options will be available to us. Were embryo flushing to become possible in humans, for instance, we could provide for pre-implantation adoptions, so that the legal relationship of the family members could be clarified at the time of embryo transfer rather than after the future child's birth. Such a provision would confirm the intent of the parties to the arrangement (the gamete or embryo donors and the planned social parents) at the earliest possible stage of the future child's development and normalize assisted reproduction as a recognized reproductive practice in society. In all cases (unless it proves to be illegal), the intent of the parties should be the basis for legal and judicial interpretation. Respecting the parties' intent ensures that the best interests of the child to be created are taken into account, and legitimizes in the eyes of the family itself and in society at large the need for assisted reproduction for many couples. It will also normalize infertility treatment and help us accept that these reproductive technologies are natural and normal ways to have a family in the twenty-first century. Through all these changes, one goal must remain clear: in all situations where these reproductive technologies and practices are used, the interests and well-being of the children to be created must be paramount.

Chapter Three

Federal Initiatives and Constitutional Jurisdiction

When thousands of Canadians banded together to call for the creation of a royal commission on reproductive and genetic technologies, few realized the speed with which these issues would develop and dominate medical-scientific research.[1] In its 1993 report, the Royal Commission on New Reproductive Technologies recommended that a permanent authority be appointed to oversee the use and development of assisted reproductive and genetic technologies and practices,[2] and proposed that certain of them be criminalized.[3] Since then, the federal government has introduced two measures — a voluntary moratorium on certain reproductive and genetic practices, in July 1995; and a Bill that would have criminalized them. The voluntary moratorium is still in place, but there is no law yet to regulate and accredit fertility clinics or deal with controversial embryo research.

Among the many technologies and research areas that are subject to the voluntary moratorium are sex selection for non-medical purposes; commercial preconception or "surrogacy" arrangements; the buying and selling of human eggs, sperm, and embryos; egg donation in exchange for in vitro fertilization (IVF) services; germ-line genetic alteration; ectogenesis (the creation of an artificial womb); the cloning of human embryos; the formation of animal-human hybrids by combining animals and human gametes; and the retrieval of eggs from cadavers and fetuses for donation, fertilization, or research.[4]

In 1996 the federal government introduced legislation to give the voluntary moratorium the force of law. Bill C-47, the *Human Reproductive and Genetic Technologies Act,*[5] would have criminalized surrogacy and certain genetic technologies. Its stated goal was to protect the dignity, health, and safety of Canadians using these technologies and to ensure the "appropriate treatment" of human gametes and embryos in research. The Bill did not create the permanent management regime promised the year before to license and accredit all fertility clinics that offer IVF and other assisted reproductive technologies, and which are the main source of embryos for research. Partly to show how seriously it took these matters, and partly because the criminal law was its main source of jurisdiction, in otherwise provincial areas of power, the federal government chose to ban and criminalize these technologies using its exclusive power over the criminal law. Many witnesses before the committee objected to the federal proposal, which, in the end, never came to a final vote as the 1997 general election was called before Parliament could decide.

The Proposed Federal Licensing Authority and the Constitution

Legislation to control fertility clinics and embryo research is again promised, and will be introduced in the near future,[6] marking the first time that all clinics will be licensed and accredited by one federal authority. All clinics that offer IVF and other assisted reproductive technologies and practices and that undertake embryo and fetal tissue research will be licensed under the new law, which apparently will be in the form of a separate statute rather than an amendment of the *Criminal Code.*[7]

Canada has two levels of government, federal and provincial, which exercise power alone or in concert with each other. Exclusive federal powers are set out in section 91 and the provincial powers in section 92 of the Constitution. Both levels of government may also share concurrent jurisdiction in certain areas.[8] Where they do, and where there is conflict, the federal legislation is paramount, unless the courts find it has interfered with a matter that lies within the provinces' exclusive domain.[9]

Can Ottawa Act Alone?

The constitutional division of power is at the heart of how we are governed. In the case at hand, can the federal government act alone, as it plans to do, to create such a national licensing authority? To answer this question, we need to be clear about who has what jurisdiction under our Constitution.[10] The Constitution assigns the main responsibility for health to the provinces. Provincial responsibilities include the running of hospitals, the delivery of medical services, the practice of medicine, and the laws governing the training and licensing of doctors and other health care personnel. On what authority, then, can the federal government act to create a national licensing and accreditation body? Two options are exclusively open to the federal government: the criminal law or the extraordinary power to legislate for the peace, order, and good government of Canada. Can it rely on either of these powers in this case?

Jurisdiction in the Field of Health

When we try to regulate reproductive technologies and practices, we will face a constitutional dilemma. Even though Canadians want to regulate these technologies and to protect all the people involved, especially the children, it is not clear who has the power to act. Canadians would be surprised to learn that the specific subject of health does not appear as such in the Constitution. This is because in 1867 health and medical services were treated as charity of a purely private and local nature.[11] Framing the Constitution to fit the reality of the time, the Fathers of Confederation did not foresee the changes that would eventually lead to a significant federal involvement in the health care field, including its introduction of medicare.[12]

At first blush it would seem that the provinces, and not the federal government, have the power to legislate in the key areas of reproductive medicine and research. In 1867 the provinces were given exclusive authority for the running of hospitals within their borders.[13] They have the power to decide which, if any, assisted reproductive technologies and practices will be covered by their health insurance scheme.[14] They also have jurisdiction over education and the regulation of the medical and health care professionals within the province.[15] This control would extend to the licensing and educational requirements of the doctors, other health care professionals, and genetic counsellors who are directly involved in reproductive medicine. Under their exclusive power to legislate with respect to "property and civil rights in the province,"[16] the provinces have the authority to establish social programs, including health insurance schemes, and to control the sale of certain food products. Finally, provincial governments have exclusive power over all matters of a local or private nature within their own provinces.[17] Although this power is not absolute,[18] the primary responsibility in Canada for matters of health rests with the provinces, including the delivery of health care services, the decision about which services will be covered as medically necessary by provincial health insurance plans, and the licensing and payment of doctors and health care workers performing reproductive medicine.

So what constitutional powers *does* the federal government have to act to regulate reproductive medicine and research? We know that Parliament, like the provincial legislatures, can pass laws in its exclusive area of constitutional jurisdiction. With few exceptions, these areas do not include health. But there are some specific domains where the federal government has special responsibilities and jurisdiction to provide health and medical services: for example, for Armed Forces personnel,[19] "Indians,"[20] "aliens"[21] in the immigration process, and prisoners[22] in federal penitentiaries. Assisted reproductive technologies offered to these classes of people within public or military hospitals would be the responsibility of the federal government. But the two most likely ways in which the federal government would seek to legislate on questions of the use of reproductive technologies and embryo research would be through the criminal law power or the general power to legislate for the "Peace, Order and good Government of Canada."[23] Are either of these appropriate?[24]

There is little doubt that there is no *national emergency* that would give legitimacy to federal intervention using the "peace, order and good government" or POGG clause. However, since the Supreme Court's decision in *R. v. Crown Zellerbach Canada Ltd.*[25] ten years ago, it has been clear that POGG also encompasses the power to enact legislation that addresses questions of *national concern*. It is arguable that under this broadened scope, the federal government could act alone to create a national licensing and accreditation authority and ban certain reproductive and genetic practices and embryo research. Certainly the Royal Commission on New Reproductive Technologies thought it could,[26] and urged the federal government to use the POGG power to legislate a national body to regulate the practice of reproductive medicine and related genetic research. I believe that the jurisdictional battle that would result if the federal government were to use the POGG power in this case would waste time and effort that are best used in developing workable solutions to the issues these technologies and research pose.

In my judgment it is equally inappropriate for the federal government to use the criminal law power to control and limit medical-scientific research. The risk to open and accountable systems, the sense of false security that this option would engender in the public, and the potential for the criminalization of doctors and scientists are some of the main reasons against making this choice. Resorting to the criminal law in this area in the first instance, and concentrating too narrowly on banning specific technologies, is short-sighted. It is not enough only to legislate against specific technologies. Most of them are moving targets; no sooner have we one within our sights then another more sensational one appears. What we need is a way for Canadians to maintain a vigilant eye on what is happening, to be part of the debate about the challenges posed by these technologies and medical research, and to recommend appropriate regulatory and public policy responses. Such a mechanism could be supple, yet effective enough to meet both anticipated and unexpected medical-scientific discoveries with a sense of calm and wisdom. To define our guiding principles first, and then to judge new technologies and practices against these is a far more effective way to prevent abuse of the public interest and individual rights than to mount a frontal attack on specific practices and technologies using the criminal law. We need a set of principles through which to identify unacceptable research and an effective national mechanism to monitor the research we do allow.

Consensus building and ongoing monitoring assume a significant involvement by the public and a transparent and defensible set of enforceable rules. Resorting to the criminal law may make *some* people feel better, but could never involve *most* people in policy development and decision-making. It would instead reduce the discussion to a few highly publicized and costly trials and leave those not directly involved fearful and concerned about what research is really being done. That was the main weakness of the last attempt at legislating these technologies. When the federal government introduced Bill C-47, it ignored the need to bring Canadians into this process, limiting the original discussion to a couple of expert round tables. When it ultimately opened the conversation to public participation in the final days of the life of the Bill, it admitted that it had underestimated the public's interest and their desire to participate in the drafting of this crucial legislation.

To avoid a repetition of this mistake, the government should commit itself to public hearings across Canada as part of the parliamentary committee's work on the Bill to ensure that the many disparate views of all interested Canadians are before Parliament when it passes the final legislation. Public involvement is not a slogan or a public relations exercise. It will help guarantee good legislation and ensure public confidence and support. It will be the key to the law's legitimacy and its acceptance by all Canadians.

Working Together

How might we accomplish this goal of working together? First, as soon as the bill is introduced, receives second reading, and is sent to committee, the members of Parliament and senators who sit as a joint committee on health should travel the country and conduct extensive public hearings. In anticipation of a real public debate, the hundreds of studies that have been prepared for Health Canada at taxpayers' expense should be made public. It is not acceptable to call for a sincere public debate without providing the background materials to help us understand what is happening and what options for action might be open to us.

Second, we need to think about the many forms that the proposed accreditation and licensing authority could take. At the very least, I believe that it must be independent of government and situated outside Health Canada, where other responsibilities are certain to raise real conflicts of interest. A body physically separate from government and the department that approves drugs for Canadians' use is essential.

Third, while the new body or commission will need to be adequately funded with federal dollars, provisions could be made for it to raise money privately, as is the case in the United Kingdom, where fees are charged by the clinics for some services and corporate interests provide research funding. We will need to arrive at a clear statement about who will control the research carried out in fertility clinics and how the new law will guarantee that the privacy of Canadian couples will be respected and their medical records protected.

A fourth consideration is that the new authority will need to be aware that it is not reinventing the wheel. We are starting from far back in this area, and many practices and trends — commercialization, for instance — have already evolved. The ways in which other jurisdictions with similar political and social values have researched and resolved certain issues should be seriously studied and used where possible to save time and money.[27]

Finally, the founding membership of the authority should be carefully chosen so that it has the capacity to provide real leadership and build consensus among the various groups and points of view that are drawn to and affected by these technologies and practices. We cannot pretend that these are purely social or medical issues. We must acknowledge that they are both — and more. This authority will need to be united in a national perspective and a firm respect for the real political and ideological divisions that exist on some of these issues — divisions that could easily jeopardize its work and future viability.

The new authority will have to overcome the suspicion that it is just one more attempt by the federal government to hijack power from the provinces in the field of health care. If we want this body to work, we will have to recognize these concerns. The need for regulation in the area of assisted reproductive technologies and direction in the area of embryo research are too pressing for us to waste valuable time in the coming months battling constitutional challenges over jurisdiction. The establishment of a body that reports to Parliament, but which is truly separate and independent from any federal government department, will go a long way towards answering the valid concern that it is just another jurisdictional intrusion. We may even want to locate it away from Ottawa to show good will. Whatever we do, we must endeavour to work together, keeping in mind our main goals — to provide the best options for those Canadians who, through disease or infertility, need assisted reproductive technologies to have children; and to protect and enhance our individual and collective rights.

Chapter Four

Embryos:
The New Frontier
of Human
Research

A ssisted reproductive technologies and practices give the infertile a chance to have children. But they do more than just create embryos for reproduction. They also ensure a supply of human embryos for research through IVF programs. In Canada, hundreds of frozen embryos end up as "extras" in fertility clinics[1] and many of them will be used for research. In this chapter we will travel to this new frontier of science, to the fascinating, yet troubling, world of embryo research where reproductive and genetic technologies meet and ethics and law face off with science. Fed in part by the love of discovery, in part by the promise of commercial gain, and most of all by ordinary women and men wanting cures to the diseases and disabilities that afflict them and their families, this kind of research is proceeding at a frenetic pace.

Many questions and controversies lie ahead of us, and in this domain also, the law will need to find ways to balance science's need to push forward with society's larger responsibility to protect human life from abuse and harm. This dual task will be difficult. Anyone who has been involved in the brutal abortion debate in North America can see what lies ahead. We can expect controversy despite the evidence that embryo research will lead to cures for disease and better health for coming generations. Parliamentarians will have to look for consensus and compromise. Canadians will have to play their part in this debate, and to reflect on the values we assign to human embryos created in the laboratory. To help in this process, this chapter will begin with a review of the present law on human life before birth and a look at the types of embryo research now under way. After some exploration of the controversial issues we need to address, we will examine current research rules and the measures the federal government has taken to date to meet the challenges raised by this research.

The Legal Status of Human Life before Birth

The public debate about the appropriate legal status of human life before birth has focused almost exclusively on the question of abortion. Historically, the fetus has never enjoyed full legal rights, although it has sometimes benefited from laws that protected pregnant women from violence.[2] Abortion before quickening was not a criminal offence at common law[3] and was considered a misdemeanour if carried out after that point.[4] In 1892 Canada's first *Criminal Code*[5] made procuring or performing an abortion a crime punishable by life imprisonment. The defence of necessity remained open to those who acted, usually during the birthing process, to save the pregnant woman's life. In 1968 the *Criminal Code* was amended to create an abortion committee system that allowed for legal abortions in certain limited situations. Although abortion was still a criminal offence, punishable by a maximum of fourteen years in prison, the amendments legalized abortions that were approved by a special therapeutic abortion committee[6] and performed in an accredited hospital. There was no requirement for a committee to be struck, however, and certain hospitals and provinces refused to appoint one. Nor were provincial health ministers required to approve hospitals so that abortions could actually be performed.

The law was challenged by Dr. Henry Morgentaler, who performed abortions in his clinics outside the parameters of the medical committee system established by the *Criminal Code*. His first challenge in the pre-*Charter* era went all the way to the Supreme Court, where it was defeated on the grounds that the amendments were a valid exercise of the federal power over criminal law. Dr. Morgentaler continued to defy the law and, in 1988, made another legal challenge to the Supreme Court of Canada.[7] By then the rules had changed, and the Justices were required to rule[8] on the constitutionality of the therapeutic abortion committee system,[9] in light of the new *Canadian Charter of Rights and Freedoms*.[10] The Court declared that the provisions requiring the abortion committee system were unconstitutional; they violated the *Charter's* guarantee of security of the person; and were not saved by section 1.[11]

Today, it is settled Canadian law that legal rights begin at birth. The embryo and fetus may enjoy a moral status as part of the human community, but can claim no legal status before birth. The *Criminal Code* states that "[a] child becomes a human being within the meaning of this Act when it has completely proceeded, in a living state, from the body of its mother." This criterion also applies to civil charges in tort law and actions under the *Quebec Civil Code*. Any right in the fetus to sue for damages caused to it while in the womb are conditional on the fetus first being born alive and viable.[12] Attempts to include the fetus within the language and protection of the *Charter* have been made and have failed;[13] and provincial laws in New Brunswick and the Northwest Territories, which include a fetus as a "child in need of protection," have not yet been challenged.[14] Although the Supreme Court has stopped short of recognizing a right to abortion in Canada, this medical procedure is now legal, and criteria for women's health, rather than those of the criminal law, apply. The decision is left to the pregnant woman alone, and is usually made in consultation with her doctor. Provinces are not required to pay for abortions performed in clinics, and some do not.[15] However, a province cannot pass laws with penal sanctions to prevent abortions being performed in clinics rather than hospitals,[16] provided they are done by a doctor using accepted medical standards and procedures.[17]

In the case of abortion, then, where there is an irreconcilable conflict between the interests of the fetus in utero and the reproductive rights of the pregnant woman, society has chosen to protect the woman.[18] But what would happen where, as is the case with IVF-created embryos, this real and physical conflict between pregnant woman and developing fetus did not exist? The current law would provide no legal status for these embryos. But should it? I will discuss this question later in this chapter, but first I want to look at the embryo research that is at the heart of our concern and on the leading edge of scientific discovery. It will revolutionize the future practice of medicine and change forever our treatment of human life.

Embryo Research: Cloning

For many of us, the word *cloning*[19] will always conjure up the image of Dolly, the Dorset ewe that made history in 1997.[20] Cloning has been tried since the 1930s and is a technology to contend with in the exciting years ahead.[21] Although even the mention of the word frightens us today, and its practice on humans is already banned in many countries,[22] it has been difficult to keep up with the reports of cloning experiments in the short period of time since Dolly. A year of animal cloning of sheep, mice,[23] calves,[24] and goats[25] was crowned by a report in December 1998 that South Korean doctors were trying to be the first to clone an adult woman by creating a genetic replica of her in embryo form.

For those among us not familiar with the science of cloning, it is important to remember that this is not a catch-all word with only one meaning. There are different types of cloning, all of which will be an integral part of medical-scientific research,[26] though each type raises a different level of ethical and legal concern.

The first type is called *molecular cloning*. It is used extensively in gene therapy, the development of drugs, vaccines, and genetic tests, and allows for pieces of DNA containing genes to be duplicated in a host bacterium. The second is *cellular cloning,* which we will look at more carefully in chapter 7, when we discuss patents on bioengineered higher life forms. This technology makes possible the creation of endless copies of cells — for example, sheets of skin for burn victims — and will be at the base of tissue engineering to make new body parts, such as ears and noses, and eventually whole organs and limbs. It is used extensively for medical research and therapies. The third is *embryo splitting,* where the embryo of an animal (or a human) is split in half to form identical twins. Already used extensively in cattle, this technology is being proposed for use on human IVF embryos in the future, for women who produce only a few good eggs for fertilization, or for couples with only a few embryos that can be frozen or used in an attempt at a pregnancy. It could also be used in pre-implantation diagnosis of IVF-created embryos: one of the identical embryos is analyzed for genetic anomalies and the others are frozen and stored while the couple wait to see if they are disease and disability-free and can be safely implanted. Embryo splitting would help couples unable to afford one or more cycles of IVF, a technology that is not covered by most provincial health insurance plans. This would save a couple from costly and physically taxing IVF cycles of drug therapy, egg retrieval, and implantation, for their embryos could be divided and frozen for future use. This technology also could offer a person a frozen living "insurance policy."[27] In this controversial practice, an IVF embryo could be split in half to create future twins. One can be implanted and the other frozen in case something goes wrong and the identical actualized child needs medical treatment such as a bone marrow transplant or a new kidney. In *nuclear somatic transfer* (NST), a fourth type of cloning, the nucleus of a cell from one animal or human is taken and placed in the egg of another individual.[28] In Dolly's case, the nuclei were frozen udder cells from an adult ewe. This is the technology that really frightens us: it is the one that Parliament should be focusing on in its legislation.[29] It could give women without ova (or any reproductive capacity if they use a surrogate), and men who cannot produce sperm, the chance to have a child identical to themselves. I am not sure it would be a good idea for parents to have a younger replica of themselves around, but we know that people will do anything to have children, especially ones that are genetically related. The greatest pressure for the use of this cloning technology will come, in the first instance, from people desperate to have genetically linked children. The potential market is huge, a fact not lost on at least two U.S. companies that are already working to clone human embryos — initially to provide embryos for research on stem cells.[30] These questions need discussion immediately, as stem cell research is not now controlled by the voluntary moratorium banning certain research.

Human Cloning[31]

While most of us find Dolly's birth an exciting, if somewhat troubling modern story, few of us would like to see human cloning.[32] The possibility of making sets of identical people repels many of us. But this reproductive cloning is only part of the purpose for exploring this technology further. At its most basic, cloning is about replication. Cellular cloning happens naturally in the body to create blood and muscle tissue. We are already using cloning methods to create human tissue such as skin and cartilage for the therapeutic treatment of burn, cancer, and accident victims. Future refinement and broader application of these cloning methods will provide a better life for millions of people. Many Canadians, for instance, die every year because of a critical shortage of donor hearts, kidneys, lungs, and other transplantable organs. What if we could actually build those organs from scratch, using our own cells and a perfected cloning technology? It is no secret that scientists are trying to do that right now.[33] Genetically engineered organs from animals such as pigs already provide parts for organ transplant and heart and other surgeries; and human tissue is regularly grown from the healthy cells of burn or accident victims. Using the patient's own cells to clone avoids rejection and a lifelong dependency on anti-rejection drugs. The options that these forms of cloning offer will greatly improve our lives in the future.

I believe that our real fear is not about *therapeutic cloning*, with all its medical promise, but about *reproductive cloning*, which would allow us to clone human embryos and, using adult cells, to create unmodified versions of ourselves.[34] Reproductive cloning is the type of cloning we need worry about as we draft laws to address embryo research. Nuclear somatic transfer technology allows us to work with these very early embryos, and the recent promising work in animals with this technology suggests that we are only a few years away from perfecting the technology for use in humans. In future, cloning of both human embryonic and adult cells may be commonplace and used for all kinds of laudable purposes: for reproduction, by the infertile and others in same-sex relationships who cannot reproduce any other way and would otherwise have to resort to donated sperm, eggs, or embryos; for medical therapy, by people who need bone marrow or other compatible tissue; or for genetic selection by those with a history of genetic disease who want a healthy child related to at least one of the partners. All these Canadians could benefit from these therapeutic cloning technologies.

Sometimes, though, we are so taken up with the technical that we forget the human implications of developing clones of ourselves or our loved ones. Try to imagine how you would feel if, having lost a beloved child in his teens, you were given the chance to clone him. Would you want him to live again in the body of another? Would the cloned child really be the child you lost or would he be a look-alike impostor? We are more than the sum total of our genes. We are also the product of our relationships and our environment. Try to imagine living with a constant physical reminder of a child you loved, replicated physically as that child, but without any of the experiences or the memories. And what would the cloned child's life be like?

Many people express personal reservations about cloning — of either human embryos or adult cells — and some refuse the technology under any circumstance. They consider it unnatural, an affront to human dignity, an attempt to play God, or a misuse of children as a means to a research or reproductive end. Some fear that we will take the perfect soldier and clone armies for dictators, or replicate the most violent criminal. Some don't want change, and fear that new family forms will be created if single women and men or same-sex couples reproduce by cloning themselves.[35] But whatever the reason, we need to remember that the word *cloning* has more than one meaning. The federal government's first attempt at banning these technologies under Bill C-47 made no allowance for the variety of purposes for which they can be used. I remember the look of surprise on committee members' faces when I first raised this concern in my presentation on the Bill. I noted how ironic it was that the type of cloning that brought us Dolly, and had triggered the introduction of Bill C-47 in the first place, would not even be covered by the proposed law, whereas other medical research on cloning would be prohibited. When we discuss this issue again in Parliament, we will have to be more careful to define what we want to ban and ensure that the beneficial applications of cloning technologies for future medical-scientific research are allowed and encouraged. How can we do this?

As a first step, we should prohibit the use of cloning technologies for human reproduction. This spectre could become reality within the next two years as a result of work in private laboratories in the United States.[36] We must move quickly ourselves and act also at the international level to ensure that humans are not cloned anywhere in the world. The other uses of cloning, for therapy and for organ and tissue development, should be encouraged. Their value to our future health and quality of life is undeniable. Finally, as we progress along this research road, we must ensure that our laws apply to *all* human embryo and adult-cell research, whether funded with public or private money.

The Tri-Council Rules on Human Embryo Research

But is that now the case? What rules currently apply to this kind of research in Canada? Are they strong enough to do the job without new legislation? Most research on human subjects is publicly funded and has required the approval of one of the three federal funding agencies in Canada.[37] With the amalgamation of the three major research agencies in Canada into a Tri-Council, a revised set of rules has been adopted to meet changing research realities, including the availability of human embryos for research.[38] These rules replace the former Canadian Medical Research Council[39] guidelines and the Social Sciences and Humanities Research Council guidelines for research on human subjects, and they complement the 1990 Medical Research Council's guidelines for somatic gene therapy research in humans. From a legal point of view the policy statement has real limitations: it applies only to research done with public money[40] and is not a legal document with set sanctions for non-compliance. It is, however, an influential ethical guide for researchers working with human subjects, and covers reproductive and genetic research involving gametes, embryos, and fetuses, which had not been the case under previous guidelines.[41] Although the creation of human embryos specifically for research is deemed to be ethically unacceptable, embryos created for reproduction can be used for research in the following situations: where the couple (or donors) have consented, where the research does not involve the genetic alteration of human gametes or embryos, where the embryos used for research are not later used for reproduction, and as long as the research takes place within the first fourteen days after their formation by the combination of gametes.[42] Research that serves a legitimate medical purpose is allowed, but ectogenesis — the cloning of human beings by any means including somatic cell nuclear transfer, the formation of animal-human hybrids, and the transfer of embryos between humans and other species — is not ethically acceptable.[43] Research involving manipulations of embryos that are not directed specifically to their ongoing normal development, such as the creation of a human-animal hybrid as a test for male fertility, is allowed provided the embryo is not intended for survival[44] or transfer to a woman's womb.[45]

These ethical guidelines are helpful as we draft new laws to deal with research on human embryos. But they depend on an approach that I believe we must question as we proceed to legislation. The foundation of the approach is the division of embryonic human development into narrow and specific developmental stages.[46] The result is the creation of an entirely new class of human life, generally called a *pre-embryo*,[47] which defines the stage from fertilization of the egg with sperm in vitro through to the end of the fourteenth day of development, when the primitive streak — the incipient spinal cord and future neural system — starts developing. Under current guidelines, these *pre-embryos* can be used for most research that can be shown to increase medical-scientific knowledge about the biology of human development, as long as they are not intended to survive. At this stage, these guidelines treat human life as no more than a mass of undifferentiated cells, and any limitation on research on the *pre-embryo* is to protect others and not the embryo itself.

My concern with the Tri-Council policy statement goes beyond the fact that it offers merely ethical guidelines, does not cover privately funded research, and carries no legal sanctions for failure to comply. What troubles me most is that it so readily endorses the international trend that treats human embryonic life as mere human tissue at its earliest and most precarious stage. Why is this trend prevalent now and why is there a need to establish a new and separate category of IVF-created human life? The answer seems clear — the need for embryos for research and the lure of spectacular future profits.[48]

In the first days after conception, embryo cells are totipotent — a source of an endless supply of stem cells. We want to do research on early human embryos to find out why they behave as they do: how and when an invisible signal commands them to take on the unique role of a lung, a kidney, or a brain cell. We want to know how a minuscule mass of undifferentiated cells can, within fourteen days of its creation, become the foundation for a human being. What is the source of these marching orders and how do the cells execute them? Why do some respond as they should, whereas others miss their cue or rebel? We want to know it all and to do this, we need very early human embryos for research.

What we learn will help us help others — the infertile, the disabled, and the sick. The answers will enable us to take charge of the programming ourselves and give directions to the totipotent[49] cells that make up early embryonic life. Scientists have already taken an adult cell and reverted it to its original totipotent state. When science masters the ability to direct the development of totipotent cells — and one way or another it will — we will have revolutionized the practice of medicine. We will be on our way to practices that allow us to make organs and body parts as needed, solving the organ donation problem in a way unheard of even a decade ago. Right now, embryo research is the new frontier and its possibilities are limitless.

In the light of what we know about embryo research, I am profoundly troubled by the Tri-Council's ethical guidelines. By defining early human embryonic life as *pre*-embryonic, they rob it of its already minimal legal status, reducing it in the public mind to no more than human tissue. They give legitimacy to arguments that legal protection for human life at its earliest embryonic stage should be reduced, not increased or even maintained. They lead to the possible legitimization of the view that these so-called *pre-embryos* are really not human embryos at all, but rather just human tissue — no potential arms, no brain, no beating heart — just a mere mass of undifferentiated human cells.[50] Science and ethics are moving this stage of life out of the continuum of human life completely. Enshrining that view in law would be just a short step away.

Failure to challenge this new notion that early IVF-created human life is just human tissue, a mere *pre-embryo*, is to condone the acceptance under the law of an entirely new category of human life. It will also open the doors to the treatment of early embryos as research *objects*, as they would no longer enjoy any protected status as human research *subjects*. There would then be little to prevent their treatment as commercial research "tools" that could be manufactured, bought, and sold. I believe that the narrow definitions these guidelines encourage will be inadequate to prepare us for the major challenges human embryo research raises. Instead, they will pave the way for more controversial research.

This view of early human life as mere human tissue should be challenged because it reduces the human continuum to no more than the sum of its developmental stages. It is as inadequate to help control possible abuse of IVF-created embryos as was the argument in the abortion context that fetal life is not really human life. Our choices in the abortion dilemma were limited by the fact that the embryo was developing within a woman's body. When the interests of the embryo and the woman were in conflict, the very physical limitation of the situation meant that only one of their interests could be satisfied and protected. That is not the case here. The dynamic has changed. With these new technologies we have the power to explore new options to protect human life at its earliest stages. We can now treat human life created by IVF outside the womb with greater care and provide it with more, not less, protection. Why would we want to do this? Precisely because what we are dealing with is human life.

We can now do all manner of extraordinary research on IVF-created embryos. But before we go the next step, we must state clearly that human embryonic life created through reproductive technologies will not be dismissed from the human family by a linguistic sleight of hand so that it can better serve the research needs of medicine and science. The question for legislators is how to do this. How can we place IVF-created human embryos within a zone of legal protection that spares them from abusive research, while simultaneously safeguarding women's reproductive rights in the context of contraception and abortion? This will be a very difficult task, but it is one that must be undertaken by all society and resolved as soon as possible.

Conclusion

Why is it important even to have this discussion? One reason is that science has already moved us irreversibly towards a new world of embryo research that requires public input and guidance from beyond its scientific and economic stakeholders. Embryo research is at the cutting edge of medicine and science. Reproductive research and technologies promise to help the infertile and the sterile have the children they so desperately want. And genetic technologies and research have pioneered new possibilities to detect and eventually correct genetic defects and disease. The image of overcoming the cruelty of disease and untimely death caused by accident or miscued genes is a seductive one. How could we fail to respond to it?

But it remains our responsibility as a society to determine the context within which these exciting developments will take place. Nowhere is that obligation more important than in our treatment of human life at its earliest stages. The value we place on human embryonic life will set the course for research in the years to come. It is, to my mind, one of the greatest challenges that awaits us in the new millennium. Science and medicine have given us the first opportunity to break the legal and political deadlock at the core of the abortion dilemma. Now we must move the agenda forward, using both law and technology as our tools. When I consider what lies ahead — from genetic enhancement to embryo cloning — I am convinced that we will need more than good will, a voluntary moratorium, or "ethical" research guidelines to protect human life in the future. We might have to accept, as in the abortion debate, that it will be impossible to achieve consensus. But we have not yet had a real public debate on these matters. The time to discuss and decide is here.

The federal health minister's commitment to legislation gives us the perfect opportunity to continue the public discussion begun a decade ago during the public hearings of the Royal Commission on New Reproductive Technologies. Many experts have been hired since then to offer their views to government on the legislative options before us. Their work was paid for by public money and their findings should now be available to the public free of charge. We need the information they have gathered to understand what is being proposed and going on in the field right now. Without it, Canadians will again be left out of the real decision-making. When the legislation to regulate human embryo research is introduced in Parliament, the federal government must commit the funds to bring Canadians to Ottawa or allow the full Parliamentary Committee on Health to travel across the country to learn how Canadians wish to regulate this research. The process followed in debating Bill C-47 was closed and limited. It must not be repeated. Open, inclusive, and informed involvement by all interested Canadians should be ensured.

We still have time to decide what we want to allow and what we choose to prohibit in embryo research. We should not be tempted to put off this essential decision-making because scientists do not yet have the technical expertise to perfect this research. When I served as a member of the Royal Commission on New Reproductive Technologies, the original majority insisted that it was precisely because most reproductive and genetic technologies were not yet perfected that we had a public responsibility to investigate their future direction and impact. Even though we were not successful in our plea at that time, we still have a chance to do so now. We must use the little window of opportunity remaining, before all these technologies and practices are locked into place, to have a large public discussion about our values and our choices. For the lesson is clear. What science can do, it will try. That is science's strength and mandate. We cannot now turn back the clock. We can, though, take charge of the public policy process that will set the rules for embryo research in the future.

Commercialization

In Part One we saw the power of reproductive technologies to create, genetically manipulate, and alter human life in the laboratory. In Part Two we will look at how genetic technologies, including genetic testing, raise the promise of cures to disease and fears both about discrimination on the basis of disability and invasions of personal privacy as the human genome is revealed and genetic engineering technologies are perfected.

Into this mix come the controversial issues raised by the commercialization of research and the patenting of life forms. Should the human body, its parts, and processes be treated as *property?* Can they be patented, bought, and sold like any other product on the market? Is a human embryo really no different than any other object, such as a table or a car, which we can own and dispose of at will?

Finally, biotechnology is one of the engines that will provide future economic growth to Canada's agricultural, food, and drug sectors. How can we ensure the safety of our food supply and earn the public's trust in genetically modified foods? How can we make the voices of concerned Canadians heard in all these decisions? Part Two tackles some of these questions.

Chapter Five

Knowing Ourselves, Protecting Our Rights

I t seems fantastic to most of us that a single drop of our blood or saliva, a skin cell, or a strand of our hair will reveal our genetic history.[1] Almost every cell contains genetic information about each person's entire being and carries an identical set of the body's thousands of genes. This pattern is contained in the DNA (deoxyribonucleic acid), the basic bearer of information in the body that is found in the nucleus of all cells. The *genome* is all the DNA, organized in chromosomes, in any living organism, from a bacterium to a human. The study of the human genome, then, is the study of DNA. The double-stranded DNA molecule is shaped like a ladder, with the base pairs the rungs and the sugar-phosphate molecules the rails, all twisted tightly to form a "double helix," or spiral. DNA is like a language and, as in any language, only some combinations or sequences have meaning. About 90 percent of our DNA does not contain meaningful "sentences."

The fact that the meaningful sentences are sandwiched among all this DNA makes their decoding a long and difficult task. A gene is a unit of information found within each cell of our body which contains the recipe for making our cells and doing the work that goes on in them. Through our genes, we pass on to our children traits that are both personal (our mother's eyes or our grandfather's nose) and universal (a brain, heart, lungs, and other major organs). A gene is like a sentence, complete with proper punctuation, that the cell can read and understand. In an organism as complex as a human there are hundreds of thousands of genes — somewhere between 50,000 and 100,000 — all of which contain a still unknown number of bases (distinct chemical ingredients) inside them. All DNA is read, or decoded, in the same way: while different organisms can have different sets of genes, they are all written in a type of universal code. Identifying each and every gene, its unique place within the genome and its role, is the task of the largest project scientists have ever undertaken: the Human Genome Project.

The Human Genome Project

The Human Genome Project, a multibillion-dollar international science endeavour, promises to identify the role and sequencing of all our genes.[2] Canada is one of eighteen countries working on this project to "map the human genome."[3] With the information they learn, scientists hope to improve the diagnosis and treatment of diseases and conditions that are caused by genetic factors.[4] In essence, these problems are caused by mutations, or small changes to our genes, which can be introduced into a DNA sequence by accident (radiation), design (pollution), or heredity (copied from a parent to child). These mutations can change the DNA sequence from its normal state, and thus affect the way a gene reads. Using a language analogy, they alter an otherwise normal sentence, giving a different message or making the sentence unreadable.

Of course, identifying each gene and its role through the Human Genome Project is just the beginning of the possibilities for science and medicine. The long-term goal is to use this information, along with new DNA diagnostic and genetic engineering technologies, to detect, turn off, cure, or replace defective genes with healthy ones.[5] We can already manipulate genes to some extent, thanks to different technologies. As we will see in the chapter on genetically engineered food, we can modify plant genes by inserting human genes into them. We can also insert human genes into animals, so they can be used as living laboratories for the production of drugs for human consumption, or their body parts used for human transplants. Canada is an active partner in the research projects of the Human Genome Project, though significant changes have been proposed in the way health research will be funded in Canada, and the existing model will be replaced in 2000 by one similar to the National Institutes of Health in the United States.[6] The first gene-sequencing centre in Canada was established in Vancouver, headed by Nobel Prize laureate Dr. Michael Smith of the University of British Columbia. Researchers there work in three main areas of DNA research: computer-generated data, mapping, cloning and sequencing, and collaborating with laboratories in France, Germany, and the United Kingdom to help identify the cell changes that lead to cancers.[7] Other research efforts include the identification and sequencing of polymorphins in human genes at the Montreal General Hospital and the identification and mapping of the seventh chromosome at the Hospital for Sick Children in Toronto.

Heredity: Genes and Discrimination

Genetic technologies give those who control them great power and those with access to them great opportunity. But what they identify and collect are some of our most personal secrets. They tell us what gene has rebelled or might terrorize or kill us. It does not matter that the predictive value of some of these genetic tests is still shaky. People are not concerned about degrees of illness: in the mind of the affected person, the boss, or the government, they have a genetic disease. In the case of late onset diseases like Alzheimer's or Duchenne's Muscular Dystrophy, for instance, genetic tests create a class of "healthy sick" — people who look well, but either might, or will, become sick as they age. Some diseases and conditions run in families: in the case of breast cancer genes, for instance, if your sister or mother has the gene, there is a strong possibility you may too. What if you do not want to be tested? Can you simply walk away from the information? Will others let you? What do you write on your application form for a mortgage or for life insurance? What lessons have we learned from the HIV experience?

The power to access this personal genetic information could lead to serious discrimination and have a negative impact on both our lives and our legal rights.[8] The question is not whether we will choose to use genetic technologies, but how they might be used against us. That is why there has been so much discussion, for example, on whether there should be broad population genetic screening or whether it should be limited to people whose family histories show they are, or might be, at risk for a known genetic anomaly. After much debate, doctors agreed in 1996 that testing should be limited not just to people whose family history has shown they may carry a genetic anomaly, but to those with genetic anomalies that can be treated or cured.[9] Yet, studies have shown that most people want to know such information even when there is no known treatment or cure, so they can prepare for the worst or, if the news is positive, get on with their lives.[10] The general rule of "no cure, no test" is not carved in stone, and testing is carried out on both a case-by-case basis and in targeted research projects. One current example involves testing for the breast cancer gene, where the only option at present is radical surgery. In most of these genetic anomalies, treatment and cure are still tomorrow's promise. In the meantime, we are grappling with the many issues that access to this extremely sensitive medical information raises.

A major, and as of yet unaddressed, consideration will be the cost of all these genetic tests to the health care system. Ontario women from families with a strong history of breast cancer have won the right to have tests paid for by the provincial health insurance scheme. The test costs almost $4,000 and is available only in Utah. Multiply this figure by even 50,000 genes and the impact of genetic testing on health care priorities and funding becomes clear. We need to bring this question out into the open and decide how to proceed. Otherwise, these decisions will be made by appointed tribunals and judges.

Genetic Testing

Genetic testing is a generic term for a process that gives us information about a person which can be used in different ways. Canada's privacy commissioner divided it into three categories: genetic screening, genetic monitoring, and forensic DNA analysis.[11] In the first two, testing identifies a person as having or being susceptible to a genetic disease or condition. In the third, scientists can identify someone for criminal investigation, paternity, or other identification purposes, such as in plane crashes or fires. The problem is that being *susceptible* to a disease is not the same as *having* it, nor can tests predict the degree of disability or the intensity of the disease. Critics of the widespread use of these technologies argue that the potential for discrimination and violations of individual and family privacy make genetic testing one of the most significant threats ever to our freedom.[12]

Over the past two decades, our wealthiest societies have been obsessed with profit and globalization. The effect of this emphasis on commerce can be seen in the Human Genome Project, where the race is no longer to *map* the human genome but to *own* it.[13] Notions of equity and collective responsibility now come second to those of profit and individual rights. Western culture has confused the mandate of commerce, which is profit, with that of government, which is people, and the result is a broadening of the reach and role of commerce in this medical-scientific project. We urgently need to extend existing laws to meet these changing realities in genetic research and to introduce new laws, where needed, to protect us from these new intrusions into our lives.[14]

Genetic testing in its various forms is different from other tools of possible discrimination.[15] It is about information that might set us apart from the mainstream and forecast ill health or death; that might send us into a kind of social and medical limbo; and, because it is about heredity, that often condemns those we love to a similar fate. The failure to introduce strict rules to protect us from genetic discrimination, laws to protect us from certain uses of genetic information in our medical records, or laws to prohibit patents on human life forms raises doubts about whose agenda matters most to governments. Genetic testing is of concern, first, because people in positions of authority and power can have access to sensitive and all-important information about us and, second, because it is always difficult to rally public support for complex issues.

Political trends in North America seem to indicate a growing acceptance of eugenic and racist tendencies, which respond well to arguments of cost efficiency and limits on the sharing of resources. Technologies such as genetic testing allow us to see who is healthy and who is not. As resources become scarcer and more limited because of actual shortages or poor public-sector fiscal management and deliberate budget cutbacks, more and more of what used to be public enterprise in Canada — health care and education, for instance — will move to the private sector, where we can expect the demand for genetic testing to continue and increase. The notion that our destiny is in our genes is just now being articulated. We need to demand that before it becomes the norm, our human rights and privacy laws be amended to protect all of us from the many discriminations that this information can create.

In Health Care

Genetic testing takes many different forms in health care. In reproduction, the new pre-implantation diagnosis technology allows us to check the cells of IVF-created embryos for known genetic anomalies[16] and to implant only the healthy ones. In pre-natal diagnosis, we can determine the same results for the fetus in utero. At birth, certain tests are performed on the newborn to check for diseases, some of which we can cure or treat through medication or diet. But in all these cases, the information we learn has an impact beyond the embryo, fetus, or child. The same applies to genetic tests for the other conditions for which we can now screen. Genetics is about the study of heredity, and the information from these tests concerns some members of every affected family, usually at random. This genetic Russian roulette puts real strains on relationships among people whose support is needed at this crisis point in a person's life. If this information is an issue now, think what it will mean when the human genome is mapped and we know the place and purpose of every gene and which ones are healthy and which are not.

In the Workplace

In his report on genetic testing and privacy in 1992, the federal privacy commissioner found that there was little genetic testing in the workplace.[17] That is good news, but in the early 1990s, when this report was published, the cost of genetic testing was high and the number of tests was limited. In the coming years, genetic testing in the workplace will increase, not just because the technology will be there, but because in a world where cutting costs is one of the key ways to remain competitive, worker performance will be more tightly monitored. Yet no one usually knows how much genetic information — especially from blood samples — is already stored on Canadians and who has access to it or control over its use. As a prelude to legislation, I recommend that the three main partners in the Canadian economy — labour, business, and government — investigate separate and collective options to solve these threats to individual rights. The recommendations of the privacy commissioner in his report provide one starting point. We need to know what genetic samples have been taken and from which individuals and groups; the extent of the existing collections and their use and purpose; and the kind of privacy protection that was in place both at the time of collection and now. This information will give us a good idea of the extent of the existing problem and the kinds of safeguards we need to include in our legislation. This can then be addressed either as an amendment to existing laws or as a new one that covers all issues involved in *genetic* testing and discrimination in both the private and public sectors.

In Life and Health Insurance

One potential source of real discrimination is the insurance industry.[18] Because I could find nothing in my research about the Canadian situation, I contacted the Canadian Life and Health Insurance Association in Toronto and presented a list of questions, the answers to which I have included in the notes.[19] In response to my question about the policy of the industry towards the collection and use of genetic information, I was told that an insurer would not require an applicant to undergo a genetic test. If one had already been done, however, access to the results would be requested, just as with any other health history. The information would be sought only with the applicant's consent, but refusal could lead the insurer to refuse the application. Genetic information is considered relevant to the granting of insurance, and failure to disclose it would make the contract voidable at the option of the insurer.

The insurance industry argues that a comparison between proposed U.S. legislation and the Canadian situation should be avoided, since the systems of health insurance in the two countries are completely different. At present, personal and medical information about an applicant or an insured is not shared with anyone without the consent of the person involved. Legislation to protect personal privacy at both the federal and the provincial levels would be welcome as long as it respects the insurance industry's particular needs to have access to all of an applicant's health information relevant to its decision-making, including genetic information. The industry is not advocating any change in existing laws governing genetic information for use in a commercial context in the private sector. However, should there be changes, they would have to be harmonized across the country and not added to the insurer's administration costs. According to the industry, consumers would probably suffer reduced services, both existing and in the future, if legislation limiting access to genetic information were introduced for the private insurance sector.

Privacy

The Protection of Personal Information in the Private Sector

The more we read about genetics and testing, the more we understand the need for strict laws to protect personal information about Canadians. There is no right to privacy under the *Canadian Charter of Rights and Freedoms* and the Privacy Acts cover only the public sector. Quebec is the only jurisdiction in North America that protects the collection and use of personal information in the private sector.[20] We desperately need new laws to recognize the novel ways technology can now invade the personal privacy of Canadians. These laws must guarantee our genetic privacy and prevent discrimination in both the private and the public sectors. The practices of genetic testing can be abused in several ways. It can be abused when researchers take samples of genetic material — blood, saliva, hair, skin, nails — from people with certain racial or health backgrounds without their consent or even without their knowledge. This has happened with some indigenous peoples in Latin America, and the genetic samples are then shared with, or sold to, other researchers in laboratories around the world. The genes are exploited for profit, often patented, and therefore legally owned by these researchers and their funding agencies, without the knowledge of the providers, who rarely share in any way in the profits of that exploitation.

In other scenarios, companies can have their own staff doctor or nurse remove blood for certain tests related to an employee's health. Other testing can also be done using these samples. Under the guise of convenience for a client, an insurance company can have a staff nurse withdraw a blood sample for testing. The resulting information could not only disqualify the person who gave the blood sample but, where a genetic disease that runs in families is discovered, his other family members too. In these cases, the laws that protect information between doctors and patients do not apply, and control of the sample rests with the company. When the human genome is mapped within the next three years, a blood sample will reveal a person's entire genetic story — good and bad. Clear and enforceable laws that identify who can demand genetic samples, for what purposes, and under what conditions must be introduced and discussed by politicians and the public now.

In October 1998, the federal government introduced legislation to protect personal information in the private sector as part of its Canadian Electronic Commerce Strategy.[21] The proposed law was to respond to similar privacy initiatives introduced in the European Union's *1995 Directive on Data Protection*. This directive prohibits member countries from transferring personal information on any of its citizens to a non-member country or to a business located there, unless it, too, guards against the misuse of personal information in the private sector. In spite of its sometimes contradictory objectives of securing privacy protection for our personal information while ensuring businesses and government departments seeking access to such information a right to do so, the proposed law, as originally drafted, could have provided a good starting point for public discussion.[22] Right now in Canada, a voluntary, private-sector privacy code is in place. It was developed under the auspices of the Canadian Standards Association three years ago and is known as the Model Code for the Protection of Personal Information. The federal government's Bill C-54 incorporates this Model Code with its ten privacy protection principles in Schedule 1, where many of the substantive provisions of the Bill are found. When passed by Parliament, the law will apply to all private commercial organizations and government departments that collect, use, or disclose personal information on Canadians for commercial purposes. The Bill originally defined "personal information" as meaning "information about an identifiable individual that is recorded in any form." Protection was severely curtailed by an amendment in Committee to eliminate the phrase "that is recorded in any form." The result will be to broaden the scope of "personal information" to include information that was not in any recorded form, such as DNA or blood samples, for instance. This is a key concern that must be addressed before Parliament votes on the Bill later in 1999.

Setting aside the question of whether sensitive information can ever be safe, once collected and stored electronically, the real debate is about what kind of personal information we really need to collect and store on each Canadian. In a health care setting, most information will be governed by provincial health or medical information laws. Certainly, information that will benefit us, such as our allergies to certain drugs, or previous illnesses, should reasonably be stored and available to doctors who treat us. In an emergency, the speed of retrieval of this information can make the difference between life and death. But what about sensitive genetic information that shows we are merely *predisposed* to a condition? Should that be kept in the same place as our other medical information or should it be kept in a more secure file, with access only after our consent in each case? We can suffer discrimination because of our genetic health, and I believe this information must be treated differently from other personal medical information. One exception might be where the health and safety of health care workers would be affected by our illness. In these cases, they have a right to know so they can protect themselves from harm. At present, most genetic conditions cannot be cured or changed. This fact alone should urge caution when it comes to the collection, use, and disclosure of personal genetic information. The onus for such activities, the provision for exemptions, and the right of access need to be strictly enforced.

Proposals for Change

Existing privacy laws cover our relationship with the federal government, but not the private sector, which increasingly collects information on our health and habits through a variety of sources. What amendments should we make to ensure that our genetic information is protected? First, at the very least, we should know what genetic information has been collected about us and for what purpose. Given the nature of the information and the real threat to our rights and well-being of its disclosure to such sources as insurance companies, banks, universities, and employers, we must be certain that this sensitive genetic information is within our total control. In terms of technical safeguards, this information must be separate from our regular medical records, for instance, and accessible only on a "need to know" basis. In keeping with our current trend towards patient autonomy, we must have complete authority over who has access and for what purposes. To deal with emergency situations, we should be required to designate a doctor or layperson to whom access is granted for our own benefit in terms of care. Each time someone wishes to access any of our genetic files, we must have the right to be notified, in writing, of the person's name and the purpose of the request for access. In the best of worlds, we should also have the power to refuse access, and computer technology may make that possible. In the meantime, we must be assured that, if we seek genetic testing, or if we or our newborns undergo this kind of testing, we will also maintain control over the resulting information. All provincial privacy legislation needs to be amended so that this principle is clear and enforceable.

Science may, in the future, be able to cure many genetic diseases and conditions. For most Canadians, that cannot happen too soon. In the meantime, we need to be realistic and appreciate the problems that discrimination on the basis of genetic predisposition could cause each of us: in getting health and life insurance, mortgages, or loans; in keeping our jobs; in receiving education and other public services; in just living our lives. Legislation to protect our genetic privacy under federal and provincial human rights laws is one place to start. Each of us can take part in this debate and argue directly to our members of Parliament for these changes. What we want is to provide all Canadians with protection from genetic discrimination and to ensure privacy and control over crucial personal information.

Chapter Six

Biotechnology: Looking to the Future

W e saw in previous chapters that genetic technologies, used alone or with reproductive technologies and practices, raise many legal issues. In this chapter we will move into another area where genetic technologies are flourishing — as a breeding and species enhancement tool for plant and animal life. We will look at the agricultural sector, where tough choices must be made to balance the needs of Canadian trade, new job opportunities, and commercial and research opportunities with the increasing public demands for a safe food supply and the guarantee that genetically engineered plants and animals will not harm our health and our environment.[1]

Biotechnology[2] will have a significant impact on the world's future food and drug supplies.[3] It uses genetic engineering technologies to enhance living organisms or to transform all or part of these organisms into something different. It is a modern-day breeding tool with great promise and is used to breed enhanced or new types of animals and plants. Genetic engineering can also be used for the same or similar purposes in humans, although that application remains controversial and has been criticized as a new eugenics tool.[4] The genetic engineering process is also referred to as gene splicing and recombinant DNA technology. It alters the basic genetic make-up of a particular plant or animal by transferring specific genetic material — often across species — from one organism to another.[5]

Why would we want to do this? In seeds and plants we want to increase their resistance to blight and disease and to enhance their appearance, nutritional value, and availability.[6] Take a tomato known as the "Flavr Savr" as an example.[7] It remains firm in shipment[8] even though genetic engineering means the farmer can let it stay an extra five days ripening on the vine. If gardeners are worried that an early frost will spoil their plants, they may be interested to know that scientists have tried (unsuccessfully so far) to solve the problem for tomatoes by genetically engineering them with a flounder fish gene, aptly called the "anti-freeze gene."[9] In the summer of 1999 tobacco plants genetically engineered to include human genes that manufacture a protein called Interleukin-10 were planted in a federal test plot in Canada. The hope is to manufacture medicines more cheaply in the future by using plants, and not just animals, to produce human proteins.[10] In animals we deliberately alter their genetic make-up, for instance by inserting human genes into pigs so that their parts and organs can be used for transplant into humans. Sheep and pigs produce valuable drugs for us in their milk, and genetically modified mice are bred to develop specific cancers for research.

In other research, a Canadian company[11] has put a completely artificial chromosome into mice embryos, giving them an extra chromosome that is then passed on to future generations. In traditional gene therapy, only small segments of DNA are added to the animal embryo. This research will allow us to more effectively produce proteins for human drugs in animal milk (such as cows and pigs) and can provide a way to actually deliver these drugs directly into a sick person's body. It can also provide a way to insert healthy chromosomes into a person suffering from a hereditary genetic condition. Can human germ-line research be far behind?

Biotechnology is already a part of our lives and can help us improve our quality of life and health. But this is just the beginning. Research now under way, for example, will use genetic engineering techniques to revolutionize how we deliver medical vaccines both at home and in developing countries. We are not just developing new drugs but novel ways to deliver them. Biotechnology is working on a first generation of "nutriceuticals" — vaccines and other drugs that are carried in basic foods that have been genetically engineered to deliver nutrition and medicine in the same bite. A genetically engineered potato can trigger immune responses to a bacterium that is the leading cause of life-threatening diarrhea in infants in developing countries and also a curse to travellers.[12] The plan now is to grow bananas to provide the same vaccine.[13] In other research, soya beans are being genetically engineered to protect against venereal disease; corn to deliver drugs against certain cancers; and tobacco to produce an antibacterial mouthwash that prevents tooth decay.[14] Nutriceuticals will revolutionize public health in many countries of the developing world, where poverty, isolation, and primitive transportation conspire with the lack of basic vaccination tools such as needles and refrigeration to leave people vulnerable to fatal bacteria and diseases. I remember vividly a meeting in Cameroon with nurses working with the late Cardinal Léger in his hospital for child polio victims. In tears, they told us of how they had pleaded in vain with a local airport official to let them transfer a Canadian gift of 40,000 vials of polio vaccine to a refrigerated truck to prevent it from spoiling in the oppressive summer heat. Precedents already exist for using food to enhance public health. In North America we fortify milk and, in the United States, orange juice, with vitamin D and calcium to help protect our bodies against the ravages of osteoporosis. Salt is iodized to eliminate goiter and cretinism, and flour and many cereals are enriched with vitamins and minerals to help us stay healthy. Nutriceuticals are yet another way to use new genetic engineering techniques to help reduce or eliminate preventable diseases. But this new process can have other social and cultural benefits, too. In most of the developing world, women grow and prepare the food their families and communities eat. Both public and private funds for public education, especially for female farmers, should accompany the introduction of these future nutriceutical foods to the developing world. This knowledge will help them maintain real control over both the food source and the local medical system, as they grow and distribute vital food nutrients, medicines, and vaccines for their families and communities. Patents on indigenous seeds and plants have had a negative impact on women and other small farmers in some developing countries. But if we are successful in finding a different legal property right that gives "ownership" to the community, rather than an individual, private corporation, or government, we will provide real economic power and opportunity to women in these countries. This is one important way that women can share in the benefits, which biotechnology promises, to help meet the world's food and health needs in the future.

Expressions of Concern

Despite its promise of future health benefits and a secure source of food and medicines, biotechnology remains controversial. In a larger sense, that is understandable. Genetic engineering of the earth's plant, animal, and human organisms reaches to the core of the natural order. It asks us to accept not just products and foods that have been genetically modified but to buy into an entirely new and unknown science. To society, this adventure is both exciting and threatening: exciting because it bears the promise of a guaranteed nutritious food supply and a new way to tackle battles against prevalent and often fatal diseases; threatening because it redefines the natural order and has created an entirely new source of economic power and control. We will deal with the critical source of that new weapon of control in chapter 7, on patents. For now, what are some of the issues raised by genetically engineered foods?

Critics of genetically modified or transgenic foods claim that there is insufficient evidence to confirm that these products will not endanger human health. They insist that the burden of proof must be met by the companies that claim they are safe, and that the evidence must include long-term follow-up health studies. This demand for stringent legislated standards backed up with sanctions, as opposed to voluntary standards set by industry, is a real stumbling block in establishing an effective process for the regulation of genetically modified foods. Class action suits for products that have injured the public are still a legal recourse, but they are expensive, take years to resolve, and are difficult to enforce. Class actions have helped in cases like breast implants, for instance, but food is not a discretionary item. Any real strategy for rules governing genetically modified foods must include a mechanism for assessment of their impact on our long-term health and a method for compensating those who suffer harm as a result of their use. These components are part of the cost of doing business and the responsibility of companies using biotechnology.

A second area where action is required involves labelling and advance notice of the introduction of genetically modified foods into our stores, where concerned consumers want clear information about genetically modified foods. Many people have become more vigilant about the food they eat and worry about the safety of the food supply, be it salmonella poisoning at a local restaurant, the fiasco of the "mad cow" disease in Britain, or dioxin scares in some European countries.[15] We assume that regulatory bodies within Health and Agriculture Canada are looking after our interests and we rely on the expertise and independence of their scientists to keep our food and drug supplies safe. Most of us consider a safe and secure food supply as our right. In the coming years, new technologies will set an even larger challenge, as we deal with genetically engineered foods.[16] Already, nearly 60 percent of the food in our stores is genetically modified, a fact lost on most Canadian consumers. Labelling of these products is essential and must be mandatory, though identification is not enough. We also have to know when genetically modified foods are coming to market. Advance notice of the introduction of any transgenic food into the marketplace must be mandatory. If the food product is safe and tasty, such advance notice can serve as an introduction to a new food option to the consumer. Most of us readily buy new food items, and are only suspicious when it appears we are being misled about their nutritional value, contents, or safety. The United States is the only country to categorically refuse these two measures, but the arguments about public health and safety remain. In Canada, in response to consumer pressure and its own leadership, the grocery industry has advised that it will consider labelling all genetically engineered foods sold in stores.

Why should we require advance notice and specific labelling of all transgenic and genetically modified foods? First, there are real health concerns, such as allergic reactions to certain added genes (for example, peanuts); increased resistance to antibiotics, especially in meats; and toxicity due to pesticide-resistant plants. Second, there is fear of an unexpected and harmful genetic expression among humans who eat these foods.[17] Third, there is real concern over threatened environmental damage caused when new genetically engineered plants or animals breed with others in the wild to create "super organisms," such as weeds resistant to all pesticides.[18] A final concern is the failure to respect the firmly held cultural and dietary concerns of certain religious groups and of vegetarians, who refuse to eat meat or foods with human or animal genes genetically engineered into them. Labelling and advance notice gives them the opportunity to avoid such genetically modified foodstuffs.

Deep cuts in public funding for research have meant that interested private corporations fund ever more research in the biotechnology sectors. Generally speaking, public-private partnerships can work to the advantage of our universities,[19] but they can also alter power relationships and research agendas. We must be vigilant to their impact on the research and other priorities these institutions are publicly mandated to serve. Two concerns in particular are worth monitoring: the potential for real conflicts of interest and the limitation of academic freedom that can come with such financial control of research agendas.[20]

In a time of increasing cynicism, when many Canadians worry that their interests about health issues are not taken as seriously as they should be, any refusal to label or warn of the introduction of transgenic foods further erodes public trust. For the biotechnology sector, this scepticism is a real problem. How the industry responds to consumers' fears will determine whether transgenic foods and genetically modified products are accepted or rejected for years to come. Biotechnology, especially in the agricultural and pharmaceutical sectors, is important to Canada's future economic prosperity, competitiveness, and international research status, and to the creation of highly skilled and well-paid jobs.[21] Aggressive policies to achieve these goals are welcome, but government and industry must realize they are not the only international goals Canadians want met.

Canada has a proud history in international development, and, to maintain this important reputation, we must consider the needs of both commerce and sustainable development. Our international track record puts Canada in a unique leadership position. Our dual commitment to economic growth and biotechnology research on the one hand and the protection of human and community rights on the other gives us moral authority. We must be willing to use this hard-earned reputation to advantage in international forums where these matters are discussed and we must be realistic about what is happening in biotechnology. The jury is still out, for instance, on whether the issue of feeding the world's people is really about increased food production or a fairer system of food distribution among the haves and the have nots. The questions that the genetic engineering of plants and foodstuffs raises are both technical (such as labelling) and legal (such as the ownership of seeds and the right to alter them, as in terminator genes, against the community's interests).

Biotech companies ask us to endorse a technology that remains a work in progress, but which touches us in the most direct way through the food we eat each day. At this basic level the public must play a larger role in shaping the future of biotechnology in Canada. Public trust is important to the forward progress of biotechnology in all sectors, but it is essential in the food sector. If North American consumers refuse to eat certain genetically engineered fruits, vegetables, and animal foods, the industry will lose one of its most affluent and influential markets.[22]

International Biosafety Regulations

Biotechnology, and its potential repercussions on both sustainable development and world trade, are matters of international concern. They force trading countries with large agricultural and pharmaceutical interests to make tough choices. Canada is no exception. Its dual role as a world trading nation and a proponent of greater influence and affluence for developing countries is not always in balance. Canada's decision in February 1999 to support the suspension until May 2000 of the international conference called to regulate the trade of genetically engineered foods is but one example of the decisions we face as we try to balance our commitments to international trade with those of human rights and economic justice. At the meeting in Cartagena, Colombia, to discuss the risks that biotechnology may pose to biological diversity and human health, Canada stood with the United States and a few other large agriculture exporters against more than one hundred other countries to argue that the scope of the proposed international *Biosafety Protocol* would result in an unacceptable restriction on international trade.[23] This decision left us all without the protections and the enforcement mechanisms that the adoption of the *Protocol* was supposed to achieve. At present, most of the developing countries are powerless to prevent the introduction of genetically modified organisms into their environment. They have no recourse against any deliberate or accidental release of genetically engineered seeds or plants into their territory. Such uncontrolled releases could wreak havoc on native ecological systems and on animal and human health.

There are several issues that must be dealt with urgently. What, for instance, does the term *burden of proof* mean? Who is financially responsible when novel plants breed with local ones in the wild and create ecological chaos? The *Biosafety Protocol* would have adopted the "precautionary principle" as the basis in deciding whether an importing country could reject a genetically modified organism. This reverse onus–type rule would allow a country to reject imports when there was insufficient evidence to show that a genetically modified or other related product was safe. The protocol is supported by most European countries, which have become more vigilant towards agricultural imports in the wake of the devastation caused by "mad cow" disease. Europeans in general now tend to be cautious about genetically modified foods. International trade in these products has become uncertain, and there is real potential for special-interest manipulation for political purposes. The United States and its supporters reject the principle not only for these reasons, however, but because they champion a different standard, referred to as "substantial equivalence." If it looks like a duck, walks and quacks like a duck, the reasoning goes, then it is a duck, even though on the inside it may be genetically engineered to be something new and quite different. In terms of food, animals, and plants, the justification is that where these genetically modified living organisms look the same as the original one and deliver a substantially similar foodstuff or animal in terms of look, nutrition, and substance, then all genetic modification and the content of the new product are irrelevant.

Why would the United States adopt this policy? It has a specific agenda, which permeates its entire policy on biotechnology. It intends to dominate the biotechnology sector worldwide and to ensure for its companies the major share of the enormous profits that the exploitation of biotechnology has promised. Success in this field is also Canada's goal. But most Canadians do not want it purchased at any cost. Critics argue that the failure to adopt the key recommendations of the *Biosafety Protocol* will serve only to cement the dominance of the American point of view and weaken the resolve of other countries, whose economies must depend on U.S. investment especially in the agricultural and biotechnology sectors.

The issue of international trade in genetically modified organisms and foods has several facets. Political and legal issues, for example, are raised by the right to patent seeds and plants, and even human genes, and by the recent decisions by international biotechnology giants to develop "terminator seeds," which have been genetically engineered not to reproduce themselves. Ironically, many of the seeds that have been genetically engineered originally "belonged" to the small and subsistence farmers who must now rely on multinational biotechnology companies for the seeds to grow crops to feed their families and ensure the life of their rural communities in developing countries.

As we will see in chapter 7 on commercialization and patents on living organisms, there is growing controversy about the use of the legal tool of patents to grant "ownership," in the proprietary sense, to higher life forms, including organisms like plants, animals, and human life. If we plan to encourage the development and sale of (transgenic) foods genetically modified for consumption, and as carriers of added nutrition and medicines, then community as well as corporate commercial interests must be factored into all the public policy decisions we take and also reflected in the laws and regulations we adopt.

Food Biotechnology: The American Response

The United States has focused its public policies in the biotechnology sector very narrowly on corporate interests. To date, the industry's successful argument to the Clinton administration that "biologically engineered foods" are the same as "natural" foods has saved these products from regulatory controls.[24] The United States refuses to require the labelling of genetically engineered foods and demands that other countries accept all such products without question.[25] Biotechnology companies decide what "relevant" information to release to the public, and, using corporate law rules as defence, argue that any further publication would adversely affect their business. This policy directly opposes previous laws that were passed to guarantee the consumer's right to know what was in food.[26]

Companies are not required to advise the public when new genetically modified food products are introduced into the marketplace, nor must they label food as being genetically altered and in what manner. Groups challenging this non-labelling decision argue that it affects them in four main areas: the First Amendment right to free speech and the consumer's right to know; public health and safety, especially for foods that can cause allergies; religious rights not to be forced unknowingly to violate dietary rules; and individual rights not to be forced to eat certain foods, such as meat.[27] Arguing that few meaningful efforts have been made to involve the public in how, or even if, agricultural and food biotechnologies should be developed, these groups demand the public registration of all new genetically modified food products to give effect to the consumer's legal right to know; the labelling of all such foods to give consumers the information they need to make an informed decision about a product's use; and testing of all such foods to prove they are safe for human consumption.[28] In my view, Canada should not follow this example. We need clear, transparent, and open systems to provide accurate scientific evidence about the safety and content of all genetically engineered foodstuffs and animals. Only then should we accept them and encourage others to do likewise.

Making Government Regulators Accountable

If we needed an example of why transparency and openness are essential to guarantee the public's trust and acceptance of new genetically modified foods and products, we have only to examine the saga of bovine growth hormone. Also known as recombinant bovine somatotropin, or rBST, this non-therapeutic drug is produced by genetic engineering and is supposed to increase milk production significantly in dairy cattle. Its long-term effects on both human and animal life are unknown, yet the U.S. federal Department of Agriculture approved its use in 1993.[29] From the time of the first application to Health Canada in 1990 for approval, controversy surrounded the hormone. On 19 January 1999, Health Canada finally announced that rBST would not be approved, but the events preceding its decision left many Canadians wondering whose interests were being served by their government when genetically engineered drugs were being evaluated for approval.

The first sign that something was not right occurred when Health Canada scientists broke an enforced silence and went public to allege irregularities in the way rBST was being treated in the required approval process. To stem criticism, Health Canada appointed an internal team to review rBST. Their report — called the "Gaps Report" — chronicled a story of missing files and insufficient scientific evidence, as one of the world's largest biotechnical companies sought to have this controversial drug approved for use in Canada. By then, Parliament had also become involved, and the Senate unanimously passed a motion urging the federal government to defer licensing rBST for at least a year, and certainly not before its impact on the long-term health of Canadians was known.[30] It also voted to authorize its Standing Committee on Agriculture and Forestry "to examine and report on the Recombinant Growth Hormone (rBST) and its effects on the human and animal health aspects."[31] In 1998 the committee held public hearings and, based on scientific testimony and other research evidence, issued its *Interim Report on rBST and the Drug Approval Process* on 11 March 1999.[32]

The report noted some of the issues that the public hearings had uncovered and made eight key recommendations. The most sensational advised Health Canada not to issue any approval for rBST until the manufacturer submitted the long-term studies identified by the review team as missing from the company's submission, and until these studies were investigated to determine any risks to human safety. Other recommendations condemned Health Canada for its slow response in providing the information requested by the committee and suggested that the federal government conduct an independent review of Health Canada's drug approval process to ensure that it fully safeguards human and animal health and safety.

Critics have worried that in matters of biotechnology, Canada often seems willing to follow the United States. The Senate's *Interim Report* makes that response less likely in future. It serves notice that our drug approval policies will be more stringent for drugs genetically engineered for human and animal use. Its findings are a direct assault on the evidence prepared, and deemed sufficient, for approval of rBST in the United States. It is likely that any future decisions made by the U.S. Food and Drug Administration will be carefully scrutinized in Canada's own drug approval process to ensure that they are scientifically sound and complete. Finally, the Senate Committee recognized the need for a larger public role in the drug approval process within Health Canada and noted the potential conflict of interest inherent in the existing process. The Senate Committee recommended the creation of an ongoing mechanism with the mandate to "stimulate public discussion on economic, trade, social, ethical and other considerations related to drugs and medical devices that are being considered by Health Canada."

This is a rare window of opportunity for Canadians interested in biotechnology and the impact of genetically engineered drugs on their health. We should not let it pass, but should move to lobby for this formal mechanism to be part of the drug approval process for genetically engineered drugs. It could take several forms, including that of a citizen's panel with a rotating national and multidisciplinary membership of informed Canadians concerned about these issues. This process would provide a better balance to the existing model, where economic considerations predominate. Public policy discussions of biotechnology require public participation and education to engender trust in, and support for, this sector that will contribute significantly to future economic growth and scientific innovation in Canada.

Consensus Conference on Food Biotechnology

One recent example of community involvement in the issues and choices raised by biotechnology was the Citizens' Conference on Food Biotechnology, held in Calgary on 5–7 March 1999.[33] Made up of informed and concerned laypeople, it provided a report to government and industry that was particularly interesting for its practical considerations, without concern for economic or political repercussions.[34] The recommendations included the following points:

- Public participation should be ongoing and in many different formats, and an independent system for gathering public opinion on food biotechnology should be put in place.
- The proposed national Biotechnology Advisory Committee should be publicly funded, independent, have equal representation from all stakeholders, and have a mandate to collect, critically analyze, and present information to both ministers and the public.
- A code of ethics reflecting Canadian values should be adopted and applied as an integral part of the regulatory process.
- Bio-safety standards and laws should be harmonized internationally, and should respect the culture and ethics of individual countries.
- The Biotechnology Advisory Committee should develop and implement an effective labelling policy.
- Interdisciplinary peer-reviewed research should be incorporated into the risk assessment process.
- The extent and the impact of concentrated control of the food industry should be publicly monitored by the federal government.
- There should be adequate public funding for the enforcement of standards, laws, and regulations.
- The Biotechnology Advisory Committee should review the current patent law and its application with respect to food biotechnology.
- The reality of public apathy should be recognized, and a public relations plan should be developed and paid for by industry, government, and producers in order to stimulate public interest in the issues raised by food biotechnology.
- Alternatives to antibiotic-resistant marker genes should be used.[35]

These recommendations will help provide transparency and accountability, which in turn should increase consumer confidence in genetically modified foods and other products by requiring mechanisms for ensuring that claims are accurate and products safe. To address this consumer concern, some companies have begun to label their products as "natural" or free from genetic modification. Some groups even promote shopping at stores that carry these products and supporting these companies, not unlike the organic or pesticide-free movements of the

1980s. The biotechnology industry has an interest in ensuring that consumers feel comfortable with genetically modified foods, not just to protect their bottom line, but to help ensure a stable and sustainable future world food supply.

Conclusion

Canada has yet to find a consistent approach that balances its two traditional goals of individual entrepreneurship and respect for a larger community interest. The make-up, mandate, and funding of the proposed national Biotechnology Advisory Committee will express the concerns Canadians feel about their future food sources. Think-tanks like the Citizens' Conference in Calgary must become routine, formalized, and publicly funded, and their role as a thoughtful and legitimate community voice must be recognized. Earning and keeping the public's trust is the best way to ensure acceptance of biotechnologies that promise us future food security. Industry will need to convince us that these new products are safe and will make our families healthy, not sick. The economic stakes are high and, as a world leader in agricultural biotechnology, Canada can use both its scientific expertise and its respected international reputation to help build both trust and markets for these foods and products at home and abroad.

Chapter Seven

The Commercialization of Life

Of the many threats that genetic engineering poses to society, the most urgent is the commercialization of human life.[1] Commercialization can take many forms, but, in essence, it involves treating human life as private property. What happens if we choose this path? Basically, human life — including embryos, gametes, reproductive capacity, human organs, tissue, body parts, fluids, and processes — would become commercial products to be bought, bartered, sold, and patented.[2] Throughout history, human beings have been treated as objects of commerce. I vividly remember walking through a fort in Ghana where people, kidnapped in the early nineteenth century from villages in west Africa, were herded into mass cells to await transport across the ocean to serve as slaves. Considered less than human because of inherent characteristics such as race and colour, they were denied basic human rights and treated as chattels to be used and abused at will. Once in the New World, they could not hold property, vote, or seek elected office. They enjoyed no legal rights and were considered as nothing more than human personal property. It is the ownership of human life and its treatment as private property, to be bought, sold, mortgaged, or even patented, that is repugnant to our fundamental values and principles of individual rights and dignity, and must be prevented.

In Canada our laws reject the treatment of human beings as personal or private property. We consider this conduct a denial of our principles of human rights and equality, and a fundamental breach of the moral value of our shared humanity. Today, there are no recognized property rights in the human body. The law allows for a quasi-legal control over human bodies, which was developed in the context of the disposal of dead bodies. It establishes responsibilities for the disposal of cadavers and provides legal options for their use for medical-scientific research. There is no property right at common law in dead bodies,[3] and the case law extends only to a right to the possession of a dead body for burial.[4] In all cases, human bodies cannot be bought and sold in Canada, and the provincial Anatomy Acts provide for the disposal of cadavers of persons who die in publicly funded institutions or public places. Bodies unclaimed after three months can be used for medical research and must then be buried. The Acts establish to whom such bodies can go for research (including medical schools), and provide that the person who accepts the body must ensure it is buried properly. Other provincial Acts, such as the Coroner's Acts, also touch on the treatment of dead bodies.

As we will see in chapter 9, on organ transplants, the issue of what, if any, proprietary or ownership rights exist in the human body was raised clearly with the first organ transplants in the mid-1950s. In response to these issues, the provinces adopted Human Tissue Gift Acts that prohibit the sale of, and dealing in, human tissue and organs, declaring such activity invalid as contrary to public policy.[5] In Canada, law and public policy are clear. Human tissue, bodies, and organs cannot be bought and sold.[6]

The American Situation

In the United States the *Uniform Anatomical Gift Act* applies the same principles. Congress passed the *National Organ Transplant Act* in 1984 to prohibit the sale of any human organ for transplant purposes. While an individual can choose whether to donate organs, the law does not recognize full property rights in human organs. Blood and sperm, considered as "replenishable tissue," are excluded from the definition of "organ." The right in dead bodies in the United States, as in Canada, is a quasi-legal one, limited to the responsibility for a body's disposal. As we will see, this principle has begun to erode as the courts declare property rights in the genetically altered "products" of our human bodies.

To treat human life as commercial matter, and our parts and processes as products to be bought or sold, contradicts our notion of ourselves as whole and special beings. It also runs counter to the laws we have developed to define and enshrine human rights. At its most basic, we believe that being human, able to reason, think, and feel, makes us special. Even those who are robbed of these faculties through disability or disease are protected. We have decided to shelter the vulnerable among us and envelop them in the same blanket of individual and human rights we have woven to cover ourselves. But with the advent of new technologies that make genetic engineering possible, human life and biological development are being compartmentalized and commercialized. This departure can cause changes in how we see ourselves and others in the human family. We looked in chapter 4 at research on human embryos and the tough task of protecting them from abuse. But other challenges are raised by genetic engineering at the cellular level, where commercialization is increasingly important. Under the banner of research, free enterprise, and profit, we are preparing the way for the next great revolution – the commercialization of human life and its treatment as private property.[7] These are the stakes as we analyze recent attempts at acquiring patents on higher life forms,[8] including human genes, cell lines, and tissues.[9]

Patents on Living Organisms

How did patents[10] come to be sought and granted on higher life forms?[11] Like most developments in this field, the process started slowly, almost imperceptibly, and just kept growing. Patents on life forms are not a recent phenomenon, except for those on higher and human life forms. For example, Louis Pasteur was granted a patent for beer fermentation using bacteria and patented vaccines; and in the 1950s and 1960s patented vaccines used live bacteria. These bacteria were usually single cell organisms, and, at the time, few anticipated our future use of living multicellular organisms, including plant, animal, and human material to genetically engineer new types of life.

It was an American case that first legalized the commercialization of living organisms. In 1980 the U.S. Supreme Court overruled the decision of the U.S. Patent Office and affirmed that a genetically engineered life form could be the subject of a patent. In the case of *Diamond* v. *Chakrabarty*,[12] which involved a genetically engineered bacterium that literally "ate" oil spills, the Court changed forever how living organisms would be considered in law and paved the way for the commercialization of higher life forms. The Court's minority stood against this change, arguing unsuccessfully that the passage of specific legislation by Congress to protect plant varieties meant that living organisms were not meant to be considered as patentable subject matter. The majority, led by then Chief Justice Warren Burger, disagreed.[13] In breaking with the tradition that no patents were awarded for "naturally occurring" products, the Court held that the genetic engineering of living organisms to create another one made them new "human inventions," the product of "human ingenuity," which could be the subject of a patent. This change in the law was made primarily to encourage scientific research, commercial innovation, and corporate profits in the United States.

Patents on Animals

This Supreme Court case quickly became the precedent for patents on other living organisms, ranging from plants to mice to human genes. Genetic engineering of one organism to create another has led to an ever growing legal battle. The stakes are high and the prize is both power and profit. The global domination of American biotechnology depends on patents, and U.S. courts have supported this public policy. From a single living organism that ate oil spills to a patent on a genetically modifed oyster,[14] the trend to legal recognition of patentable rights in genetically engineered living organisms was formalized in 1987 with a key policy change by the U.S. Patent Office to allow patents on "non-naturally occurring non-human multicellular living organisms, including animals."[15] Within the year, Harvard University successfully sought a patent on a genetically engineered mouse. This "oncomouse" made history as the first mammal to be patented for use in cancer research, and, for the first time, animals became patentable subject matter. This decision created a huge controversy in Europe, but the language of ethics had no force against the power of commerce. Since then, the American standard, definition, and practice has been generally accepted.

So far Canada is the exception, but there is no assurance how long this resistance will last. After receiving a patent in the United States, Harvard University sought a patent for the oncomouse in Canada. The application to the Canadian Intellectual Property Office was refused, and the appeal failed. In March 1998 the Federal Court refused the second appeal and upheld the decisions of the CIPO and the commissioner of patents.[16] Leave will be sought to appeal this decision to the Supreme Court of Canada.

Patents on Human Life

The Moore Case

Genetic engineering at the cellular level can be done in most living organisms. Inevitably, then, it was only a matter of time before someone sought a patent on living *human* organisms. The *Moore*[17] case records the first time a patent was awarded on a genetically engineered human organism. Moore had a cancerous spleen and seemed doomed to die. His doctor agreed to remove the spleen, but also planned with a researcher colleague to use cells from it to develop a new genetically engineered cell line. They did not tell Moore of their plans or of the commercial potential of the cell line they planned to create using his cells. The operation was successful and saved his life, but after several trips to Los Angeles from Seattle for what were billed as extensive postoperative check-ups, Moore became suspicious. After confronting his doctor, he discovered that the superior treatment and first-class tickets were not about post-operative care but about research — and that he was the source of cells that were being genetically engineered to create a new cell line (appropriately called the "Mo-line"), worth billions of dollars. Furious at the deception, Moore wanted a part of the profit and argued that, had he known the doctor's plans, he would have insisted from the beginning on being a partner and in sharing the vast profits the new cell line would earn. He may have consented to the surgery, he argued, but not to the commercialization of his genetically engineered cancerous cells. He *owned* his body, Moore contended, and the doctor had *stolen* the cells from him. The court disagreed.

Moore's arguments were refused on the grounds that the new cell line was so different from the original cancerous spleen as to be an entirely new living organism. The court found that this genetically engineered cell line had required sophisticated scientific skill, research, and ingenuity. All Moore provided was the original material, which he had "abandoned" at the time of surgery, thereby ending his legal rights to it. He had suffered no damages. The doctor's skill and care had cured his fatal cancer and he was healthy. To head off further suits by patients whose cells or tissue might be removed and commercialized in the future, the California Supreme Court stated that the "use of excised human cells in medical research does not amount to a conversion."[18] In an astounding reasoning, it found that Moore did not "own" his body and could hold no proprietary rights in the new cell line. Researchers and their universities or companies that genetically altered his cells, in contrast, *could own* the "new" product and be given a patent on it. The court made clear that even in situations where the patient could not have known that his cells were to be used without his consent for lucrative biomedical research, corporate and medical research interests would prevail. It refused to recognize and enforce the right for a person to sell his own body tissue for profit, but left the question open to the legislature to require consent and sharing of profits where a person's cells were used to create a profitable new biotechnology product, such as a new cell line. It found that the tort of conversion is not necessary to protect patients' rights, and that, regardless, the protection of researchers (described as "innocent parties who are engaged in socially useful activities")[19] takes precedence. The justices agreed that the doctor had breached his fiduciary duty to Moore in the doctor-patient relationship, but found only a lack of consent.

This decision, more than any other, has opened the floodgates for future patent applications for genetically engineered human cells and tissue. The justices did raise the question of new laws to handle these kinds of situations, but offered no suggestions for reform. One judge recommended a licensing scheme that established a fixed rate of profit to be shared between the researcher and the person "donating" his or her cells. Insisting that they had the best interests of patients as their primary concern, the justices refused to find that individuals have a right to *ownership* in their own biological material — cells, tissue, and organs — saying that, if they did, biomedical research would suffer and sick people would be put in the impossible situation of accepting to "donate or sell" cells, tissue, or organs, even if they did not agree, for fear of being denied treatment. Better that doctors and medical researchers be able to help themselves to tissue and cells that would otherwise be destroyed as medical waste.

The Sale of Body Fluids

In the United States the sale of replenishable body fluids, including blood and sperm, is still allowed. Where legislation exists, it treats these sales as the provision of a service, rather than a sale of goods. Barring negligence or fraud, suppliers and donors are free from claims under products liability legislation — for instance, tainted blood. While sales of "replenishable human tissue in non-vital" amounts is allowed, the *Moore* decision makes it clear that in the absence of new statutory or judicial recognition of property rights in the human body, only companies or institutions (for example, universities or governments) paying for research that will be commercialized can claim proprietary rights in human material that has been genetically engineered, such as human genes, cell lines, and tissues. Although this case denies individual ownership of our bodies, it gives this right to companies, universities, governments, and others involved in the research to genetically engineer a new commercially viable product from human tissue, fluid, and cells.

This key decision sets the stage for a new approach to corporate and governmental control over the commercialization of the human body — its cells, cell lines, parts, tissues, organs, fluids, and processes. We saw in chapter 5 that the U.S. government has sought patents on the genes that have been discovered in government-funded laboratories as part of the international Human Genome Project. The *Moore* case gives strength to the U.S. government's actions by recognizing a right to ownership by companies and governments that fund research which results in the commercialization of genetically engineered human material. There are indications that this rush to patent human genes, cells, and other material will not be easily stopped. A more complicated and ethically unacceptable practice is that of the U.S. National Institutes of Health, which is patenting genetic material from indigenous people in other parts of the world. On 14 March 1995, for instance, the U.S. Patent Office issued a patent to the National Institutes for an unmodified cell line drawn from an indigenous person from Papua New Guinea.[20] After a diplomatic incident, a previous patent on a gene found in a Guaymi Indian woman in Panama was withdrawn. That patent had been for a virus found in the woman's blood which was said to have had potential in AIDS and leukemia research. The virus, though, was preserved in a line of blood cells that had also been patented for future research and commercialization. In the meantime, patents have been granted in the United States for recombinant animal and human DNA.[21] And, following the landmark decision in the *Moore* case in California, genetically altered human processes can be patented there as well. The American courts and Patent Office have accepted that human genes, cell lines, and tissue that have been isolated and genetically engineered in the laboratory to produce a human organism not found in nature can be patented.

What results can we expect from this decision? The most obvious is a lessening of trust, which is at the heart of the doctor-patient relationship. The decision in *Moore* should put us on our guard whenever we have surgery, give blood, or sign a donor card. The second may be a decline in our willingness to volunteer and donate. Individuals should not be expected to stand by and receive nothing when their bodies are being used as raw material sources for the development of new and highly profitable biotechnology products. Sharing of patent rights and financial rewards will be expected. Finally, adopting this approach will mean legal conflict and judicial intervention. In the absence of specific legislation, these situations will be resolved in the courts. Therefore, the training of judges and lawyers in science, medicine, and ethics is essential.

The reason this massive change is taking place now is primarily because technology has moved us into an entirely new sphere of possible research. Genetic engineering allows us to manipulate and alter existing organisms at the cellular level, whether they be from bacteria, plants, animals, or even humans. Historically, the law has not had to respond to these kinds of challenges. In Canada we generally managed to agree that certain products and practices were necessary for the public good and would not be legally owned or controlled by any government, individual, corporation, or public institution. Medical techniques are one example of this tradition. In cases like *Moore*, new situations have to be faced thanks to biotechnology, but the basic importance of the public interest and the collective good remain the same. Legal tools such as patents are the excuse, not the reason, why we have moved along the road so far towards the commercialization of human life. It arises from the culture of commerce, which, under the banner of free enterprise, has promoted the acceptance of a view that every thing must have a price.

Steadily and aggressively, practices that have treated plant and animal life as a commercial commodity have crossed the species barrier and are accepted and used on human life. Commercial definitions and practices apply to this growing and highly lucrative market in genetically engineered life.[22] This trend is not going to change unless we demand other solutions that respect the integrity of human life and ban the use of the human body, its parts, and processes as objects of commerce. Identifying human genes, whether through scientific research or their collection from indigenous tribes or local families suffering from genetic disorders, is not about "discovery" in the sense that the patent laws anticipated. Even if it were, there are certain matters that must always be above the clutches of commerce. Human life and the human body fall within that category. We should be sure that our laws state clearly that these values and human rights must be recognized and respected.

Options for the Future: A Canadian Way?

In light of these cases and practices, we must ask if we are doomed to become no more than the commercial sum of our human parts. Patents on living organisms are recent. They recognize the power and promise of the biotechnology sector to the economies of the future. In my view, no legal solution will be effective unless we recognize the commercial nature of the new technologies that allow us to genetically engineer new living organisms, from oil-spill-eating bacteria to human embryos. But the economic considerations are not the only ones; and before we give over our human bodies and parts, we must search for options that balance commercial interests and human integrity.

How might we do this? In some ways, our courts have already begun to develop a "Canadian way."[23] By taking a stand against the tide of commercialization in the Harvard mouse case,[24] the Federal Court has ensured that Canada can recognize other values and approaches as we shape biotechnology to respect a larger societal agenda than just commercial profit. The Court also put a hold on expected applications for patents on DNA sequences on our chromosomes that scientists will identify as part of their participation in the international Human Genome Project. It has given the federal government the breather it needs to seek out workable alternative solutions to patents on human life. It has given Canadians a chance to resist the tidal wave which has been unleashed by our southern neighbour and which marks a sea change in the values of human integrity and non-commercialization of life.[25] It is now up to Parliament to act on this fundamental question. Will we uphold our traditional value that human beings are not objects of commerce? Our challenge is to build quickly on the opportunity we have been given. We can begin by looking for other legal tools that protect the specific economic needs of commerce in the field of biotechnology, while respecting the collective value of the non-commercialization of human life. We need an ongoing mechanism to make this process a reality. Perhaps it should be started by a standing committee of Parliament, a task force, royal commission, or citizens' advisory team. But whatever method we choose, we must move as quickly as science is progressing right now, and must start from the non-negotiable premise that humans are special and must never be treated as objects of commerce and profit. This choice is not about denying profit to companies and investors. It is, though, about denying them the right to legal property rights in human life. Our challenge is to be as creative with law as we have been with science. The legal profession has a responsibility to be more than the handmaiden of commerce. Lawyers must also be creative in meeting these new legal issues and accept their larger responsibility to protect and respect society's interests and collective rights.

Consent

Canadians have come a long way from the medical paternalism that marked most of the twentieth century. With our new autonomy has come the responsibility to make difficult decisions: about donating our organs, tissue, and limbs for transplant; about refusing treatment, even though without it we will die; about assisted suicide and euthanasia; about the very meaning of life and death.

In Part Three, the issues of consent and control in medical decision-making are explored. Keeping control over our major life decisions is key for all of us: from living wills to the requirement to consent to medical treatment to the right to refuse it for ourselves, our children, and others in our care. What are our rights and responsibilities in this area, and is the law keeping up with the changing realities science and medical technology offer? These are some of the tough choices we will look at in the last part of this book.

Chapter Eight

Keeping Control

I n providing us with the tools to prolong life, technology has created a profound human dilemma. We may live longer and often
healthier lives, but at what cost to our personal autonomy and to
society's other health care priorities? As we age, technology's reach
makes urgent a better understanding of the purpose and extent of individual autonomy in a health care setting and prompts inquiry into the
ways in which we can maintain our control over major life and death
decisions. We know that these are deeply personal matters, but they
also have a huge impact on health care systems and priorities and finite
health care resources. In this final part, we will look at several current
and often controversial issues regarding autonomy, including the right
to refuse treatment, organ and tissue transplants, assisted suicide, and
euthanasia. Through the lens of law, we will examine some of the rules
that now apply[1] and ask which of them need updating to reassure and
protect us in the years ahead.

The success of the patients' rights movement during the past two
decades has allowed us to forget the struggle that gave us the power

we enjoy today to make vital decisions for our families and ourselves. Until quite recent years, the doctor dictated and the patient obeyed. As patients fought to be included in decision-making, this attitude slowly evolved and changed. Today, patient autonomy and individual rights have become an established part of the doctor-patient relationship. As this evolution took place, other social and legal changes acknowledged greater individual rights and responsibilities. Legal frameworks such as those provided by the *Canadian Charter of Rights and Freedoms* have set a new legal standard for the protection of individual rights. The patients' rights movement opened the door for greater and more meaningful individual involvement in health care decision-making. Our responsibilities will increase even more as we become heath care advocates for ourselves and our families in the future.

The Requirement for Consent

Individual autonomy engenders two key rights in the health care context: first, the right not to be interfered with against our wishes, which is at the root of the legal requirement for consent to medical treatment; and, second, the right to refuse treatment, even when refusal will lead to our death.[2] Except in an emergency,[3] every competent adult must consent to medical treatment, and for such consent to be valid, it must be voluntary and informed,[4] free from coercion and fraud, and be for the treatment proposed. Consent can be written or verbal and can be withdrawn at any time. Doctors and health care professionals who provide treatment against a competent person's objections face charges of assault and battery.[5]

In obtaining a legal consent to treat, physicians and other health care professionals must meet a tough standard. They must provide the patient with information that is complete, understandable, and relevant to the person making the decision.[6] They must answer the subjective question: "What information would this particular patient reasonably consider relevant in agreeing to, or refusing, treatment? In practice, the patient should know what the proposed treatment or surgery entails; what its probable benefits, material risks, and expected side effects are; what alternatives are available; and what would happen if the proposed treatment were not followed.

In deciding a course of treatment for cancer, for example, a patient may be presented with a recommendation for surgery to be followed by chemotherapy. When seeking consent, in addition to telling the patient that the proposed treatment is *objectively* an approved medical procedure for this cancer, the doctor should probe further and see if the proposed option is the one that *subjectively* best suits that patient. This consideration does not require doctors to be mind readers, but it does require them to explain in detail the choices, their benefits and harms, and other alternatives to the treatments proposed. And it requires that doctors take time to listen attentively to their patients' concerns. This new approach accepts that treatment options are as much personal as medical decisions.

When consent to treatment is given, it covers only the treatment agreed to or one reasonably related to it. For instance, if a patient has agreed to a lumpectomy and the doctor discovers another lump during the course of surgery, her consent to the original procedure would also include consent to remove the second lump. It could even be interpreted to include a valid consent for a follow-up surgery or treatment for the same or a closely related cancer. It would not, however, in an analogous situation, include an appendectomy, under an agreement to have a gall bladder removed.

Valid consent for treatment requires very specific information. But who is eligible to give such consent? What defines the capacity to consent? In Canada, there is a refutable presumption that a person who has reached the age of majority is competent to give a valid consent to medical treatment.[7] But consent can be refuted by evidence that shows that a patient lacks the mental capacity to understand what is being proposed. This incapacity could result from a mental disease or condition that has robbed a person of reason and decision-making powers. One author has put it this way: "The best test of a person's capability to understand the relevant information is to determine if the person can, in fact, understand the relevant information presented in a way that is appropriate to the person's education, culture, language and special needs."[8]

On Behalf of the Vulnerable

Consent to medical care for children has been given special provision in law.[9] To protect children and minors, the *Criminal Code* places a legal duty on parents and legal guardians to provide medical treatment for their children or others under their care.[10] This includes medical treatment such as surgery, and in ambiguous cases, errs on the side of treatment, on the assumption that preserving life at all cost is in the best interests of the child. Parents enjoy authority over their minor children, and retain the right and responsibility to consent to medical and other health-related treatments on their children's behalf. However, this right is not absolute,[11] and a parent's religious beliefs, for example, will not be allowed to endanger the health and life of minor children, especially infants.[12] As part of its historic role, the court always maintains its *parens patriae* jurisdiction when children and the vulnerable are involved.

In line with our growing respect for individual autonomy, however, courts have become increasingly reluctant to define competence strictly by age, except for infants and the very young child.[13] Generally, legal capacity to make important decisions, including those involving health care, increases with age.[14] To be treated as a mature minor, a child must show that he or she has "the capacity to understand the nature and consequences of medical treatment" and can make independent medical decisions about appropriate care.[15] Where youth are declared mature minors for health care decisions, they are treated as adults and the court loses its *parens patriae* jurisdiction, as there is no longer a "child in need of protection."[16] Generally, then, an infant would never be able to consent, while a competent adolescent on the eve of an eighteenth birthday could enjoy full legal status for health care decision-making. The theory (although not always the practice) of the law respecting minors in medical decision-making makes good common sense: it follows the current trend towards treating maturity as a point on a continuum and respects the increasing autonomy of youth moving towards adulthood. A mentally competent mature minor (judged to be so by a finding of fact by the court based on expert advice) could accept or reject medical treatment, overriding parental objection.

But what happens when persons are incompetent through disability, age, or disease and cannot give a valid consent?[17] Who decides whether to treat or refuse treatment? As a general rule the decision is made by those closest to the patient, a parent or spouse, for example, or the person with the legal responsibility of deciding on care and treatment. Vulnerable adult patients fall into two distinct categories. In the first are patients who have never been competent and will never be able to make their views known. They can neither consent to nor refuse medical treatment. In these situations, the law treats such adults as it would children. Each person's case is studied and the court tries to determine the individual's level of mental capacity. As in cases involving children, this judgment will be a finding of fact by the court, based on expert advice. Even within this group of mentally disabled adults, the court will find different levels of mental ability and make every attempt to invite individuals to speak for themselves, so their wishes can be known. In the second group are previously competent persons who have lost their capacity to make decisions about health care and other financial and personal matters for themselves. They have a distinct advantage over the first group because they can maintain their control over health care and other decisions by drafting an advance directive.[18] They can make their wishes known in writing in accordance with provincial laws and can give authority to a family member, physician, or friend to act on their behalf to fulfil those wishes.

The Right to Refuse Medical Treatment

The right to refuse oneself any and all medical treatment even when to do so will result in death is an extension of the requirement for consent. This is a key right, and one that will become more important as medical technology extends its capacity to keep us alive for long periods after a serious accident or debilitating disease. Hospitals and care facilities grapple daily with the issue of futile treatment and express concern about family members' reactions to the tough decisions about initiating, extending, or withdrawing treatment that must be faced in these cases. The debate about the appropriate use of finite health care resources will be one of the hottest issues to confront the boomer generation.[19] Making our voice heard and our views about our choices known through an advance directive will be essential. However, given the current practice of allowing families to veto otherwise legal advance directives, the ultimate challenge will be to have our final wishes respected.

Some cases capture the public imagination and come to symbolize an issue of popular concern. The case known simply as "*Nancy B.*"[20] was one such case. It crystallized Canadians' concern about protecting the vulnerable and respecting individual rights and dignity. The story of Nancy B., a twenty-five-year-old Quebec woman suffering from Guillain-Barre syndrome, was both tragic and heroic. A nerve disorder had left her paralyzed from the neck down and unable to breathe on her own, and she did not want to live out her days as a captive of technology. After two years on a respirator, she recognized her condition was irreversible and asked to have the respirator removed, knowing that she would die. As a respirator is considered "medical treatment," she was doing no more than exercising her right as a competent person under the *Quebec Civil Code* to refuse treatment.[21] The hospital was concerned about negative publicity and feared being sued for performing an assisted suicide, which is a criminal offence.[22] The *Criminal Code* also prohibits anyone from consenting to have death inflicted upon them[23] and places a duty on doctors to do everything reasonably possible to save a human life.[24]

Although the right to refuse treatment was already established in Quebec at the time the decision was taken, Quebec law requires that such cases be heard by a superior court judge on an individual basis to ensure that there is no abuse of the patient's rights. Quebec is the only province in Canada where this legal requirement applies, but were the same question to be raised in other jurisdictions, the result would be the same, as the right to refuse medical treatment such as respirators, technical and medical interventions, and drugs is well established all across the country. The only issue for the law in similar cases is to ensure that the patient is competent and that his or her decision to refuse or end treatment is informed and voluntary. In supporting Nancy B.'s right to refuse medical treatment, the superior court judge reaffirmed the rights of all competent adult patients to make their own informed decision about whether to start or continue treatment that has been deemed futile under accepted medical standards. The judge distinguished this case from one of euthanasia and noted that in cases where death can logically be attributed to the disease (no matter how young the patient) and life-sustaining technology is really just a tool to prolong the dying process, patient autonomy in health matters and the right to self-determination will prevail.[25]

Confronting the Ultimate Decision

Two issues arising from patient autonomy must be discussed and resolved in the near future. We have seen that there is a right to refuse treatment; but does a patient have a corresponding right to demand treatment in all situations? Does the legal right to care include futile treatment other than recognized palliative care? In most individuals' lifespans, the greatest amount of care is needed during the last weeks of life, and because the resolution to these issues involves the allocation of health care resources and the protection of the vulnerable from abuse and untimely death, they are as much public policy as legal issues. In the absence of a valid advance directive and power of attorney for personal care, family members must assume responsibility for health care decisions. Is there a limit to what they can demand?[26] When a patient enters a coma or loses the ability to express his or her preferences in these medical cases, should the presumption be that the person would have chosen a peaceful death or heroic and ultimately futile medical interventions?

Above all, we must think about humane treatment at the end of life as well as the use of modern technology merely to extend life. Humane treatment demands that the *quality* of an individual life be considered as well as its *length*. While most people would choose life over death in normal circumstances, can we assume the same when being kept alive is merely a prolongation of dying and could even be described as a "living death"? These large ethical questions about end-of-life decisions and the present laws on euthanasia and withdrawal of treatment have important implications for legal reform. Questions for future public policy consideration abound. What is the appropriate use of finite health care resources? How can we protect the individual rights of the incompetent and vulnerable? How can we balance the rights of family members with the responsibilities of the medical teams who must make these tough human decisions in intensive care units every day?

Obviously, if we want to keep a measure of control over the quality of our living and dying, we need to take action while we are well. As technology dictates medical responses in situations of crisis and prolonged dying, more and more Canadians are drafting advance directives and living wills. During the last two decades, advance directives and living wills[27] have grown in importance, and most provinces have moved to codify them.[28] Ontario, for example, has codified the right of a competent person to appoint one or more people to make health and medical care decisions on his or her behalf[29] and provides a way in which persons judged mentally incapable to decide on their own treatment can appeal that judgment. These provincial statutes give teeth to Canadians' right to full autonomy in accepting or refusing medical treatment or other forms of care, and they broaden the scope of autonomy to include decisions involving commitment to a nursing home or psychiatric hospital.

These laws help clarify process, but the onus is on us to use them. We must tell others, especially our family, what we value in life, how we want to live and die, and whom we want to speak on our behalf when we can no longer do so for ourselves. Few of us want to be kept alive when further treatment would be futile, or when accident or disease has robbed us of our dignity and purpose. Seeing parents and friends die has forced many of us to confront the fact of death. It has also encouraged us to reflect on our own priorities and what the power of technology to keep us alive in a state of living death would mean for us as we age in the new century. If we want to maintain control we must act now to make our wishes known. What are the values that guide us every day? What matters most to us in life, without which we would find being alive unbearable? These are intimately personal preferences, but we must make them known now.

Most of us cherish our freedom. Having the right to choose is what sets our society apart from those where human rights and personal freedoms are restricted or denied. Individual autonomy, especially in health care decision-making, is a cherished value for most Canadians. Knowledge of the legal rules can help guide our decisions in preparing for the future. Even though it is awkward to talk about dying, and many believe to do so brings bad luck, we should all try to raise the subject with our families. It is far better to talk about death when we are healthy than when we are ill or in a medical crisis.

Advance decision-making can also save the lives of others, as technology perfects the ability to successfully transplant human tissue, organs, and limbs — the issue to which we now turn.

Chapter Nine

Organ and Tissue Donation: An Urgent Need

T hanks to modern medical technologies and practices, successful organ and tissue transplants are increasingly common.[1] It
is now possible even to transplant limbs,[2] and researchers are
moving towards growing living, artificial human parts, nicknamed
neo-organs. The new discovery of how to isolate stem cells, which
can grow into any of the body's cells, promises to help doctors repair
all kinds of damaged tissues. At a time of acute shortage of organs for
transplant, these discoveries add interest to an already hot research
area.[3] But as the more complex techniques and clinical research on
perfecting organ transplants still face obstacles, and actually growing
organs and limbs for transplant is still some way off, people who
need tissue and organ transplants *right now* must rely on organ donation for life-saving procedures.[4] Today, organs including the kidney,
liver, heart,[5] lung,[6] pancreas, and small intestine, and tissue including
the cornea, skin, bone marrow, skin, sperm, ova, and heart valves can
be successfully transplanted. Research towards transplanting tongues
and other parts is proceeding rapidly.[7] All are needed by Canadians

on waiting lists for one or multiple transplants. In addition to saving lives, transplants can be more economical than the long-term care they replace.[8]

The Human Tissue Gift Acts

In Canada the provinces regulate the donation of human tissue and organs through Human Tissue Gift Acts.[9] Certain tissue, including skin, bone, blood, and other regenerative tissue replaceable by the natural process of repair, is not covered by the laws. The purpose of the provincial Acts is clear — to ensure access to those in need of tissue and organ transplants donated either *inter vivos* (during life) or *post mortem* (after death). The process is closely regulated to eliminate abuse, and to reassure potential donors that they are protected from organ piracy, coercion, and the fear that medical care will be withheld if they refuse to donate.

Generally speaking, all the provincial Human Tissue Gift Acts provide a process for the donation of organs.[10] They set out the consent provisions for donations *inter vivos* and *post mortem*; define which organs are covered and which are not; and set out sanctions for failure to comply with the Acts' provisions. Organ donations within each province are handled according to the provincial Acts and are administered by not-for-profit provincial bodies in cooperation with local hospitals.[11] Although each provincial law varies slightly in its wording, generally the Acts provide for similar definitions of vital terms and the same basic legal requirements and safeguards.[12]

A crucial question in organ donation is: "When is a person legally dead?" Regenerative tissue, like blood, can be donated easily while the donor is still alive; and certain regenerative tissues are therefore specifically excluded from the requirement for statutory consent and other provisions of the provincial Human Tissue Gift Acts.[13] Retrieval of these tissues is done according to accepted medical practice, and the normal rules of consent, substituted consent, tort, and contract apply.[14] But while regenerative tissue and even an organ such as a kidney can be donated *inter vivos* on a routine basis, most organs, notably the heart, can only be removed after a donor or potential donor is legally dead. When the viability of human organs is measured in hours, timely access to them is essential. At one time, legal death occurred when a person's heart, breathing, and circulation had irreversibly stopped. Today, technology allows us to keep people alive for extended periods on respirators. In light of new technological realities,[15] the traditional definition of death has been extended to include *brain death.*[16]

The Canadian Medical Association has established strict guidelines for the diagnosis of brain death.[17] According to its definition, brain death occurs when all of the following medical criteria have been met: there has been an event or accident that could cause brain death, and the possibility of other conditions to reverse it no longer exist; the patient is in a deep coma and does not respond within the cranial nerve distribution to stimulus to any part of the body; there are no brain-stem reflexes; the patient does not breathe for at least three minutes after being removed from the respirator, and when reassessed after a period of time, all the above conditions persist.

To respond to a fear on the part of the public that hospitals might declare people brain dead to be able to harvest their organs[18] rather than try to save their life, all relevant provincial laws require that two doctors who do not perform organ and tissue transplants certify that a person is brain dead before any hospital can start to remove the organs that person has donated.

Just as the donation of specified regenerative tissue is not covered by the rules in the various provincial laws, neither are human eyes that are to be used for cornea transplants. As the Acts are worded,[19] none of the required rules governing the donation of organs apply to eyes for cornea transplants. In law this means that a person's eyes could be removed without following the consent provisions of the Act, where there is a valid organ donation card. In practice, however, the legal consent rules for *post mortem* organ and tissue donation are followed. Some hospitals include the normal hierarchy for next-of-kin consent in their rules for consent.[20] Because eye removal is a simple process, many doctors have been trained to perform eye retrieval to supply eye banks with resources for much-needed cornea transplants.[21] Eye banks generally operate independently but share tissue, resources, and information locally, nationally, and internationally.[22] Standards for their operation are being set by the Bureau of Biologics, and education of hospital staff about eye retrieval donation is ongoing.

Most of the provincial Acts include clauses specifically banning the direct or indirect purchase, sale, or other dealing in any tissue for transplant or any body part or parts for therapeutic purposes, medical education, or scientific research.[23] Blood, blood constituents, and semen are exceptions. The purchase, sale, or barter of human organs is invalid as contrary to public policy in Canada. These restrictions reinforce the Canadian societal value that the human body, its parts, and its processes are not personal property in the regular sense and should not be treated as objects of commerce to be bought and sold. They also codify the respected humanitarian principle behind donation of human organs and tissue. Should a market in organs and tissue ever develop in Canada, however, it is unlikely that existing sanctions under provincial laws would be strict and onerous enough to prevent such abuse. Manitoba is the only province whose legislation specifically includes human embryos, fetuses, and gametes in its definition of tissue. This means that, in the absence of overriding legislation, these human tissues could be bought and sold in Canada.

The transplant procedure itself is a carefully orchestrated series of events. Generally, once brain death has been declared by two physicians not involved in the transplant, and consent to donate is confirmed through a valid donor card, living will, or permission of the next of kin, the medical transplant team will begin to test the organs for viability and health. Certain tests, including blood tests and tests for viruses such as HIV and hepatitis will be performed. Organs can be subjected to x-rays and/or ultrasound. Meanwhile, the waiting list of people in need of a specific organ transplant is searched for a compatible recipient. In keeping with the respected Canadian principle that those in the greatest medical need should "go to the head of the line," and to ensure maximum trust in the system, recipients with the most urgent need are given priority. Generally, the potential recipient is someone who has less than forty-eight hours to live without a transplant. During this time the donor's body will be kept functioning on a respirator to maintain the health and viability of the organs and tissue to be donated. Once a compatible recipient has been found, the donor will be operated on to remove the designated organs and tissues. The body of the donor is then released to his or her family for burial and the donated organs are transplanted into matched recipients. In all these situations, no one is permitted to divulge identifying information about the donor or the recipient, unless legally required to do so, or unless the donor, the recipient, or their next of kin consents in writing to the publication.[24] In all situations, legislation dealing with organ and tissue donation do not affect the requirements of the various provincial Coroners Acts or the operation of the Fatality Inquiries Acts where they exist.

Finding Eligible Donors

Organ, tissue, and limb donations are currently topics of intense debate, and reports from the frivolous to the fantastic abound in the popular and scientific press. Here are some of the issues regarding the eligibility of donors that will appear on public policy and legislative agendas in the months to come.

The present definition of brain death as "whole brain death" automatically excludes categories of people who have suffered only "higher brain death." This is an important distinction. A person who suffers whole brain death cannot breathe spontaneously and does not respond to light, pain, or sound stimuli. A person suffering higher brain death (as in the precedent-setting Karen Quinlan case[25] in the United States) may be in a persistent vegetative state, but still retain sufficient brain stem activity to be able to breathe spontaneously and respond to certain external stimuli such as heat or light.

The status of anencephalic infants[26] is another example of the legal dilemmas parents and doctors frequently face in considering eligibility for donation. Today, prenatal diagnosis can identify anencephaly — a fatal condition — prior to birth. Parents must then decide whether to abort the pregnancy or carry it to term and consider donating the fatally flawed infant's organs. In the latter case they risk being charged with infanticide because their infants do not meet the criteria for whole brain death. Public reaction is divided on these options. Should we amend the law to allow for exceptions to the whole brain criteria where families consent to the donation of an anencephalic infant's organs and tissue for transplant? Should we amend the *Criminal Code?* Amending the present legal status of these infants is the only way to allow for the donation of their organs while they are viable. It is the only way to protect parents wanting to consent to donations, the health care professionals and institutions that help them, and ultimately the families of the infants who would receive the donated organs. The Law Reform Commission of Canada studied this issue in 1992 as part of its research on the procurement and transfer of human tissues and organs, and recommended against any change in the current legal definition of whole brain death.[27] But in our ongoing debate about these issues, I believe we need to revisit these definitions, to be sure they are still relevant today and in fact represent the community consensus.

Another problematic area in need of attention is that of donations among children in a family (*inter vivos*). Under all the provincial laws governing human organ and tissue donation, only competent adults can donate *inter vivos*. Parents can consent to the *post mortem* donation of their child's organs for transplant, education, or research, but cannot give a substituted consent for *inter vivos* donations. This restriction makes sense in principle and supports our historic rules protecting children from abuse and acting in their best interests. But in the case of certain illnesses, family members are often the first to be identified as suitable donors. What can a family do in a situation where one child needs a kidney transplant, for example, and another minor child has two healthy kidneys and is a compatible donor for the fatally ill sibling? Under existing law, minors cannot consent to donate their organs. Should their parents or legal guardians be permitted to do so on their behalf? Or should younger children be protected, even if that means their sibling will die? How would we protect children from abuse in such cases? Does the court's *parens patriae* power to protect children afford a possible solution in such cases? I believe this issue of parental consent for the *inter vivos* donation of organs among minor children within a family will become a growing issue as medical technology perfects organ transplants. It raises troubling legal and ethical questions, but we all know that when it comes to the lives and health of our children, most of us would go to any length to help them. Genetic diagnosis at the pre-implantation and prenatal stages allows us to detect disease at an embryo's earliest stages and will eventually allow us to alter and enhance embryos and to correct genetic anomalies. Early in the new millennium we will be able to grow human organs as we do certain tissue right now, and the questions that technology forces us to face now may be quickly overshadowed by others. But in responding to the current challenge to craft laws that balance human need with human rights, we should give the present law governing organ and tissue donation among children in the same family a second look.

As our respect for the autonomy and intelligence of younger people increases, legal definitions are changing and becoming more nuanced and realistic. Where once only adults could offer a valid legal consent for health care, today increasingly younger persons have the intellectual capacity and maturity to do so too. The category of *mature minor* is well established and calls into question the complete ban of organ donation *inter vivos* by minors in most of the provincial Human Tissue Gift Acts. I predict that growing respect for the decisions of young people who are mentally mature and competent will mean these provisions are changed.

Mentally disabled adults cannot consent to donate their organs and tissue under the Acts. Should this provision be changed? If so, how can we ensure an informed and valid legal consent? I believe that the Acts' exclusion of such persons should be maintained to protect the mentally vulnerable from abuse and engender trust in the transplant system. Unlike a mature minor, whose capacity is increasing with age, mentally disabled adults will never have the capacity to make an informed decision to donate, or be able to give a valid legal consent. The legal principle of informed consent is the one way we can protect the vulnerable from abuse. There are really only three options in these cases: continue to prohibit all donations from the mentally handicapped, change the law to allow them in all cases, or change the law to allow them in certain limited cases where the potential donor can demonstrate to a judge's satisfaction the capacity to provide a valid legal consent.

The option of redefining the degrees of incapacity seems the most promising, but it would require discipline within the system and a firm set of criteria. Some criteria have already been judicially developed as we enlarged the previously monolithic class of children to include mature minors. In some cases, where the lack of capacity is recent, due to injury or illness, and where the person was once competent and able to make his or her views known, doctors and family members can be guided by the potential donor's previously expressed wishes. Today, any rule that automatically excludes from donations whole classes of persons (in this instance those suffering from a mental disability) is out of keeping with both our current understanding of the continuum of ability and disability experienced by individual mentally disabled adults and with our ever-evolving respect for individual autonomy in health and medical care decisions. While the protection of the vulnerable should prevail over the need to harvest organs for transplant, persons previously excluded from donating their organs *inter vivos* on the basis of mental disability alone should be reconsidered, and their cases should be reviewed according to recognized legal principles by a judge or by a specially appointed community-based advisory board on a case-by-case basis.

Most Canadians would be startled to learn that even if they have a valid advance directive, few hospitals would respect their decision to donate their organs *post mortem* for transplant or research if their family objected. In spite of increased respect for individual autonomy and the great need for human organs and tissue for transplant, a recent parliamentary report on the question recommended that family members maintain their right to veto a donor's legally valid decision.[28] There are several important reasons for resolving this issue. We must ensure that valid consents for *post mortem* donations are respected; that urgently needed organs are made available for transplant; that doctors, other health care personnel, and hospital administrators are protected; and that the transplant system is reinforced. Respecting written consent will in turn weaken the present pressure to introduce *mandated donation,* a system under which we would be deemed legally to agree to donate our organs and tissues unless we opted out in writing in a prescribed form.

Overcoming the Shortage of Organs for Donation

Despite the intent of the various provincial Acts to make organ and tissue donations legally possible in specific situations, Canadians in need of an organ for transplant die each year because of the shortage of available organs. In British Columbia, for instance, about 25 percent of people needing an organ in 1997 died before one could be found. Canada's organ donor rate is less than fourteen per million population,[29] one of the lowest among industrialized countries, and fewer than half of all Canadians eligible to do so have signed donor cards. How can we overcome this shortage? Several suggestions have been made. Organ transplant agencies and related non-profit organizations must undertake a more pro-active communications role. An education campaign is essential to raise awareness of donor consent.[30] Lawyers in estate and family law practices who draft wills and counsel clients preparing their financial affairs can also help, and the profession should discuss how it can encourage colleagues to raise the issue of organ and tissue donation. A positive onus on lawyers practising in this area would have a real impact on the number of Canadians who agree to organ donation. Raising the matter of donations in a formal and non-threatening way well before a medical crisis could also decrease the practice of family veto of *post mortem* donation.

Creating a Cord-Blood Registry

Other issues in organ and tissue donation are on the horizon. One involves blood from the umbilical cords of newborns. In December 1996 Canadian researchers[31] announced that they had identified blood stem cells, the "parent" cells that make all the types of blood cells. Using laboratory mice genetically engineered to be born without an immune system, they identified the stem cells, which look like most other cells and are one in a million in the bone marrow. This research opens up new options for medicine in the treatment of certain cancers, such as leukemia, and other genetic conditions and diseases of the blood and the immune system. Stem cells, also called the "progenitor" cells, develop and produce the three basic types of blood cell. Three current sources for stem cells are the umbilical cord of newborns, bone marrow, and the bloodstream. Until now, bone marrow has been the main source of stem cells, but the potential of cord-blood stem cells as a virtually unlimited source of future stem cells could change that. Cord blood is much richer in these essential cells than the adult bloodstream, and they have not yet built up the antibodies that could cause rejection or disease in transplants. Blood removed from the umbilical cord at birth can be stored in liquid nitrogen for future medical uses either by the newborn or a matched family member or, more generally, by needy strangers with a matching tissue type. Regulating the procedure and ensuring that specialized cord-blood banks are public and accessible to everyone should be a priority.

The handful of cord-blood banks already in existence can help us develop workable models, and new regulations should apply to both public and private banks. Donation, rather than commercial profit, should be the basis for the collection and use of cord blood, just as it is for blood generally, and the usual rules governing consent should apply for the parents of all newborns. Because donated cord blood is tested for infectious diseases, legislation must strengthen privacy laws to protect family members from disclosure should the tests reveal diseases that could affect immediate family members. The issues raised in regard to cord blood are similar to those raised by genetic testing. Integrating the process of drawing cord blood from all newborns into perinatal routines in Canadian hospitals could provide us with an ample supply of stem cells for use in the treatment of blood-related cancers and immune system disorders. A national registry would ensure a coordinated approach and make available safe cord-blood samples for medical research.[32]

Mandating a Request for Donation

One option is that doctors and medical personnel on duty at the time be legally required to ask all competent patients "in their last illness" (or to ask their family if they are incompetent) to donate their organs and tissue for transplant. A fine or loss of funding to the hospital could be imposed for failure to do so. However, in no province is there an enforcement mechanism to ensure that a required request is actually made, nor are sanctions imposed for failure to do so. At most, failure to conform with the Acts' provisions could mean the loss of points for hospitals in the accreditation process, a matter of little concern for hospital administrators in the turbulent throes of health care restructuring. The federal Standing Committee on Health addressed this question and recommended professional training of health care professionals on ways to approach families for donation requests and the development of systems to monitor hospital processes.

Offering Incentives for Being Pro-Active

A second option is the one adopted in Quebec; it gives a financial incentive for hospitals to seek out donors and provide transplant services. In 1997 their legislation rewarded hospitals by providing $500 for every donor a hospital identified and an additional $4,500 for every organ the hospital transplanted. Some Canadians would object to this measure, but in the short term it would increase awareness of the need for donation, create teams of specialized health care professionals able and willing to provide accurate and helpful information to the public, and clearly formalize the donation process. The Parliamentary Committee that studied this question recommended this second option to encourage pro-activity.[33]

Quebec's payments to hospitals for identification of potential donors and actual organ transplants carried out within a hospital are considered to be different from a private sector trade in human bodies and body parts, which is banned by the various provincial Human Tissue Gift Acts. The Quebec program is a controversial one, even though its purpose is not to trade in organs for profit but rather to help to respond to the need for human organs and tissue for transplant and to recognize the cost to a hospital in providing this service to the community it serves. Covering the legitimate costs of "donating," as we do in the case of sperm donations, for example, is a well-established practice in Canada. As long as all existing rules and laws involving freely given and informed consent are followed, and the potential donor's medical care is not compromised, it would be practicable to institute a legal protocol that combines required request with reimbursement to the health care system of the legitimate costs of identifying donors and removing and transplanting organs and tissue.

Asking Earlier

As pro-active policies increase public awareness of the need for organs and tissue for transplant, more and more doctors will make requests during routine check-ups, rather than during a patient's last illness. As in the case of lawyers, this kind of protocol can be introduced by their profession's governing body and be included under negotiation for billing purposes. But there is no reason why this task should be left exclusively to doctors and nurses. While the legal requirement to ask could be maintained, the onus could shift from the doctor and medical staff to specially trained professionals such as pastors, counsellors, or patient advocates who would be supported by volunteers knowledgeable in matters of transplant and able to provide clear answers to the potential donor's questions. Distancing the medical and hospital staff from the request for donation could prove beneficial in other ways. It breaks the direct link between a potential donor and the doctor (who is seen as an interested party), thereby decreasing the possibility of a patient feeling that a refusal could jeopardize his or her medical care in the final hours or days of life. The use of trained persons to assist with required requests recognizes the need for specialized skills to handle the emotions that can interfere with our normal ability to assess the pros and cons of our actions at a time of medical crisis. To agree to a *post mortem* organ donation when you are in the hospital is to acknowledge that you or your loved one is close to death. Few of us can handle such situations with equanimity. The assistance of a person who can address consent to donation in a compassionate and humane way at this critical time will contribute far beyond the mere acquisition of organs for donation. It will offer a patient peace of mind and increase confidence in the entire organ donor system.

Mandating Organ Donation

Some countries have a system of *mandated donation*,[34] a reversal of the usual donating system. All are *deemed* to have consented to have their organs and other human tissue removed after death and used for transplant or research, unless they opt out of the system. Countries such as Spain, France, and more recently Brazil have such systems.

Mandated donation is controversial; the Parliamentary Committee studying the question recommended against it, insisting instead on greater public awareness and education. Australia has already chosen the latter option and sends specially trained teams of doctors to intensive care units around that immense country to educate staff and patient families on donation. It now has a donation rate of forty per million, more than twice Canada's rate of approximately fourteen per million. The results seem worth the effort. Texas and Spain have pushed the educational component even further so as to provide a professionally trained counsellor who asks families about donations at every hospital. In British Columbia a new registration system has been introduced and is being closely monitored by other provinces.

While it has some support in Parliament,[35] mandated or required "donation" should, I believe, be a legislated option of last resort. The key to donation is gaining the confidence of Canadians in the system, not in pitting them against the medical profession. Doctors already allow families to veto otherwise valid legal consents to donate, and I doubt that they would proceed to retrieve organs if the law made donation mandatory, especially if patients were not even aware that the law required them to opt out. Education and heightened awareness seem the better way to address the shortage of organs and tissue for transplant. I argue that a law mandating or requiring donation is incompatible with our established legal principles of individual autonomy and informed consent and should not be adopted in Canada.

Xenotransplantation[36]

Recent developments in growing human tissue and organs for transplant offer a new solution to the serious issue of donor shortages.[37] Researchers' focus has been directed to the transplantation of genetically altered animal tissue and organs into humans, a process known as *xenotransplantation*. For years, our immune system was an effective bar to successful transplants, even when the donor was a human.[38] Today, new genetic engineering technologies and effective anti-rejection drugs combine to make even xenotransplants possible. By using genetic engineering techniques, scientists basically "humanize" animals. They insert human genes into animal embryos to create animals that are genetically prepared to serve as organ donors for humans. By the time this book is published, for instance, the world may well have witnessed the first human transplant using the heart of a genetically altered pig.[39] In the meantime, one American company has already been granted Food and Drug Administration approval to treat six patients suffering from a severe form of epilepsy with brain cells from fetal pigs.[40] Results seem encouraging, but as with all medical-scientific breakthroughs, xenotransplantation poses real dangers and raises several troubling issues.[41]

Just as human-to-human transplants created controversy about public health and safety[42] when first performed, so xenotransplants of organs such as hearts, kidneys, livers, and lungs, and tissue such as pancreatic islets, neural tissue, bone marrow, skin, corneas, and blood,[43] will continue to provoke heated public debate well into the twenty-first century. One of the most crucial challenges for law and medicine will be to put in place legally defined and enforceable standards, protocols, and rules to ensure that xenotransplants protect the public's health and safety, and that those who suffer from them have a legal recourse.[44] These standards would require guarantees, not just promises, that genetically altered animals[45] would be free of viruses and other pathogens that could be transferred unknowingly along with the organ.[46] Like all these technologies, their impact on public health and safety extends well beyond the individual to the larger community; and our professional rules and laws must reflect the seriousness of this potential threat to society's interests.[47] While medicine and science must ensure that xenotransplants are technically safe,[48] the law must protect individual and community rights.

Canada has sponsored a national forum on xenotransplantation to study the clinical, ethical, and regulatory issues[49] it raises, and Health Canada has also proposed a risk management framework for discussion on the safety of tissues and organs for transplantation in Canada.[50] International cooperation and regulation are high priorities. The World Health Organization (WHO) has issued a report in its consultation on xenotransplantation that recommended guidelines for the future surveillance and control of emerging and other communicable diseases introduced by cross-species organ and tissue transplantation.[51] The most extensive investigation of the issues surrounding xenotransplantation is the 1996 *Nuffield Council on Bioethics Report,*[52] which concluded that xenotransplantation was ethically justifiable, but that care must be taken to institute legal and medical safeguards for the future.

The treatment and use of animals in scientific research is another matter of increasing concern to members of the public concerned about animal rights. A public inquiry in the United Kingdom led to the most thorough discussion to date of the ethical issues raised for animals as transplant objects for xenotransplantation.[53] The report that followed found that it is ethical to use animals for research and transplant, and outlines areas where regulation will be required, including the limitation or prohibition of the creation of transgenic animals, and the care and maintenance of animals for exclusive use in xenotransplantation.[54]

Towards an Independent Transplant Network

In April 1999 Parliament addressed the questions of organ and tissue transplant directly. Its mandate[55] arose from a private member's motion and a request by the health minister for advice[56] on the appropriate federal role in addressing the issue of a shortage of donated organs. It also responded to a growing activism by transplant agencies and advocates to raise awareness among the public of the desperate need for organs for transplant.[57] As part of its work, the Parliamentary Committee held two months of public hearings and submitted a final report[58] in April 1999.

The committee recommended creating a Canadian Transplant Network.[59] Health Canada would have jurisdiction to set all standards, provide education and preventive health programs, approve all research in the field, and monitor and enforce compliance by the provinces with the *Canada Health Act*. It would also have the final power to create the network, which initially would have four permanent programs each overseen by an expert advisory group to deal with the process of donation, from obtaining consent through to the procurement of organs, their actual transplant, and related follow-up data. The committee urged that specific pediatric data be kept to help determine the unique requirements of children in need of organ and tissue transplants, and that a special award be offered to recognize the contribution of donors and their families and to increase awareness of the urgent need for donors of all ages.

A controversial recommendation involved the requirement for the consent of the next of kin, even where there was a valid legal consent to donate an organ or tissue. The committee insisted that this consent was essential to respect the interests of the family. I disagree completely with this approach. Where a person has expressed the wish in writing to donate organs and tissue, this decision should be respected. The committee's paternalistic approach flies in the face of Canadian principles of individual autonomy and choice, and should be avoided.

The final recommendation surrounded the issue of brain death. Rather than use this opportunity to begin a new public debate about the present definition of brain death, the committee reinforced the existing definition. It did so in spite of evidence of new medical technology that can determine when a person is in an irreversible coma with no hope of ever regaining consciousness. Instead, it recommended measures to police doctors and nurses more closely, requiring additional account-ability for each and every diagnosis of brain death and for extra training about brain death. I believe that refusing to recognize the current advanced state of medical diagnosis in this area will delay even further any meaningful public discussion of the question of brain death. This question has many facets, from the use of finite health care resources to the legal protection of doctors and nurses from charges of murder. It is a controversial and current question Canadians must face and resolve.

Conclusion

The Parliamentary Committee would entrench the federal Health Minis-try in all aspects of organs and tissue donation and transplantation. While this involvement would provide a kind of one-stop shopping for those in the system, I believe that it would also create real conflicts of interest within the department, federal-provincial conflict over jurisdic-tion, and a needless concentration of power and decision-making in the federal government. The provinces already have procurement and education systems in place that should be enhanced rather than elimi-nated by yet another reshuffling and federal intervention in the health care field. The recent announcement by the federal health minister that he plans to forgo a federally run national transplant network in favour of working with the provinces and territories to develop a truly inte-grated and more affordable Canadian network will respect provincial jurisdiction and existing efforts. If the federal government wants to help, it should provide much needed funds to existing provincial systems to allow them to create a linked national or international system. That would leave the federal government free to act in new areas.

For instance, the next stage of organ donation research and activity involves xenotransplantation and the use of new genetic engineering technologies to use stem cells to grow new organs, all of which will require great transparency to ensure the public trust. But in the present procurement system, any new national transplantation network should be built upon existing provincial strengths, and be independent of government, situated outside any federal government department, operating with it at arm's length. It should build upon existing agencies and expertise and could present annual reports to Parliament for public scrutiny and study, if the parties involved at all levels agree.

Most of the provinces have established non-profit agencies and organizations working in this area, and many are advanced in their process. British Columbia, for example, has already moved actively to establish a computerized provincial organ donor registry, run by B.C. Transplant, which also oversees donations and transplant services for the government. Professional training and reporting of imminent death of donors in a hospital setting is already required.[60]

Leadership for this exciting and essential initiative should come from several fronts, including the public, private, and volunteer sectors. It will be families living in local communities who play the determining role in promoting greater donations of human tissue and organs. Any *government* action and funding should ensure that people at the local level have the information they need to make organ donation a community priority and responsibility.

Chapter Ten

A Right to Die?
Assisted Suicide

W e have seen that, in response to the patients' rights movement and the advent of modern medical technologies, the
principles of personal autonomy and consent have been
clarified and legally recognized. We must consent to be treated and we
have the right to refuse medical treatment, even where that rejection will
lead to our death. A broad definition of *treatment* applies which covers
drugs, respirators, and other technologies used to keep people alive.
But how far does this right extend? Can we seek the help of others, such
as doctors, to help us die? If suicide is not illegal,[1] does that mean we
have a constitutional right to die? Clearly, we do not, and counselling or
helping someone to commit suicide is a criminal offence.[2]

The question arises whether this prohibition is always justified.
Recent cases suggest that Canadians are concerned that the present
Criminal Code provisions are too blunt and inflexible and need to be
reconsidered. Three recent cases, one on assisted suicide and two on
euthanasia, highlight areas where more public discussion is needed on
these difficult human problems. In the Sue Rodriguez case, an other-

wise competent adult was denied the right to assistance in suiciding. Her disease made it impossible to carry out this otherwise legal act alone.[3] In the Tracy Latimer case,[4] a mentally and physically incompetent child was killed by her father, who claimed it was a mercy killing and in her best interests to end the pain and suffering she had experienced since birth. The case is before the Supreme Court of Canada. Finally, the case of Dr. Nancy Morrison,[5] a Halifax doctor who was originally charged with killing a terminally ill patient in her care, reminded Canadians of the thin line between medication for palliative care and euthanasia, and demonstrated the difficult circumstances that doctors and intensive care nurses face in their work with terminally ill patients.

Chapters 10 and 11 will analyze whether our current criminal laws are able to address these real-life dramas. How might we resolve the dilemma of respect for personal autonomy for the terminally ill and the protection of the vulnerable? This question is addressed in these last two chapters.

Competent Adults: The Case of Sue Rodriguez

Are there cases where use of the criminal law so limits the individual autonomy of a competent person that it in fact creates a legal injustice? This question was at the centre of the Sue Rodriguez case, a story containing all the elements of an important legal precedent and a tragic human tale. A once physically active British Columbia mother in her early forties, Sue Rodriguez suffered from amyotrophic lateral sclerosis (ALS), commonly known as Lou Gehrig's disease. The prognosis was clear. This fatal neurological disease, marked by progressive loss of all muscle control and eventual death, would make it impossible for her to end her life by her own hand. She refused to commit suicide while she could still enjoy life with her young son, but she did not want to die by suffocation or end her life in a drugged or vegetative state. She argued forcefully before the courts that it was only the disease that prevented her from performing the otherwise legal act of suicide at a time of her own choosing, and she treated the doctor as merely the means by which she could carry it out.

This devastating disease had already started to erode her body by the time she began her legal battle for the right to have a doctor help her die. She challenged the constitutionality of subsection 241(b) of the *Criminal Code*, which makes assisted suicide a criminal offence, and argued that it violated her section 7 *Charter* right to life, liberty, and security of the person;[6] her section 15 equality right not to be discriminated against on the basis of disability;[7] and her section 12 right not to be subject to cruel and unusual punishment.[8] She sought an order from the Supreme Court of British Columbia declaring the section invalid to the extent that it prohibited terminally ill and disabled persons access to physician-assisted suicide to perform the otherwise legal act of suicide. As the media reported her appearances in court and her rapid physical deterioration, the B.C. Supreme Court dismissed her application,[9] a decision that was upheld on appeal by a majority of the B.C. Court of Appeal.[10] With little time left to her, she sought and was granted leave to appeal to the Supreme Court of Canada, which in a 5–4 decision refused her arguments.[11] In dismissing her appeal, the majority upheld the *Criminal Code* provisions that make assisted suicide a crime.

The Supreme Court's Decision

The Supreme Court Justices were deeply divided on what interests were in greatest need of protection and how to achieve them. The majority[12] argued that the fundamental interest at stake in assisted suicide was the sanctity of human life and the protection of the vulnerable. The minority opinions were each slightly different, but generally defined individual autonomy and self-determination as the key interests at stake.[13]

The majority ruled that the right to security of the person could not include a right to end one's life. Delving into legal history, Mr. Justice Sopinka noted that suicide[14] and assisting death have been crimes, at least until recently, and insisted: "At the very least, no new consensus has emerged in society opposing the right of the state to regulate the involvement of others in exercising power over individuals ending their lives."[15] The majority agreed that criminalizing assisted suicide deprived Sue Rodriguez of personal autonomy and caused her physical and psychological pain that affected her personal security, but they also held that this prohibition was accomplished in accordance with the principles of fundamental justice and that subsection 241(b) should stand.[16] That is because the section 7 right is really the right not to be deprived of life, liberty, and security of the person, *except* in accordance with the principles of fundamental justice. This means that section 7 would involve a two-step analysis: first, to identify whether a person has been deprived of any of the three listed rights, and second, whether they were deprived in accordance with the principles of fundamental justice. Only where there was a denial of fundamental justice would there be a finding that a section 7 right was violated. In its reasoning in this case,

the majority held further that respect for human dignity is not a principle of fundamental justice.[17] They pursued this particular approach in
denying her claim that criminalizing assisted suicide violated her section 12 right to be free from cruel and unusual treatment or punishment.[18] They refused to address the equality issue,[19] holding that,
regardless, the challenged section was saved under section 1 of the
Charter.[20] They decided that because the ban on assisted suicide
applied to every Canadian, and not just disabled ones, it did not violate
the rights of the disabled[21] — a reasoning that had already been abandoned by the same Court in *Charter* analysis before.

The dissenting opinions in the *Rodriguez* case addressed most of
these questions and founded their decisions on respect for the principles of individual autonomy and choice. In their judgments, they
offered legislative options for the future consideration of Canadians.
The Chief Justice[22] decided this case on the issue of equality and concluded that disabled persons who are unable as a result of their disability to commit suicide, an otherwise legal act, suffer discrimination
contrary to section 15 of the *Charter.*[23] Although not underestimating
the real vulnerability of *some* people in society, he noted the real difference between a competent, disabled person like Sue Rodriguez, who
has made an informed decision and seeks assistance to carry it out, and
others, who are not competent to consent or could be unduly influenced to agree to kill themselves. He believed we could be astute
enough to tell the difference on a case-by-case basis and refused to
accept that legislation was futile to prevent an inevitable abuse.[24] He
urged the adoption of the criteria outlined by Mr. Justice McEachern in
his dissent in the B.C. Court of Appeal, which we will discuss below.

In her judgment on the dissenting side, Madam Justice McLachlin
refused to consider *Rodriguez* as an equality case,[25] choosing instead to
treat it "as a case about the manner in which the state may limit the right
of a person to make decisions about her body under s. 7 of the *Charter.*"[26] She found that subsection 241(b) was arbitrary and violated Rodriguez's section 7 right to the liberty and security of her person and the
principles of fundamental justice.[27] Like the Chief Justice, she did not
shy away from offering options for Parliament and the medical profession to consider,[28] and she argued forcefully that existing criminal provisions and judicial review could protect society from abuse. She urged a
legal change to prevent the hardship that subsection 241(b) imposed on
people like Rodriguez and to recognize that the key issue in assisted sui-

cide was that of ensuring informed consent. In seeking other options, McLachlin joined the Chief Justice in urging the adoption of a process of judicial review of each request for assisted suicide.[29] This accountable and enforceable process would maintain the present criminal prohibition as a general legal principle, but would allow a judge of a superior court to tailor a remedy to the needs of the particular applicant, as McEachern had done in the lower court in this case. This protection is essential to ensure public trust in the system, and to protect the vulnerable and those influenced to end their lives for whatever reason.

So what do we learn from this case? First, that the law in Canada on assisted suicide remains. The Supreme Court's decision reinforces the law that denies competent but physically incapacitated Canadians from seeking assistance to end their lives, even where other physically capable Canadians can end their lives without fear of any criminal prosecution. Second, this case provided the best example of the injustice the current law can cause a terminally ill Canadian in Rodriguez's situation. It confirmed the need for greater discretion and flexibility in these situations to ensure that the vulnerable are not doubly discriminated against by their illness and their disability. The *Rodriguez* case contained all the elements needed to make politicians and the public sit up and take notice: Rodriguez was a competent and compelling advocate, the issue was both current and controversial, and there was no consensus on its resolution. The narrow division of the Supreme Court's final decision reflected the rifts that exist in the larger Canadian public. Third, Rodriguez's case challenged Canadians to rethink their views on this subject. She took the argument that the vulnerable would be put to death against their will if the law were changed and turned it on its head, refusing to be a victim and demanding the same treatment as an able-bodied Canadian would enjoy in this case. She convinced many that physically incapacitated or disabled people are not necessarily more vulnerable or less able to make valid and informed choices than any other group, and that the protection they need is not against themselves or their caregivers, but against an overly paternalistic state that refuses to respect their autonomy in these matters.

The Court's decision left Sue Rodriguez with two options. She could die a "natural" death by suffocation or pneumonia, conscious or drugged, hospitalized and completely dependent on others, or she could commit suicide by her own hand well before she would want to and before her fatal disease made it impossible for her to accomplish. She could not have assistance in legally ending her life. Ironically, she died as she had wished in spite of the law. When the time came that she decided her life was unbearable, friends ensured that she could commit suicide. They broke the law, but for lack of evidence as to what actually happened that day and by whom, no charges were laid for assisting a suicide. Rodriguez started the national debate. We have a responsibility to carry it on and to arrive at some consensus for others like her in the future.

At a most basic level, Sue Rodriguez forced all of us to ask a question we hope we will never have to face: "If that were me, what would I choose?" For most of us, the answer is not clear. Few of us have experienced her level of pain, anxiety, and suffering, but we can imagine it. And sometimes, like fear itself, the imagining is worse than the fact. The individuals I asked in my own small poll all answered that they would choose suicide. People care passionately about these questions, but as things stand now we rarely talk about them. As we will see in chapter 11 on euthanasia, doctors and nurses in intensive care units and the patients they care for don't have the luxury of ignoring this discussion. For them, the tough choices must be made now. For a variety of reasons, Sue Rodriguez and the Supreme Court precedent her legal challenge established force us to decide some of these questions. We must face the fact that, in this kind of case, individual autonomy is a phrase with little to offer those who cannot physically carry out their choices themselves.

The Recommendations of the Senate Committee

The coverage of the *Rodriguez* case and the intense public interest it created forced political consideration of the issue of assisted suicide for physically incapacitated Canadians. As in the past with such highly controversial questions, the Senate took up the challenge and appointed the Special Committee on Euthanasia and Assisted-Suicide, which adopted a broad mandate to examine the legal, social, and ethical issues relating to euthanasia and assisted suicide. The senators held public hearings across Canada and, in their final report, echoed the judgments of the Supreme Court Justices in both their divisions and their reasonings.[30] In their report, entitled *Of Life and Death*,[31] the majority recommended that the criminal offence of counselling suicide be maintained. A minority recommended amending section 241 of the *Criminal Code* to exempt from criminal sanction those who help another person commit suicide in very specific situations and to provide procedural safeguards both before and after an assisted suicide.[32]

Other private members' bills have been introduced since the publication of the Senate Report, but no government action has been taken and the law on assisting a suicide still stands.[33]

Legislative Options for the Future

If we were to accept that the key difference between assisted suicide and euthanasia is a person's competency to consent and make informed decisions to seek assistance to end his or her life, what special rules would be required to determine a patient's mental competency, so we can protect mentally vulnerable Canadians from abuse? Thanks to the courts, we already have some suggestions to consider as we start our public discussion. In his judgment in the B.C. Court of Appeal in the *Rodriguez* case, Mr. Justice McEachern outlined conditions that would apply in all cases of requests for assisted suicide or voluntary euthanasia.[34] These terms were later cited with approval by the minority decisions in the Supreme Court of Canada.

- The person seeking assisted suicide must be mentally competent to make a decision to end her life.
- Mental competence must be certified by two physicians, one of whom is her treating physician and the other an independent psychiatrist who has examined her during the twenty-four hours prior to putting the technical arrangements in place to allow her to end her life.
- She must commit suicide by her own hand.
- One of the doctors must be with her when she ends her life.
- The doctors must certify that she "truly desires to end her life," that it is a decision reached without pressure or outside influence and of her own free will.
- They must make sure she has not changed her mind and ensure that she knows she can change her mind at any time.
- They must certify that she is terminally ill, near death, and without hope of recovery, suffering unbearable pain or severe psychological distress, or would be were it not for drugs.
- They must certify the time when she would likely die.
- The regional coroner must be given three days' notice of the original psychiatric assessment and be present personally or through a medical doctor representing him.
- Once the arrangements have been put in place to allow her to end her life at a time of her choosing and she is aware of the availability of palliative care at that time, a psychiatrist must re-examine her

daily during the thirty-one-day time-limited period for evidence that she has not changed her mind.

- Following her suicide, one of the doctors must confirm in writing to the coroner that she had not changed her mind.
- The arrangements to allow a person to end her life expire and must be made inoperative if they are not used by the end of thirty-one days.
- If the patient has not committed suicide within the thirty-one-day period, it will be assumed that she has not made up her mind to commit suicide, or that she has changed her mind or lost the competence to decide.

What would it mean if we were to follow these rules? First, people who are terminally ill, without hope of recovery, and suffering either unbearable pain or severe psychological distress, whether or not they are on medication and receiving palliative care, could seek assistance to commit suicide. Second, rules for the actual process of assisting a person to commit suicide would be formalized, and doctors and coroners would be legally accountable. Third, the person who is dying and seeking assistance to end her life would be placed in control to the extent that she can direct the time and place of that death. Finally, by making the procedure public and requiring its record as an assisted suicide in these specific situations, the secrecy of a terminally ill person's death would be eliminated and the odour of crime would be removed.

The Law in Oregon

In addition to the issues the Canadian judges have identified, we should also examine other legislative examples.[35] No country makes assisted suicide legal,[36] although we will see in chapter 11 that the Netherlands has announced that it will formalize in law the system that has been in place there for some years. This system frees doctors from criminal prosecution for performing assisted suicide and euthanasia in certain specific situations. In North America the only jurisdiction that has a legal regime to allow assisted suicide is the state of Oregon, where doctors are free to provide medication for use by a person who wants to "die with dignity." Quoting from its *Death with Dignity Act*,[37] "[a]n adult who is capable, is a resident of Oregon, and has been determined by the attending physician and consulting physician to be suffering from a terminal disease, and who has voluntarily expressed his or her wish to die, may make a written request for medication for the purpose of ending his or her life in a humane and dignified manner in accordance with this Act."[38]

A mentally competent person suffering from an incurable and irreversible disease, which doctors say will lead to death within six months, may request in writing "a prescription for medication to end his or her life in a humane and dignified manner."[39] Several conditions apply, including a long list of specific responsibilities to be carried out by the attending doctor; the requirement of a second opinion by another doctor; the need for counselling to determine mental competency and the absence of depression or disease that would affect the patient's ability to make a valid request; the need to prove an informed consent; a requirement that the family be notified by the person seeking assisted suicide before the prescription is written; the necessity for repeated requests for a prescription; the repeated reminder to all people seeking a prescription of their right to rescind their request at any time; and the establishment of a fifteen-day waiting period between the original request and the actual writing of the prescription. All these steps must be documented, along with the patient's medical record, and reported to Oregon's Health Division. Existing insurance contracts,[40] wills, and other contracts and statutes[41] must not be affected by a person's decision to request medication to end his or her life. The Act covers only those situations where a competent and terminally ill person decides to seek medication to end his or her life. In effect, it does not qualify such deaths as suicide, and the usual charges associated with it, including assisted suicide, mercy killing, or homicide do not apply in these cases. The Act makes it clear, though, that where the physician or any other person becomes the active agent of death, charges will be laid. This situation occurs when a physician or other person ends a patient's life by lethal injection, mercy killing, or active euthanasia.[42]

As would be expected, even though the other relevant laws about homicide, assisted suicide, and suicide remain in force, and this Act applies only in a narrow and specific band of situations, the legislation was highly controversial. In fact, the people of Oregon were required to vote twice on the matter before it was finally enacted.[43]

Conclusion

I began this discussion with assisted suicide, including voluntary euthanasia,[44] because it covers the kinds of cases we might resolve by treating them as an extension of our current legal right to refuse treatment. I believe the carefully considered decisions of competent, terminally ill Canadians about how and when they want to die should be honoured. Such recognition reconfirms our respect for fundamental individual choices and supports enforcing them through advance directives and living wills. It acknowledges that, for many people, physical life at all cost is secondary to a full and independent life; and puts that profoundly personal decision in their control. The case scenarios extend well beyond those in *Rodriguez* and are formidable in their complexity. This public debate about control at the end of life will be controversial, but deserves attention to either change or reconfirm existing law on assisted suicide.

Substituted consent cases also need to be addressed. For instance, parents now must legally consent to treatment for their children. Should they be able to ask for assisted suicide for their terminally ill children if these minors fall within the categories set out for competent adults? Would we think differently if the child were mentally incompetent? What if the child refused and wanted to live? And, finally, what about the cost to the health care system? Should this factor ever be a consideration, and, if so, when and why? Throughout this book, we have seen that in all these issues raised by modern medicine and technology, our biggest challenge is to balance two competing interests: individual autonomy in personal health decision-making and the protection of the vulnerable from abuse. In assisted suicide, the elements exist for us to do both. This suggestion is not necessarily to argue for a "right to die" — which I would oppose — but to respect the wishes of a competent person in specific situations of terminal illness to end his or her life in a "humane and dignified manner" and to have access to the medication to do so, as is provided for in the Oregon law.

The main arguments presented against assisted suicide and euthanasia are clear. One is religious: it holds that all life is sacred and that its beginning and end must be dictated by God alone. The other one is procedural: it holds that under no circumstances can we avoid the "slippery slope" that will see us killing the vulnerable and the incompetent among us. Support for the rights of competent people to *choose* to die is just the beginning, the argument goes, and in the end it will lead us to a modern-day killing ethic founded on eugenic considerations about whose life is worth living and whose is not. We are right to worry about "what if" scenarios, perhaps for no other reason than it keeps us vigilant to possible abuses. We cannot make some people less subject to the influence of others, but we can have mechanisms to try to ensure that potential manipulation is minimized. The majority in the *Rodriguez* case argued that no legislative scheme has yet been found to prevent such abuse, so we must maintain the law and deny competent but physically disabled Canadians the right to control over their lives as guaranteed under the *Charter*.[45]

Is that what the majority of Canadians believe? Even if there is no constitutional right to die,[46] there *is* a constitutional right to life, liberty, and security of the person. Is it correct to argue that disability and disease that lead to a painful and struggling death affect not just our individual comfort and security but also our basic definition of ourselves? If we believe that our own human dignity depends on our physical and mental independence, should that view not be respected? Madame Justice McLachlin argued that our right to life, liberty, and security of the person is violated when state action prevents a person, on fear of criminal prosecution, from exercising that right. Is there a better legal principle than personal autonomy in health care and life decision-making on which we should found future action? If so, what might it be?

My own research and reflection on these questions have raised more questions than answers. I believe that the law — if we decide that assisted suicide and euthanasia are different in practice and legal effect — must consider mental competence as a key factor. As an advocate for greater individual autonomy in health care and related decision-making, I prefer legal recognition for individual choices that ensure that terminally ill, competent Canadians can keep control at the end of their lives. It will not help us directly with some types of cases, such as those that involve substituted consent for now incompetent adults or for young children and infants, or for those who have never been mentally competent. These are cases in law's grey area: achieving consensus on them will be difficult and will require more public discussion than has gone on so far. I believe, though, that there is room for real legal innovation as we face these situations in the coming century. I also believe that cases such as *Rodriguez* highlight current human dilemmas at the end of life, and demonstrate real differences between cases where a competent patient exercises an otherwise legal option to kill herself and one where a doctor or relative takes it upon herself or himself to kill another. In this, assisted suicide is truly different from active euthanasia, the subject to which we now turn.

Chapter Eleven

Euthanasia

I n chapter 10 we addressed the question of assisted suicide, including voluntary euthanasia, where a competent and terminally ill person seeks assistance to die. We saw this choice as a possible extension of our existing legal right to refuse treatment (even where lack of treatment would lead to our death), and the fact that it is not illegal to commit suicide. It is clear that not all health care scenarios are the same and that, unlike the relatively straightforward case of Sue Rodriguez, the matter of substituted consent will require serious consideration. In this chapter we will look at euthanasia and analyze some of the key issues through the lens of two well-known cases: those of Tracy Latimer and Dr. Nancy Morrison.

In the *Latimer* case,[1] we will look at the debate about euthanasia from the side of the children and the disabled who will be killed and who cannot give a valid consent or even understand what is being proposed. We will also consider the views of the parents or caregivers who believe they are acting in the best interests of the child or the incompetent disabled person, and ask to be treated differently by the criminal law. The question is straightforward: Should we move away from the absolute ban on killing others? If the answer is yes, should we amend the *Criminal Code* to create a category that would carry a lesser sentence for "mercy killing" than exists now?

In the *Morrison* case,[2] we will analyze the current debate about the protection of doctors and nurses working in hospitals and other health care settings, where their use of drugs for palliative care and pain management can hasten death.

Euthanasia is defined most frequently as a deliberate act undertaken by one person with the intention of ending the life of another person to relieve that person's suffering, where that act is the cause of death.[3] This category includes all situations where a patient has not expressed, or is not competent to express, a wish to die because the person is an infant or a child, is incompetent through disease, disability, or accident and unable to make his or her wishes known, or has not left a valid legal directive or living will that speaks to the health care scenario in issue. In Canada[4] euthanasia is illegal[5] and is treated as homicide, a crime that involves one person causing, either directly or indirectly, the death of another person.[6] Homicide may be either *murder*, where death is caused intentionally, or *manslaughter*, where it is caused negligently. Euthanasia is usually considered criminal homicide, punishable as first- or second-degree murder or manslaughter, which may in certain circumstances be prosecuted as other kinds of offences.[7] The *Criminal Code* [8] makes it clear that no one can consent to be killed, and even if the person did agree, that consent would not provide a defence from criminal responsibility to the person inflicting death.

The practical legal challenge at present, as we will see in the *Latimer* case, is how to take into account a person's motive in these cases.[9] Our criminal law considers only a person's intent. If a man intends to kill someone and does, he is guilty of murder and liable for imprisonment for life. The *Code* allows considerations of motive for parole purposes, but in cases that are sometimes labelled as "mercy killing," the fact that the accused may face life imprisonment with no chance of parole for ten or twenty-five years has been a powerful reason for juries not to convict. This reasoning is especially prevalent where the stories are tragic and the person killed was in terrible pain. Cases of euthanasia usually fall into two categories: the first involves family members killing a terminally ill or seriously impaired relative, and the second involves ending a patient's life in a hospital or other health care setting. These cases are all profoundly sad human dramas, and the argument that it was an act of mercy to liberate the sick, disabled, or dying person from misery can be compelling. For public policy, the difficult issue is whether the law should be amended to allow greater judicial discretion in these cases and, if so, in what situations. Two cases that contain all the elements of the dilemma are the *Latimer* and the *Morrison* cases.

Disabled Children: The Tracy Latimer Case

As this book goes to print, the Supreme Court has agreed to hear an appeal in the 1993 case of Robert Latimer, the Saskatchewan farmer who killed his severely disabled twelve-year-old daughter Tracy by putting her in the cab of his truck and asphyxiating her with carbon monoxide.[10] He argued that it was a mercy killing, the act of a loving father who no longer wanted his child to suffer pain. Although he was convicted of second-degree murder in the case, the sentence was reduced by the Saskatchewan Court of Queen's Bench to two years less a day, half of which was to be served in a provincial institution and half on his farm. The court granted him a constitutional exemption[11] from the mandatory life sentence with no chance of parole for ten years. In November 1998 the Saskatchewan Court of Appeal overturned the lower court's decision and reinstated the mandatory minimum sentence. The Supreme Court of Canada will be asked to review both the conviction and the sentence, as well as the use of the constitutional exemption in this case. Latimer will argue that he acted out of necessity when he killed his daughter — another novel defence. Our highest Court will have to clarify the law but amending the *Criminal Code* will be the responsibility of Parliament.

This case clearly raises the two key questions of the rights of children and the disabled and the inflexibility of the *Criminal Code* provisions concerning sentencing and homicide. Tracy Latimer was doubly disabled. She was a child who would never be able to give a valid legal consent, or even understand or speak to the options before her. She was at the complete mercy of her family, who had cared for her and loved her since her birth. In their turn, they believed that their dedication to her and the fact that she was their daughter gave them the right to decide what was in her best interests. The fact that she was severely disabled and in considerable pain was justification enough, to Robert Latimer, for his action. From his point of view, the law was unfair and arbitrary, and it should be changed to allow for killing as an act of mercy. As such, it would carry a minimum sentence.

This case also raises serious questions about the historic responsibility of the state to protect the best interests and rights of children. It also challenges the *Charter* guarantees of non-discrimination against the disabled. Any scheme that is adopted by Parliament must respect these legal precedents. Public opinion is clearly divided on euthanasia, expressed as "mercy killing" in this case. In a *Globe and Mail*/CTV poll, however, a large majority (73 percent) of Canadians expressed the view that the mandatory minimum sentence was too harsh in the *Latimer* case, and 41 percent said that "mercy killing" should not be illegal.[12] Other cases involving the killing of family members have been treated differently.[13] There is clearly a need for more guidance on these questions and for real public consensus-building about the values we want to respect and the practical options for possible reform. The upcoming Supreme Court ruling will allow us to discuss the many issues this case raises and to see what our next steps might be.

Health Professionals

We have reviewed one situation where a person is killed by a family member to end pain and suffering, but the more usual case arises in a hospital setting.[14] The scenarios are legion, but the most common is that of an incompetent patient who is in a terminal stage, frequently in pain, under heavy medication, and close to death. There are also cases where a person is irreversibly unconscious or in what is called a persistent vegetative state. In this situation, the question is whether to withdraw treatment, or nutrition and hydration, in order to hasten death. In Canada, to hasten death through the use of increasing doses of drugs (morphine, for instance) is not a crime, provided it can be shown that the primary purpose of the medication is to ease pain or make the patient more comfortable. In most of these cases, the issue of the futility of further treatment, including resuscitation, has already been discussed with the patient or the family, where the patient may or may not be aware of what is happening. It is this kind of situation that causes the greatest anxiety and offers the most risk of abuse for either economic or other personal family reasons.

There is also considerable confusion and concern among the medical and nursing personnel faced with these issues on a regular basis. Some recommend greater training of doctors in palliative care and pain management generally.[15] What do we want done in these situations, and how can we ensure that our laws protect not only the vulnerable but also the doctors and nurses charged with making these medical decisions? The case involving Dr. Nancy Morrison,[16] a Nova Scotia respirologist accused of murdering a terminally ill patient while he was in hospital, raised again the precarious position of doctors and nurses, and the need for greater guidance and legal clarity in such end-of-life situations.

The Canadian Medical Association

Since 1922 the Canadian Medical Association (CMA) has advocated clarification of the *Criminal Code* concerning the provision of palliative care treatment that may shorten life. In its policy summaries, available on the Internet, the CMA has offered one on *physician-assisted death*[17] in which it has lumped both euthanasia and assisted suicide into one category. The CMA supports neither, but excludes from its definitions "the withholding or withdrawing of inappropriate, futile or unwanted medical treatment or the provision of compassionate palliative care, even when these practices shorten life." These measures would include progressive increases in dosages of medication that suppress breathing and induce total sedation. The CMA defines *euthanasia* as "knowingly and intentionally performing an act that is explicitly intended to end another person's life and that includes the following elements: the subject is a competent, informed person with an incurable illness who has voluntarily asked for his or her life to be ended; the agent knows about the person's condition and desire to die, and commits the act with the primary intention of ending the life of that person; and the act is undertaken with empathy and compassion and without personal gain." It defines *assistance in suicide* as " knowingly and intentionally providing a person with the knowledge or means or both required to commit suicide, including counselling about lethal doses of drugs, prescribing such lethal doses or supplying the drugs."[18]

The definition of euthanasia provided here excludes the practices most commonly referred to as *involuntary passive euthanasia,* where an incompetent patient whose wishes are not known is "allowed" to die. The largest "grey area" is in this category, and deliberately excluding it from the definitions is not helpful and can even suggest that it is not viewed as euthanasia at all. An illusion is maintained that these situations are beyond the reach of the law and that doctors and health care professionals should feel free from criminal sanction if they engage in these practices. Society often acquiesces in this activity, but it would be wrong for doctors and others to think that because their professional association has defined euthanasia as assisted suicide for their practitioners, they will always be free from criminal charges and prosecution in every case. Until the law is changed, or amendments are made specifically to exclude situations of terminally ill, elderly, and incompetent patients, with or without a legally valid advance directive, then a doctor or anyone else who "causes, either directly or indirectly, the death of another person" could be considered for charges of homicide. For instance, the *Code*[19] makes a person criminally responsible for causing death even where the treatment or action taken only accelerated an already irreversible process of dying. Generally speaking, the difference in law is between actions that merely avoid prolonging the dying process and those that actually kill a patient. It is because these distinctions are often blurred that confusion arises and mistrust can breed. For doctors and nurses, the sanctions for moving beyond those limits are extreme — possible life imprisonment for homicide. Both the limits themselves and the penalties for breaching them need to be clearer in order to protect health care personnel and maintain the public's trust.

The Report of the Special Senate Committee

After the Supreme Court of Canada announced its decision in *Rodriguez*, the Senate appointed a Special Committee on Euthanasia and Assisted-Suicide. It studied the issue of palliative drug therapies and recommended that treatment aimed at alleviating pain, but that also shortened life, be considered legal for competent patients and for those with a valid advance directive. The same criteria were considered appropriate for the practice of total sedation.[20] Where the patient's wishes were not known, the committee recommended that the doctor and the health care providers make every effort to consult the family or other appropriate surrogate decision-makers and proceed on that basis to ease or eliminate pain.[21] Where these wishes were known, they should be respected. If treatment is carried out against the patient's wishes, the legal recourse is an action for assault and battery under section 265 of the *Criminal Code*.[22] To quote the Senate Report: "The Committee recognizes that providing treatment aimed at alleviating suffering that may shorten life is legal."[23] Total sedation of a patient is legal when it is done with the consent of the patient or the designated health care surrogate. Although these measures are already in practice, the testimony before the Senate Committee makes it clear that there is a great deal of confusion about the criteria on which the medical profession makes its decisions and what the general public think are their rights. In the end, the committee voted by a majority of one to maintain the *Criminal Code* unchanged as it relates to both assisted suicide and euthanasia.

In 1996, in the wake of the Special Committee Report, Senator Sharon Carstairs, seconded by her Senate colleague Dr. Wilbert Keon, a world-renowned heart surgeon, introduced a Bill to protect health care providers in situations of euthanasia and assisted suicide.[24] The Bill would have amended the *Criminal Code* to shield health care workers[25] from criminal liability if they acted upon a request to withhold or withdraw treatment in certain circumstances. The request would have to be made by a competent person who was suffering from a "life-threatening condition" or anticipated one. It would have to be made before or while life-sustaining medical treatment was in place, and made verbally or by signs in the presence of at least one witness. Any other request, including one by an incompetent person, would have to be in writing by the person involved or by a substitute decision-maker pursuant to a valid advance directive, or by the person's legal representative or a "relative who is most intimately associated with the person." In all these circumstances, a valid advance directive would always take precedence.

The Bill provided a comprehensive definition of *life-sustaining medical treatment* and covered doctors, nurses, and others working under the doctor's direction. It protected health care providers who administer pain-relieving medication to a person to alleviate or end that person's physical pain, even where that medication is provided in doses that may shorten the person's life. The Bill assumed that most people have not made a valid advance directive, nor have they expressed their wishes to their family and friends in the event that they are faced with a terminal condition, disability, or injury that robs them of their ability to speak for themselves. The view set out in the Bill is that individual autonomy is important, but that decisions of this kind have an impact on both the family and the health care system. Although the first preference would be to respect the individual's choice, others have the right to act on that person's behalf, including the prescription of drug therapy for palliative care and for total sedation, where no opinion has been expressed. The Bill's definition of *life-sustaining medical treatment* is wide and may startle those unfamiliar with hospital and nursing home care at the end of life. It was defined as meaning "any medical or surgical procedure or intervention that uses mechanical or artificial means to sustain, restore or supplant a vital function in order to postpone death including, without limiting the generality of the foregoing, artificial hydration and nutrition."[26] The Bill was debated in the Senate, but was defeated.

Palliative Care: Drugs

The Ontario coroner has further clarified the position on euthanasia by finding that palliative care that results in death will not be considered criminal if the following four conditions are met:

- The palliative care is intended solely for the relief of suffering.
- The care or treatments are administered in response to actual or observed signs of suffering.
- The care and medication are commensurate with the suffering.
- The treatment is not undertaken deliberately to cause the patient's death. The care and medication have to be documented, and it must be shown that the doses of drugs administered were increased progressively and not given in one massive dose.[27]

The paucity of case law leaves these issues open to speculation, but the federal Justice Minister's statement before the Senate Committee and the *obiter* of Mr. Justice Sopinka, speaking for the majority in the *Rodriguez* case,[28] give us some indication of the legal defence we can expect in future where a patient dies pursuant to a doctor's treatment for pain using high, or even lethal, dosages of drugs. In no case is futile treatment mandatory. In his testimony before the Senate Committee, then federal Attorney General and Justice Minister Allan Rock stated: "The *Criminal Code* does not require futile treatment, nor does it require capable patients to accept treatment they do not want. Similarly, necessary palliative care which is carried out in accordance with generally accepted medical practice is not prohibited by the Code whether or not this treatment results in the death of the patient."[29]

The Dutch Approach

It is useful to look at other jurisdictions[30] as we wrestle with these questions at home. While euthanasia is illegal throughout the world,[31] one country — the Netherlands — has moved formally beyond the narrow confines of criminal law to address this practice in certain situations. The Dutch government has implemented carefully constructed guidelines that will soon be the law and, if followed, protect a doctor from prosecution for euthanasia and for assisted suicide. These guidelines allow doctors to respond to their patients' request to die, as in assisted suicide and voluntary euthanasia, but also allow euthanasia where the patient is incompetent.[32] Concerns about this are highlighted by recent evidence that the class of persons seeking help from doctors to kill themselves include the emotionally ill, and not just physically ill people suffering from terminal disease.

The history of the Dutch debate on both assisted suicide and euthanasia has been controversial. In January 1990, after three unsuccessful legislative attempts to set criteria for euthanasia in both the *Penal Code* and the *Medical Practices Act,* the Dutch government established the *Remmelink Commission* to inquire into medical practice surrounding euthanasia. To ensure a full hearing, legal immunity was given to doctors who testified. An interim notification procedure to be followed in all cases of euthanasia and assisted suicide was adopted by the Royal Dutch Medical Society, and these guidelines were later legally codified. The new law amended the *Burial Act, 1995*, and came into force on 1 June 1994. It established a mandatory regime to be followed by doctors involved in what was described as an "unnatural death." Amid controversy about the inevitable slip towards unfettered killing of the old and infirm, involuntary euthanasia was later covered by the guidelines.[33]

How have the Dutch managed to get consensus on euthanasia and assisted suicide? Some of the reasons are unique to that country and could probably not be replicated elsewhere. In the Netherlands, for instance, health care is publicly financed and its social systems are extensive and well developed. It also has an advanced system of nursing homes, supported by nursing staff and doctors specially trained in geriatric care.[34] Politically, the Netherlands is a unitary state, a small country with strong local government, a sound economic infrastructure, and one of the most culturally cohesive populations in the developed world. This homogeneity makes it easier to achieve consensus for political decisions than in Canada or the United States, for instance, with their diversity of cultures and points of view. The Netherlands has traditionally been in the vanguard of social change and experimentation, and the Dutch are willing to discuss and tackle divisive questions other countries choose to ignore.

But perhaps as important is the Dutch legal system, which can be adapted to serve the needs and policy choices the people want. This system allows them to act on principles that recognize and respect the collective good, which often takes precedence over North American notions of individual rights. Euthanasia and assisted suicide still remain criminal acts under the *Penal Code*. Euthanasia is defined as intentionally ending the life of a person at his or her request, and assisted suicide as inciting or assisting another person to end his or her life.[35] Refraining from action or stopping treatments do not qualify within this definition, and the need for a request by the patient excludes such vulnerable patients as newborns and the comatose. As in Canada, the use of drug therapy for palliative care to reduce pain (as opposed to ending life) does not constitute a criminal offence, even where the ever-increasing doses have the effect of shortening the patient's life. Criminal proceedings may only be instituted by the Department of Public Prosecutions, which has significant independence.[36] The public prosecutors are not legally bound to prosecute unless they have been ordered to do so by a court of appeal, the justice minister, or the procurator general. This broad discretion moulded the Dutch public policy response to euthanasia and assisted suicide and made the present model possible. Doctors are assured that no prosecutions will be initiated if they follow the specific rules established to handle all euthanasia and assisted-suicide cases.

This process could not happen in Canada, where it is the responsibility of a provincial Crown prosecutor to lay a criminal charge. If a criminal act, such as euthanasia or assisted suicide, has taken place, the Crown prosecutor has no discretion not to lay a criminal charge on the grounds of public interest if there is sufficient evidence for a conviction.[37] To complicate matters, if the accused in Holland is compelled to action by *overmacht* (roughly translated as *necessity*), the Dutch *Penal Code*[38] allows this defence to a criminal charge. It must be a *medical* necessity, so it covers only those cases where doctors are involved. A second kind of medical necessity arises in situations of medical emergency. In the Netherlands, where a doctor is faced with ending the life of a consenting patient or letting that patient live in terminal pain, he can evoke the defence of "situation of medical necessity" and actually commit an illegal act, such as ending that patient's life. Where a doctor is faced with a competent patient in unbearable pain who wants to die and for whom there is no other way to end the pain, the rationale holds, he can chose euthanasia, even though doing so is against the law. It should be clear that the Dutch model goes much further than any situation that has been considered in Canada, and its potential for abuse is significant.

In all these cases the doctor would be required to follow the procedures established in 1994, and the following substantive and procedural criteria are required by the guidelines:[39]

- The request for euthanasia must be made by the patient and be entirely voluntary, informed, and persistent.
- The patient must be adequately informed about his medical condition, its prognosis, and alternative available treatments.
- There must be intolerable suffering with no prospect of improvement, but the patient need not be terminally ill.
- Other alternatives must be explored and shown to have been ineffective or rejected by the patient.
- In those districts of the country where it is required, the physician must wait a full twenty-four hours between the repeated request and the act of euthanasia.
- The euthanasia must be performed by a physician after consultation with a colleague.
- The physician must exercise due care and keep a written record of the case.
- The death must be reported to the local medical examiner as a death by euthanasia and never as a natural death.
- The physician involved may seek guidance from the state inspector for health, the Royal Dutch Medical Association, the local district attorney, or the medical examiner.

In testimony before the Canadian Senate Committee studying euthanasia and assisted suicide, one Dutch expert set out three issues of greatest concern with their existing system: "first the substantial existence of cases of unrequested termination of life and a related gray area; second, the reporting of cases of euthanasia to the public prosecutor; third, the need for improvement of the quality of the medical community's views and performance regarding the end of life."[40] Recently, concerns over broadening the category to include non-terminally ill patients suffering from depression has caused considerable debate. In one of the most publicized cases on the capacity of psychiatric patients to request euthanasia, a middle-aged Dutch social worker whose two sons had died through suicide and cancer decided that she wanted to end her life, which, she insisted, had no further meaning for her and had become unbearable. She refused all medical treatment for her depression, although she did see her psychiatrist for several therapy sessions. Colleagues reviewed the sessions and the journal she kept as part of the therapy and concluded that the lesser evil was to provide her with the means to commit suicide painlessly and with as little violence as possible.[41]

Other key concerns will have to be addressed as we search for a public consensus on these questions. For instance, is the principle of full mental capacity and competence undermined when mentally ill or depressed patients are allowed to request euthanasia? Although few would disagree that mental pain can be as acute and destructive to one's dignity and person as physical pain, there is little doubt that in terms of legal capacity, the two are different. Allowing mental suffering to be treated on an equal footing with physical pain, without additional safeguards, can undermine the very notions of mental capacity which legitimize informed patient decisions about whether to undertake or continue treatment. When, in this case, the decision means the death of the person, caution is essential. In setting legal boundaries, we must also understand the impact on the public's perception of doctors, nurses, and other health and care givers if they alone were given the legal authority to make life and death decisions for us were we to become incapacitated, for whatever reason. Public confidence in the medical and health care professions is essential in our society, and any laws and amendments to existing rules to allow euthanasia in whatever circumstance must take full account of this point.

The Dutch model gives exceptional power over these questions to doctors. This kind of paternalism would go against the trend in Canada and the United States towards lessening the all-powerful grip of the medical profession on major health care decisions in favour of an expanded and more dominant role for the patients and their families. Patient preference, reliance on better palliative care and pain management alternatives, and demands for individual autonomy in health and life decisions are part of the modern Canadian way. Every attempt should be made to broaden the role and to respect the rights of individual Canadians in these complex situations. As the educated and articulate generation of Canadian baby boomers ages, the question of the acceptability and accessibility of both euthanasia and assisted suicide will grow in importance and public appeal. Lawyers working in this area will be asked to help to balance the concerns of the public with the protection required for individual Canadians and the doctors and nurses who care for them.

Why is it so important to address these problems as they affect health care providers as well as the individual? Two reasons come to mind. First, to provide doctors and nurses with a measure of protection against legal action; and, second, to reassure the public that their lives and those of their loved ones will be protected when they are in the hospital and seriously ill. The case of Dr. Nancy Morrison in Halifax is proof of the need for effective and enforceable procedures to protect patients as well as the professional reputation of doctors and nurses who work daily with seriously and terminally ill patients. This reason alone should encourage us all to come up with some practical and acceptable options for legislative reform.

Canadian Considerations

What might some of the legal requirements be to protect doctors and nurses from criminal charges in these cases? This process is now in effect, and it should be formalized in law as part of any reform we may consider. First, it must be established, that a patient is suffering severe pain and has agreed to a program of palliative care (or at least has not refused); second, the drug used must be appropriate in the circumstances and the treatment acceptable medical practice; third, the dosages should be increased progressively to meet the increased intensity of the pain; and finally, the treating physician's actions should be intended mainly to alleviate the patient's pain.

We must agree on a set of procedural guidelines that could provide guidance to doctors and nurses as well as comfort to families. One way would be to have a judge of a senior court review each case to ensure that the procedural requirements noted above have been met, and to provide reasons if necessary. The doctor and nurse could then proceed within the confines of the legal ruling, following the standards and medically accepted practice norms of their professions. Thought should be given to whether this process can be triggered by the family or the patient, or only by doctors and nurses. Once this process is complete, doctors and nurses would be free from prosecution and criminal charge.

This model need not be the only option for Canadians to consider, and we may want to try something different. We might want to create small panels with special responsibilities, from whose decisions an appeal could lie to a higher court. Such a system would ensure that the decisions are made "closer to the people" — as in jury trials. It would also confirm that these are fundamental issues that have an impact on all of us, not just on the people involved at the time.

If the real concern is that there will be abuse and that innocent and unwilling people would be put to death, we will want to craft a dynamic and truly open system for decision-making. Some principles are firm. Where possible, we must encourage and promote life as a fundamental societal value. All other choices will be a deviation of this norm, and those seeking other options will be required to make compelling arguments why this value should be challenged and changed. In either case, there is no doubt that the fabric of the status quo is ripping at the seams and needs to be either mended or changed for a new piece entirely. Modern medicine is the reason we need to discuss these matters and search for solutions that meet new technological realities and changing societal attitudes. Law will be the tool that allows us to define the elusive balance between the collective good and our own individual interests.

Conclusion

Should euthanasia be legal? In my view it should not, for at least two reasons. First, society has an interest in protecting its members from harm. This obligation includes protection from having death inflicted upon them, even where the stated purpose is to end their suffering.[42] The responsibility is even larger when it involves children and the physically and mentally vulnerable. Laws with appropriate sanctions are the only effective way to express our rejection of the deliberate killing of people in our society. The sentencing provisions may need to be made more flexible to ensure convictions and to allow judicial discretion in sentencing at the trial stage, but that should never mean that, as a value, we condone killing. Even in the Dutch and Oregon laws, as they stand right now, the changes presume that the historical ban on killing remains. Moreover, we have adopted human rights and criminal laws to protect the vulnerable and historically disadvantaged from discrimination and abuse. The very fact that we need such laws indicates that some groups are vulnerable and could be treated as less valuable members of society because of their sex, age, race, or physical or mental disability. This bias is already at work in how we view disability generally, and we must be cautioned against any further erosion of the rules against killing others. Euthanasia may indeed be the one area where we can justify the concern that no law can truly protect the weak and vulnerable and ensure their protection against abuse. Canadians have to help parliamentarians address this issue.

At first glance, continuing the present criminal prohibition of euthanasia raises other questions. Does this mean, for instance, that we must die a miserable death or be kept alive on a machine? As we have seen in chapter 10 on assisted suicide, it need not. Advance directives for health care are increasingly sophisticated methods of expressing our individual autonomy and choices. They allow us to make certain personal values and choices clear, and to express our legal right to refuse treatment, including life support, even where that decision will lead to our death. These legal tools give us real power. The challenge is to ensure that they are respected by family members and health care professionals who are there when they would come into effect. The tradition and practice of doctors and nurses is to act to save people's lives, to assume we would choose life over death. These attitudes are normally positive and should be encouraged. But where we have specifically decided otherwise, our views should be respected. The purpose of increased patient autonomy and involvement in our own health care decisions is to end the traditional paternalism by doctors and to ensure that we all take more responsibility for our lives. It would not be right to encourage people to take charge, provide them with the legal tools to make tough end-of-life and treatment decisions, and then ignore their choices. Paternalism is still the dominant value towards old and sick people, especially if they have lost their ability to speak for themselves. With the best of intentions, we all think we know better than elderly or sick relatives or friends what is best for them. But if they have spoken, while competent to do so, to express their values and choices, we must respect these wishes and act according to what *they* wanted, not according to what *we* think is best.

Respect for individual autonomy in medical decision-making and protection of the vulnerable from potential abuse must both be assured in any change to the existing criminal law. This is an urgent and profound problem. As we age, we worry that health and medical care resources will not match the demands of a large elderly population. Economic arguments about limited health care resources are compelling and will affect public policy in the future. There has to be a way to ensure that we will neither be put to death against our will nor denied our freely formed and competent decision to refuse treatment — even where that will result in death. As a starting point, more, not less, attention should be paid to the protection of the vulnerable — the elderly, sick, and mentally incompetent. Judicial review on a case-by-case basis is one way to achieve this goal. Assisted suicide and euthanasia are not issues that will go away in the coming years. We need to find ways to discuss them as we ourselves age and care for others.

Conclusion

Some Final Thoughts

A ll through this book, the connecting theme has been the need for us to create new and effective ways in which we can join the public debate on medical and scientific technology that will both enhance and haunt our living and dying in the coming century. I hope this book will be a starting point for the many Canadians who, until now, have felt these issues too distant and new to join in their discussion.

What I have tried to do with this book is to set out in one place some of the key issues we will be asked to address in the first years of the new millennium. All of these will affect most of us in some way and go to the core of how we define ourselves as human beings. The decisions we make now will set the course for the future path for the use and development of many of the technologies, research, and practices covered in this book. We need to remember that this will happen whether or not we participate. But I believe that we will have better public policy — and therefore better laws — if we are all at the tables where these matters are discussed and decisions taken.

The public decision-making processes are not set in stone. They require some updating, and new ways to involve more Canadians in informed discussion are always welcome. They will need to take account of the ever-moving and changing targets that are at the heart of the massive technological and scientific revolution now under way to ensure that our public policy is sensible and strong. In this process, each of us must accept a role and responsibility. It is up to all of us to ensure that, in the tough choices that lie ahead, we achieve the benefits science and medicine promise and still protect our societal interests and human rights.

Glossary

Allograft: a transplant between members of the same species.

Amniocentesis: a form of prenatal diagnosis where a needle is inserted into the amniotic sac to remove a small amount of amniotic fluid for screening for genetic and other fetal anomalies.

Artificial insemination (AI): the injection of collected sperm from a partner or donor into a woman's uterus to fertilize an ovum (egg).

Assisted reproduction: where reproduction is achieved other than through regular sexual intercourse; usually refers to AI, IVF, or one of its variants and relies on donor gametes or embryos.

Autograft: a transplant (usually of skin or bone) from one location in an individual to another location.

Autosome: a chromosome other than a sex chromosome. We have forty-four autosomes (or twenty-two pairs).

Azoospermia: absence of living sperm in the semen.

Bank: a place where a supply of human tissues and other human materials such as blood, sperm, and skin are kept for future use.

Blastocyst: a stage of development of the zygote; a fluid-filled sphere of cells that will give rise to embryo and placenta.

Bone marrow: the soft tissue of the inner cavity of the bone, responsible for the production of blood cells.

Brain death: the stage when the whole brain, including both the higher and lower brain, has ceased activity.

Chimera: an individual whose cells derive from different zygotes of the same or different species, occurring spontaneously or produced artificially.

Chorionic villus sampling (CVS): a method of prenatal diagnosis, where fetal tissue is obtained for genetic and other testing of the fetus.

Chromosome: a thread-like structure in the nucleus of a cell, containing DNA, the hereditary material (genes); a human has forty-six chromosomes: forty-four autosomes and two sex chromosomes.

Cloning: the process of producing a group of cells all genetically identical to the original cell that they started from. In gene technology, cloning is the process of producing multiple copies of a single gene or segment of DNA, as in skin or cartilage cloning.

Congenital anomaly: an anomaly present at birth caused by genetic factors, injury, or infection, before or at birth, or by other environmental or unknown factors.

Cryopreservation: freezing to extremely low temperatures, for example, of sperm, ova, and embryos for later use in reproduction or research.

Deoxyribonucleic acid (DNA): the genetic material, in the form of a double helix or spiral contained in the chromosomes, which codes for hereditary characteristics.

Direct ovum and sperm transfer (DOST): a method of assisted reproduction, where the washed sperm and ova are transferred to a woman's uterus through a small tube (catheter) for fertilization.

Egg donor: a woman who provides ova for reproduction purposes for another couple, whom she may or may not know.

Egg recipient: the couple or woman who receives the ova.

Egg retrieval: the process by which ova are removed for insemination in vitro.

Embryo: the stage from two to eight weeks in human development, following the zygote stage and before the fetal stage.

Embryo donation: the process whereby embryos are donated to couples who may be unable to produce their own, for use in reproduction.

Embryo flushing: a flushing or lavage of the uterus to recover an ovum or zygote.

Fecundity: the capacity to either conceive or impregnate.

Fertility: the ability to produce children.

Fertilization: the union of the sperm and ovum.

Fetal tissue research: the use for research of fetal cadaver tissue obtained from abortions, ectopic pregnancies, miscarriage, or stillbirth.

Fetus: the stage of human development between eight weeks and birth.

Follicle: a fluid-filled structure within the ovary that contains the developing ovum.

Gamete: the mature male and female reproductive cell, which contains one set of twenty-three chromosomes.

Gamete intrafallopian transfer (GIFT): a method of assisted reproduction whereby sperm and egg are introduced together into the woman's fallopian tubes.

Gene: the physical and functional unit of heredity.

Gene alteration: changing the structure of a particular gene in a controlled way.

Gene therapy: treatment to cure a disease or condition caused by a defective gene.

Genetic engineering: the isolation of genes so as to alter their structures and relationships to the rest of any genetic material in a controlled way; and includes cloning.

Genetic screening: use of tests in families or other groups to acquire genetic information about them, such as their susceptibility to certain inherited diseases.

Genetic testing: identifying an abnormal gene (such as the breast cancer genes) through a specific test.

Genetics: the study of the structure, regulation, expression, transmission, and frequency of genes.

Genome: all the genetic material contained in the chromosomes of a person's cells, containing as many as 100,000 genes.

Germ cell: the cell or cell line that produces sperm or ova for reproduction and through which genetic traits or changes can be passed from one generation to the next.

Implantation: the process by which the zygote becomes imbedded in the wall of the uterus between the sixth and fourteenth day following fertilization.

Infertility: diminished ability to impregnate, conceive, or bring a fetus to term.

Intracytoplasmic sperm injection (ICSI): a process of assisted reproduction for severe male infertility or sterility, where a single sperm is micro-injected directly into the ovum.

In vitro fertilization (IVF): a technique of assisted reproduction that is at the base of most of the other interventions; it involves the "mixing" of sperm and ovum (fertilization) in a petri dish in a laboratory to create a zygote, the future embryo, to be transferred to a woman's uterus for gestation and birth; in vitro means "in glass."

Ovaries: paired female sex glands in which egg cells are developed and stored and the hormones estrogen and progesterone are produced.

Ovulate: to release an ovum (egg) from the ovary.

Ovum: the female ovum or oocyte, formed in the ovary.

Preconception contracts: better known as surrogacy contracts, where a man or a couple enter into an agreement for a third party to have a child and give it up to them after its birth.

Pre-implantation diagnosis: the testing of a zygote created through IVF for known genetic anomalies.

Prenatal diagnosis (PND): the testing of a fetus in the uterus before birth for known genetic or other anomalies.

Semen: the fluid containing the sperm that is emitted during ejaculation.

Sex chromosome: the X and Y chromosomes that determine sex; XY is male and XX is female.

Somatic cell: any cell in the body that does not become a germ cell (ovum or sperm).

Sperm: the male reproductive cell produced by the testes.

Stem cells: primordial, all-purpose, and undifferentiated cells from which all the body's tissues develop. Human embryonic stem cells can develop into any of the body's 210 types of cells.

Superovulation: the production of abnormally large quantities of ova during the estrous cycle, usually achieved through the use of superovulatory drugs.

Surrogate: a woman who carries a pregnancy to term for another. The ova used to create the embryo may be hers, or that of the contracting female partner, or of a donor, known or stranger to all of them.

Transgenic: having genetic material artificially introduced from another species.

Ultrasound: high-frequency sound waves focused on the body and reflected to provide a video image of internal tissues, organs, and other structures; used in the assisted reproduction technologies such as IVF to retrieve ova and in prenatal diagnosis to identify the sex of the fetus and the state of its major organs and other visible structures.

Xenotransplantation: cross-species transplantation of genetically altered animal tissue and organs into humans.

Zona cutting or drilling: process used in ICSI to place sperm directly into the ovum.

Zona pellucida: the outer layer of the egg that protects the ovum and allows in the sperm for fertilization.

Zygote: the earliest stage of human development from fertilization to the end of the second week.

Zygote intrafallopian transfer (ZIFT): a form of assisted reproduction where a zygote is transferred to the fallopian tube for implantation.

Note: These definitions come mainly from the Royal Commission on New Reproductive Technologies Report and the Parliamentary Report on Organs.

Notes

The Web site and e-mail addresses in this book were current at the time of publication.

Introduction

1. Ian Kennedy, *Treat Me Right: Essays in Medical Law and Ethics* (Oxford; New York: Clarendon Press, 1991) at 119.

Chapter 1: Reproductive Technologies: Challenges for Regulation

1. Artificial insemination with frozen semen has been used in the cattle industry for over half a century and has a success rate equal to that of natural insemination. "Straws" of frozen semen can be stored indefinitely in containers of liquid nitrogen and then thawed to coincide with a female animal's, or woman's, ovulation. Drugs can be used to time ovulation to suit others' schedules if need be. For an excellent analysis of these issues in animal breeding, see Emily Kilby, "Breeding's Brave New World," *EQUUS* 255 (January 1999): 25. For related readings, see "Succeed When You Breed," *ibid*. at 231, and "Genetic Engineering," *ibid*. at 173.

2. While the purchase of human eggs is banned under the federal voluntary moratorium introduced in 1995, recent media reports make it clear that some fertility clinics are regularly advertising in university papers and on the Internet for young women to "donate" their eggs in return for $2,000. Clinic spokespersons insist that the money is to cover costs and that they are therefore not breaking the moratorium. See "Web site offers $2,000 to human egg donors," *Globe and Mail*, 13 May 1999, A8.

3. The Canadian Fertility and Andrology Society is a voluntary organization of some 400 physicians, scientists, and other health care professionals concerned with reproductive medicine and research. Its mission is "to promote education and research of female and male reproductive health, to provide accreditation expertise and processes for measuring outcomes of therapy, and to respond to social needs with regards to human reproduction." For further information, contact the Canadian Fertility and Andrology Society, 2065, Alexandre de Sèvre, Suite 409, Montreal, Quebec, H2L 2W5; phone (514) 524-9009, fax (514) 524-2163, or at <http://www.cfas.ca>.

4. For access to Statistics Canada's age-specific fertility rates, see <http://www.statscan.ca/english/Pgdb/People/Health/health08.htm>.

5. *1996 Guidelines for Therapeutic Donor Insemination*, Canadian Fertility and Andrology Society, May 1996, at 5. In about 40 percent of these cases, infertility is due to a male factor.

6. *Proceed with Care: Final Report of the Royal Commission on New Reproductive Technologies*, vol. 1 (Ottawa, 1993), lists extensive reading material on infertility. See in particular chapters 8–15, 162–358 inclusive. Other groups offer support and educational seminars to the public, including the Infertility Network at phone (416) 691-3611, fax (416) 690-8015, and e-mail <102137@compuserve.com>.

7. For definitions of current assisted reproductive technologies and practices, see the glossary in this book.

8. *Proceed with Care*, vol. 1, above note 6, chapter 10.

9. In the flurry of activity surrounding Bill C-47 in 1997, the Alberta Heritage Foundation for Medical Research (AHFMR) published a report on IVF to determine its effectiveness in producing pregnancies and healthy babies. See Paula Corabian, "In Vitro Fertilization and Embryo Transfer as a Treatment for Infertility," AHFMR, March 1997. For further information, contact AHFMR at 1-888-259-0066.

10. For a list of fertility clinics in Canada, contact the Canadian Fertility and Andrology Society. See note 3 above.

11. The lack of quality control standards and reporting requirements was highlighted in May 1999, when it was learned that a woman and her husband who were patients at the London, Ontario, fertility clinic were suing the hospital. Their embryos had been accidentally implanted in the womb of another woman, who fortunately had not become pregnant. The hospital attributed the incident to human error and the person responsible was fired. See Gloria Galloway, "Embryo mix-up underscores 'need for legislation,'" *National Post*, 27 May 1999, A3.

12. For an excellent overview of the issue of regulation of new reproductive and genetic technology (NRGTs) and the perspective of experts from the United States, United Kingdom, and Canada, see Warren H. Pearse, ed., "Assisted Reproduction: A Process Ripe for Regulation?" *Women's Health Issues* 6, no. 3, (1996).

13. The British Human Fertilisation and Embryology Authority is the most advanced and all-encompassing model. It would be suitable for Canada in terms of its mandate and actual work. For a copy of its *Code of Practice*, and for excellent research and policy discussion papers, see HFEA's Web site at <http://www.hfea.gov.uk>. It is expected that the Canadian government will choose the British model as its guide for legislation. This is a medically driven model, which grew out of the voluntary licensing authority established in the mid-1980s by the British Medical Association. It has a broad mandate, including the licensing of clinics and enforcement of the regulations. But it also has a larger role in education and policy, that we should consider as we develop our own regulatory model for running fertility clinics and conducting research on human embryos created through IVF in these clinics.

14. *The Human Fertilisation & Embryology Act 1990*, U.K. 1990, c. 37, created the permanent Human Fertilisation & Embryology Authority (HFEA). It provided for the enforcement of a code of practice, defined terms and made provisions for the creation, use, and development of human embryos and for their use in reproduction and research; public dissemination of information and research involving human reproduction and research; and the amendment of other laws, such as the *Surrogacy Arrangements Act 1985*, U.K. 1985, c. 49.

15. "CFAS and similar organizations in other countries have created practice guidelines to assist physicians and allied health personnel. CFAS is working with the Canadian Council on Health Services Accreditation to develop accreditation procedures for infertility treatment centres. These procedures can form the basis of licensure requirements by the Provincial and Federal Governments." *Response to Bill C-47: Human Reproductive and Genetic Technologies Bill* (Canadian Fertility and Andrology Society, 25 September 1996) at 11.

16. The countries with some form of legislation include Australia, Austria, Brazil, Czech Republic, Denmark, Egypt, France, Germany, Hungary, Israel, Mexico, The Netherlands, Norway, Saudi Arabia, Singapore, South Africa, Spain, Sweden, Taiwan, Turkey, and the United Kingdom. Countries with guidelines for assisted reproductive technologies include Argentina, five states in Australia, Egypt, Finland, Ireland, Italy, Japan, Poland, South Korea, Switzerland, and the United States. Canada has a voluntary moratorium that prevents certain reproductive and genetic practices; and plans legislation to ban certain reproductive and genetic practices, and to establish a licensing authority. Belgium, Greece, Hong Kong, India, Jordan, and Portugal have neither guidelines nor legislation. *Globe and Mail*, 25 May 1999, A1.

17. The International Federation of Fertility Societies (IFFS) has a mandate to contribute to the standardization of terminology and the evaluation of both diagnostic and therapeutic procedures used in medically assisted procreation (MAP). For their text on "assisted reproduction techniques" (ART), approved by the Executive Committee of IFFS on 22 September 1995, in Montpellier, France, see <http://www.mnet.fr/iffs/a_artbis.htm>.

18. On 27 July 1995, then health minister Diane Marleau announced a moratorium on nine reproductive technologies and practices, including sex selection for non-medical purposes, commercial surrogacy arrangements, the purchase or sale of gametes and embryos, egg donation in exchange for IVF, germ-line genetic engineering, ectogenesis (the creation of an artificial womb), the creation of animal-human hybrids, and the removal of oocytes from an aborted fetus or cadaver for use in donation, reproduction, or research.

19. Bill C-47, *An Act respecting human reproductive technologies and commercial arrangements relating to human reproduction*, 2d Sess., 35th Parl., 1996, was the first legislative attempt by the federal government using its criminal law power to ban the practices and technologies covered by its earlier moratorium in 1995. Like the moratorium, the Act, which would have been cited as the *Human Reproductive and Genetic Technologies Act*, would have banned the following practices: commercial surrogacy, the sale, purchase, barter or exchange of human gametes, zygotes, embryos and fetuses, post-mortem insemination, cross-species fertilization, the fusion of human and animal zygotes and embryos, implantation of a human embryo in an animal and vice versa, germ-line genetic manipulation, use of gametes from aborted fetuses or cadavers for reproduction or research, sex selection except "for reasons related to its health," ectogenesis, and the use of IVF to create embryos for research. The Bill died on the Order Paper when the government called the 1997 general election.

20. The *Globe and Mail* ran a series of articles on infertility clinics at the same time that the federal health minister was advising that he planned to introduce legislation in the fall of 1999. See Anne McIlroy, "Only the market rules Canadian clinics," *ibid.,* 22 May 1999, A1; "Fertility clinics face curbs," *ibid.,* 25 May 1999, A1; Sean Fine, "Playing the odds on conception," *ibid.,* 24 May 1999, A1; Sean Fine, "U.K. regulatory body likely to be used as model for Canada," *ibid.,* 25 May 1999, A4; Sean Fine, "Living quietly with the pain of infertility," *ibid.,* 27 May 1999, A4. See also Gloria Galloway, "Embryo mix-up underscores 'need for legislation,'" *National Post,* 27 May 1999, A3.

21. On 25 June 1998, in the case of *Bragdon* v. *Abbott,* 524 U.S. 624 (1998), the U.S. Supreme Court ruled that a person is protected from discrimination under the *Americans with Disabilities Act* of 1990 (Pub. L. 101-336, 104 Stat. 327 (1990)), if he or she has a physical or mental impairment that substantially limits reproduction. In the case at hand the woman had HIV, and the Court had been asked to rule on, inter alia, whether or not reproduction is a major life activity. This case could have far-reaching effects on access to assisted reproductive technologies in the United States, where health care is so closely linked to employment. It could mean that employers can no longer discriminate against infertile workers in terms of health insurance benefits covered for their employees or refuse them time off for infertility treatments. See Pamela Prager, "The Impact of *Bragdon* v. *Abbott* on persons affected by infertility" at <http://www.inciid.org/bragdon-abbott.htm>.

22. Estimates from Ontario, where most IVF clinics are situated, are that each treatment cycle of IVF costs the Ontario Health Insurance Plan (OHIP) an average of $1,000–3,000. Included in this estimate are egg retrieval, embryo transfer, consultations, and related procedures such as ultrasound, blood work, and laboratory costs. Other costs, such as fertility drugs, the freezing and storage of sperm, embryo freezing and thawing, and pre-implantation karotype screening are paid for directly by the patient.

23. IVF is not funded in Canada, with the exception of Ontario, in cases where women suffer from "complete bilateral anatomical fallopian tube blockage that did not result from sterilization" (R.R.O. 1990, Reg. 552, subs. 24(1)(23). In 1988 the health ministers of the provinces and the territories (Quebec excepted) agreed to a process of reciprocal billing and payment according to established tariffs. Among the listed exempted services were IVF and artificial insemination. In 1998 a claim by a Nova Scotia couple to have the costs they had incurred out of province for IVF and ICSI paid by the provincial health insurance plan was denied. See *Cameron* v. *Nova Scotia (Attorney General)* (1999), 172 N.S.R. (2d) 227 (S.C.), aff'd [1999] N.S.J. No. 297 (C.A.), online: QL (APJ).

24. Ontario is the only province whose health insurance covers IVF. Health insurance there is legislated by the *Health Insurance Act,* R.S.O. 1990, c. H.6, and Regulations; and until 1 April 1994, IVF was an insured service under the Act. After that date, IVF was delisted and now is only paid for in limited circumstances. IVF is not covered by OHIP except "for the first three treatment cycles . . . that are intended to address infertility due to complete bilateral anatomical fallopian tube blockage that did not result from sterilization" (Reg. 552, s. 24). Several cases have been heard in Ontario by the Health Services Appeal Board, challenging the Regulation as it relates to other assisted reproductive technologies and the narrow category of people who can have access to public funds for IVF treatments.

25. In a recent case before the Ontario Health Services Appeal Board, five couples suffering from male factor infertility appealed separate decisions of the General Manager of OHIP that denied each of them the public insurance funding required to pay for intracytoplasmic sperm injection with IVF. Their appeal was dismissed. All five had been told by their doctors that this was the appropriate treatment for their male factor infertility. All five couples had been refused on the grounds that IVF is not funded in Ontario for male

factor infertility and sperm injection is not a service listed in the Schedule of Benefits under the Act [see Reg. 552, subs. 24(1), para. 23, *Health Insurance Act,* R.S.O. 1990, c. H.6, as amended], which funds IVF only for infertile women suffering from "complete bilateral anatomical fallopian tube blockage." This appeal to the Board raised the constitutional question whether the Act offended the *Canadian Charter of Rights and Freedoms,* Part I of the *Constitution Act, 1982,* being Schedule B to the *Canada Act 1982* (U.K.) 1982, c. 11 [hereinafter *Charter*]. The Board found that the challenged section of Regulation 552 infringed the rights of the five couples to equal benefit of the law without discrimination based on sex, but not based on physical disability. It also found that the challenged sections were a reasonable limit under s. 1 of the *Charter.*

26. According to Dr. Renée Martin, a medical geneticist and professor of pediatrics at the University of Calgary, men with conditions that severally decrease or eliminate their sperm production have increased chromosomal abnormalities compared with the general population. She reports that studies show a fourfold increase in sex chromosome abnormalities among babies born as a result of intracytoplasmic sperm injection (ICSI) (1 percent compared to 0.25 percent in the fertile population), and that, although the world literature reports no increased incidence of congenital birth defects, the risk remains higher among this group. She also found an increase in autosomal abnormalities in the sperm of infertile men, which she noted may increase their risk of producing a baby with Down's Syndrome or other autosomal chromosomal problems. *CFAS Communiqué,* January 1999, at 3.

27. The main risks of IVF to women's health are associated with ovarian hyperstimulation and include infection, vaginal bleeding, and multiple pregnancies. Other risks include ectopic pregnancies, spontaneous abortions, premature births, an increased rate of Caesarean sections, and a possible increased risk of breast cancer.

28. Other studies suggest that, given the high rate of multiple births with IVF, children conceived through IVF have an increased rate of congenital malformation, a lower average birth weight, and a tendency to require more prenatal care. In a recent study of HFEA statistics, it was concluded that "among women undergoing IVF, the chances of a live birth are related to the number of eggs fertilized, presumably because of the greater selection of embryos for transfer. When more than four eggs are fertilized and available for transfer, the woman's chance of a birth is not diminished by transferring only two embryos. Transferring more embryos increases the risk of multiple births." *New England Journal of Medicine* 339 (1998): 573–77. This conclusion should mean that the new licensing authority can move to limit to two the number of embryos transferred in each treatment cycle.

29. For example, Nkem Chukwu, twenty-seven years old, gave birth by Caesarean section to eight babies in Texas on 20 December 1998. She had been given fertility drugs and refused selective reduction. This was the first set of octuplets to be born alive. One died, and at birth all were in critical and premature condition. The estimated cost to keep the surviving babies alive during their hospital stay was U.S. $2 million. Lawrence K. Altman, "For surviving octuplets progress comes in ounces," *New York Times,* 17 January 1999.

30. See Health Canada, *Food and Drugs Act,* R.S.C. 1985, c. F-27, subs. 30(1), *Processing and Distribution of Semen for Assisted Conception Regulations,* Schedule No. 721, c. F-27, subs. 30(1), 1 June 1996.

Chapter 2: Issues of Legitimacy and Inheritance

1. The Royal Commission on New Reproductive Technologies (NRTs) recommended that this be the only medical situation for which IVF be publicly funded. In other cases, it was

to be treated as research. Royal Commission on New Reproductive Technologies, *Proceed with Care* (Ottawa: Minister of Government Services, Canada, 1993) at 526. Since 1 April 1994, Ontario has paid for IVF only in this context.

2. In their presentation before the Parliamentary Committee on C-47, the Canadian Fertility and Andrology Society argued that "such a system [of non-anonymous, altruistic semen donation] will potentially reduce the supply of safe, high quality semen, leading to health risks in women seeking other sources of sperm. . . . CFAS is not against a non-anonymous *alternative* to the current system for families that wish this approach, but it should not replace anonymous semen donation as an option. . . . it is inappropriate, and possibly dangerous, to introduce a system of semen donation that is not evidence-based and has not undergone successful pilot studies. Systems of solely non-anonymous semen donation have yet to prove successful in the few countries that have attempted this approach." *Response to Bill C-47: Human Reproductive and Genetic Technologies Act,* presentation of the CFAS Government Relations Committee, 25 September 1999, at 9.

3. The Canadian Fertility and Andrology Society, *1996 Guidelines for Therapeutic Donor Insemination* (Montreal: CFAS, 1996). Health Canada's Health Protection Branch has issued Regulations in respect of the use of donated or purchased sperm that is used or intended to be used on a woman seeking to achieve a pregnancy through AID, IVF, or other assisted reproductive technologies or practices. Schedule No. 721, *Food and Drugs Act,* R.S.C. 1985, c. F-27, subs. 30(1), "Processing and Distribution of Semen for Assisted Conception — Regulations." In other developments, we can now freeze sperm stem cells, which can produce both sperm and new sperm stem cells in the future, making a man immortal through the storage of his genetic material over the years. The ethical questions remain, as do the legal issues of inheritance and legitimacy. Michael D. Lemonick, "The sperm that never dies," *Time,* 10 June 1996, 69.

4. On 25 July 1999, the day that Louise Brown, the first IVF baby turned twenty-one, the British government announced its intention to give AI children the right to know the identity of their biological "parents" — the men and women who donated the ovum and sperm that led to their conception. Only people who donate sperm or ova *after* the law comes into effect will be required to have their identity revealed. This will follow the example set in the adoption process, where children can learn the identity of their biological mother, but usually only if she agrees to the release of this information. A consultation on the matter is expected in fall 1999. *Globe and Mail,* 26 July 1999, A1.

5. The need for greater access to relevant medical information on sperm, ova, and embryo donors will increase as the link between genetics and disease becomes better known.

6. The main reason for banning sperm mixing was concern about abnormalities in the future child potentially created by the presence of additional genetic material at the point of fertilization. In sperm mixing, the sperm of the infertile man and that of the donor were literally mixed and then used to try and fertilize in vitro the ovum of the infertile man's partner. Recent articles show that a similar practice is happening with women, where the genetic material of two women (usually an older and much younger woman) is joined in one ovum. Normally, the ova of the older woman are too imperfect for fertilization and a small amount of the younger woman's genetic material is placed in the ovum of the older woman's to make fertilization more likely. As of May 1999, three boys and two girls had been born using this technique, and five other women were pregnant. Lois Rogers, "Eggs of two moms make one baby," *Calgary Herald,* 16 May 1999, A1.

7. For a brief outline of a real case, see the following article: Paul McKeague, "Born into a legal limbo," *Edmonton Journal,* 29 May 1999, H3.

8. *Criminal Code,* R.S.C. 1985, c. C-46, s. 155.

9. *Convention on Protection of Children and Co-operation in Respect of Intercountry Adoption*, 29 May 1993, 32 I.L.M. 1134, Can. T.S., 1997/12.

10. Using British Columbia as an example, the regulation under the *Adoption Act*, R.S.B.C. 1996, c. 5, set the fine at a maximum of $10,000 and/or six months in prison. Reasonable expenses to the birth mother are provided in the Regulations (B.C. Reg. 293/96), as are legal and medical fees relating to the adoption. See s. 84.

11. *In re Baby M*, N.J. 396, 537 A.2d 1227 (Sup. Ct. 1988).

12. The consent form used by the GOAL Program at the Ottawa Civic Hospital is an example of such a consent form. For a copy of their form, contact the GOAL program at (613) 761-4865.

13. In the United States the *Uniform Parentage Act* has been interpreted in surrogacy arrangements to cover the social mother and father who are genetic strangers to the embryo that a gestational surrogate carries for them. The California Court of Appeal for the Fourth Appellate District has held in a surrogacy arrangement using a donated embryo that the intended social parents were the legal parents: see *Buzzanca* v. *Buzzanca*, 61 Cal. App. 4th 1410 (1998). Its decision was based on the rule that parental relationships may be established when intended parents initiate and consent to medical procedures, even when there is no genetic relationship between them and the child. It also found that the intended father could not opt out of his responsibilities, reconfirming the law that parents cannot agree to limit or abrogate a child's right to support. Finally, it could allow intended social parents to be declared parents to the embryo that a surrogate is carrying for them at the time of implantation. This decision would end the uncertainty about legal status and legitimacy of the future child, and reduce the cost, delay, and uncertainty of a step-parent adoption after the birth of the child. See Andrew W. Vorzimer et al., "*Buzzanca* v. *Buzzanca*: The Ruling and Ramifications" at <http://www.inciid.org/buzzanca-case.html>.

14. R.S.C. 1985, c. C-46, ss. 214, 215, & 280–86.

15. *R.* v. *Brooks* (1902), 5 C.C.C. 372 (B.S.S.C.).

16. R.S.C. 1970, c. D-8, s. 2, and R.S.C. 1985 (2d Supp.), c. 3, as amended.

17. As of 1 May 1997, the *Divorce Act* also contains the new *Federal Child Support Guidelines*, SOR/97-175.

18. The term *parens patriae* means that the court acts as the child's parent for decisions affecting its health and well-being. This historical power in the court to protect children means that while parents have the prime responsibility for the care of their children, the courts can always intervene where evidence shows that the child is suffering or will suffer from parental actions or inaction.

19. For Ontario examples see A.H. Oosterhoff, *Oosterhoff on Wills and Succession*, 4th ed. (Scarborough: Carswell, 1995); and Brian A. Schnurr, *The 1999 Annotated Ontario Estates Statutes* (Scarborough: Carswell, 1999).

Chapter 3: Federal Initiatives and Constitutional Jurisdiction

1. The Royal Commission on New Reproductive Technologies was formed by order in council on 25 October 1989, with a broad mandate "to inquire into and report upon current and potential medical and scientific developments relating to new reproductive technologies, considering in particular their social, ethical, health, research, legal and economic implications and the public interest, and recommending what policies and safeguards should be applied." There were seven members originally: Dr. Patricia Baird (Chair), Dr. Bruce Hatfield, Martin Hébert, Grace Jantzen, Maureen McTeer, Suzanne Rozell Scorsone, and Louise Vandelac. Two additional members, Bartha Maria Knoppers and Susan McCutcheon, were later appointed, in part to break the deadlock that existed

between the majority of the Commission's members and the Chair. When the original majority of members asked the Federal Court to intervene to clarify their legal status and the legality of a subsequent order in council giving complete authority to the Chair, they were dismissed from the Commission. The Commission reported at the end of 1993.

2. "To ensure that new reproductive technologies are provided in a safe, ethical, and accountable way within these boundaries, we recommend that the federal government establish an independent National Reproductive Technologies Commission, charged with the primary responsibility of ensuring that new reproductive technologies are developed and applied in the national public interest." *Proceed with Care: Final Report of the Royal Commission on New Reproductive Technologies,* vol. 2 (Ottawa: Government Services Canada, 1993) at 1023.

3. *Ibid.* at 1022.

4. Hon. Diane Marleau, "Health Minister calls for moratorium on applying nine reproductive technologies and practices in humans," Health Canada, Release 1995-57, 27 July 1995.

5. *An Act respecting human reproductive technologies and commercial transactions relating to human reproduction* received First Reading on 14 June 1996. It died on the Order Paper when the 1997 federal general election was called.

6. "Body to regulate genetic, reproductive technology," Mark Kennedy, *National Post,* 14 May 1999, A2.

7. Anne McIlroy, "Fertility clinics face curbs," *Globe and Mail,* 25 May 1999, A1.

8. An example of the concurrent jurisdiction would be the administration of justice in criminal matters, where the federal government has exclusive power over the criminal law but the provinces are charged with its administration.

9. See, for example, inter alia, *Attorney General for Ontario* v. *Attorney General for the Dominion,* [1896] A.C. 348 (P.C.) (Liquor Prohibition Appeal, 1895); *Attorney General for Ontario* v. *Attorney General for the Dominion,* [1894] A.C. 189 (Assignment for Benefit of Creditors Case); *Tennant* v. *Union Bank of Canada,* [1894] A.C. 31 (P.C.); *Citizens Insurance Co.* v. *Parsons* (1880), 4 S.C.R. 215.

10. *Constitution Act, 1867* (U.K.), 30 & 31 Vict., c. 3, ss. 91 & 92. For further reading about constitutional law, see Peter W. Hogg, *Constitutional Law in Canada,* 4th ed. (Toronto: Carswell, 1997).

11. "In 1867 the administration of public health was still in a very primitive stage, the assumption being that health was a private matter and state assistance to protect or improve the health of the citizen was highly exceptional and tolerable only in emergencies such as epidemics, or for purposes of ensuring elementary sanitation in urban communities. Such public health activities as the state did undertake were almost wholly a function of local and municipal governments." Canada, *Report of the Royal Commission on Dominion-Provincial Relations,* (Chairmen: N.W. Rowell and J. Sirois), Book II (Ottawa: J.O. Patenaude, printer to the King, 1940), 32–33 [hereinafter *Rowell-Sirois Report*].

12. In the *Rowell-Sirois Report,* the Commissioners reconfirmed the provincial predominance in the health care field. "Dominion jurisdiction over health matters is largely, if not wholly, ancillary to express jurisdiction over other subjects. . . . Provincial responsibilities in health matters should be considered basic and residual. Dominion activities on the other hand, should be considered exceptions to the general rule of provincial responsibility, and should be justified in each case on the merit of their performance by the Dominion rather than the province." *Ibid.,* 34. In *Schneider* v. *The Queen in Right of British Columbia,* [1982] 2 S.C.R. 112, a challenge of British Columbia's *Heroin Treatment Act,* S.B.C. 1978, c. 24, this view was adopted and clarified.

13. *Constitution Act, 1867* (U.K.), above note 10, subs. 92 (7).

14. Only Ontario provides any coverage, funding women with completely blocked fallopian tubes for three attempts at pregnancy using IVF.

15. *Re Shelly* (1913), 4 W.W.R. 741 (Alta. S.C.); *Ex parte Fairbain* (1877), 18 N.B.R. 4 (S.C.); *Re Stinson and College of Physicians and Surgeons of Ontario* (1910), 22 O.L.R. 627 (D.C.); *Re Heyward et al.,* [1934] O.R. 133 (S.C.).

16. *Constitution Act, 1867* (U.K.), above note 10, subs. 92(13).

17. *Ibid.,* subs. 92(16).

18. "[T]he true test must be found in the real subject matter of the legislation: if it is such that it goes beyond the local or provincial concern or interests and must from its inherent nature be the concern of the Dominion as a whole . . . then it will fall within the competence of the Dominion Parliament as a matter affecting the peace, order and good government of Canada, though it may in another aspect touch on matters specially reserved to the provincial legislatures." *Attorney General for Ontario* v. *Canada Temperance Federation,* [1946] A.C. 193 at 205 (P.C.).

19. *Constitution Act, 1867* (U.K.), above note 10, subs. 91(7).

20. *Ibid.,* subs. 91(24).

21. *Ibid.,* subs. 91(25).

22. *Ibid.,* subs. 91(28).

23. *Ibid.,* s. 91.

24. I would like to thank Prof. Sujit Choudhry of the Faculty of Law at the University of Toronto for his helpful comments on matters raised on jurisdiction in chapter 3 and the scope of section 7 of the *Charter* in chapter 10.

25. [1988] 1 S.C.R. 401, 48 D.L.R. (4th) 161, [1988] 3 W.W.R. 385.

26. *Proceed with Caution: Final Report of the Royal Commission on New Reproductive Technologies* (Ottawa, 1993) at 108.

27. The 1998 annual report of the Human Fertilisation and Embryology Authority (HFEA) in the United Kingdom highlights the current issues involved. Among these issues are the following: genetic testing of embryos; the number of embryos transferred in each treatment cycle and multiple births; the welfare of the child; payment to sperm and egg donors; pre-implantation genetic diagnosis; cloning; cryopreservation (freezing) of sperm and ova; storage and use of testicular and ovarian tissue; intracytoplasmic sperm injection (ICSI); and improvements to the research licensing process. The HFEA has also dealt with other issues, and many of their excellent research and organizational materials are available on the Web, which has links to other infertility and research organizations in the United Kingdom, minutes of the HFEA Board's meetings, a glossary of terms, data and research findings, and policy updates. See <http://www.hfea.gov.uk>.

Chapter 4: Embryos: The New Frontier of Human Research

1. This happens when couples have no further need for their frozen embryos because they have completed their family, divorced, or died. Embryos that are unsuitable for transplant or cryopreservation (freezing) are also used for research. Most clinics require couples to agree on what will be done with "extra" embryos and ask that they be donated either for someone else's reproductive needs or for research. The couple can also ask that they be destroyed. Most clinics here will transfer an embryo only to the female partner of the couple whose gametes were used to create the embryo in the first place. Both members of the couple must agree a second time in writing before a transfer of a thawed embryo is made. This is a double check on the couple's marital status at that moment and ensures two things: that the couple are still together and agree on becoming parents; and that the practice of surrogacy will be very limited.

2. *Criminal Code,* R.S.C. 1985, c. C-46, s. 223.
3. For further historical background on abortion in Canada, see Law Reform Commission of Canada, *Crimes against the Foetus,* Working Paper 58 (Ottawa, 1989), 5–13.
4. *Blackstone's Commentaries on the Laws of England,* Book 1, 129–30.
5. S.C. 1892, c. 29, ss. 272–73.
6. After 1968, subs. 237(4) and (5) of the Canadian *Criminal Code* provided the only legal option for a pregnant woman wanting an abortion: see *Criminal Code,* S.C. 1954, c. 51, s. 237, as am. by *Criminal Law Amendment Act,* 1968–69, S.C. 1969, c. 38, s. 18.
7. *R.* v. *Morgentaler,* [1988] 1 S.C.R. 30, 44 D.L.R. (4th) 385.
8. After the advent of the *Charter,* the power of judicial review changed and grew. To quote Dickson C.J., "Canadian courts are now charged with the crucial obligation of ensuring that the legislative initiatives pursued by our Parliament and legislatures conform to the democratic values expressed in the *Canadian Charter of Rights and Freedoms.* As Justice McIntyre states in his reasons for judgment, 'the task of the Court in this case is not to solve nor seek to solve what might be called the abortion issue, but simply to measure the content of s. 251 against the *Charter.*' It is in this latter sense that the current *Morgentaler* appeal differs from the one we heard a decade ago" (at 46).
9. The first two constitutional questions were as follows:
    "1. Does section 251 of the *Criminal Code* of Canada infringe or deny the rights and freedoms guaranteed by ss. 2(a), 7, 12, 15, 27, and 28 of the *Canadian Charter of Rights and Freedoms?*
    2. If section 251 of the *Criminal Code* of Canada infringes or denies the rights and freedoms guaranteed by ss. 2(a), 7, 12, 15, 27, and 28 of the *Canadian Charter of Rights and Freedoms,* is s. 251 justified by s. 1 of the *Canadian Charter of Rights and Freedoms* and therefore not inconsistent with the *Constitution Act, 1982?*" (*ibid.* at 31)
10. *Canadian Charter of Rights and Freedoms,* Part I of the *Constitution Act, 1982,* being Schedule B to the *Canada Act 1982* (U.K.), 1982, c. 11.
11. Section 1 reads: *"The Canadian Charter of Rights and Freedoms* guarantees the rights and freedoms set out in it subject only to such reasonable limits prescribed by law as can be demonstrably justified in a free and democratic society." This guarantee allows for legislation that would otherwise be declared *invalid,* because it contravenes one of the rights and guarantees provided in the *Charter,* to be declared *valid* instead. The limit is one that has been shown to be justified and even necessary to protect larger societal interests and prevent larger societal harm. An example would be libel and slander laws that limit a person's freedom of speech but protect others from having their reputation diminished by deliberate falsehoods.
12. See *R.* v. *Prince* (1988), 44 C.C.C. (3d) 510, [1989] 1 W.W.R. 80 (Man. C.A.), which held that a person who attacks a pregnant woman whose fetus in utero is injured and later born alive, only to die from the injuries, will be guilty of at least manslaughter.
13. See, inter alia, *Minister of Justice of Canada et al.* v. *Borowski,* [1981] 2 S.C.R. 575, 130 D.L.R. (3d) 588; *R.* v. *Sullivan & Lemay,* [1991] 1 S.C.R. 489, 55 B.C.L.R. (2d) 1; *Tremblay* v. *Daigle,* [1989] 2 S.C.R. 530, 62 D.L.R. (4th) 634.
14. This change in the legislation of New Brunswick and the Northwest Territories allows child welfare authorities to apprehend addicted pregnant woman in legislatively defined circumstances. The change was made to address the serious problem of substance abuse among some pregnant women, resulting in children born with fetal alcohol syndrome. For a discussion of the issues raised by such intervention, see S. Martin and M. Coleman, "Judicial Intervention in Pregnancy," *McGill Law Journal* 40 (1995): 947–91.
15. Only four provinces — Newfoundland, Ontario, Alberta, and British Columbia — pay for abortions performed in clinics. Abortion is considered a medically necessary procedure under the *Canada Health Act,* qualifying it for payment in both hospitals and clinics.

16. *Nova Scotia* v. *Morgentaler* (1989), 93 N.S.R. (2d) 202, 64 D.L.R. (4th) 297 (N.S.S.C.).

17. Following the Supreme Court's decision, s. 287 of the *Criminal Code* was of no force or effect. To fill the perceived vacuum, the Mulroney government introduced a Bill (C-43, *An Act Respecting Abortion*, 2d. Sess., 34th Parl., 1989) whose legislative purpose was defined as being to protect women's health by requiring that all abortions be carried out by qualified doctors. But the real effect of the Bill would have been to recriminalize abortion in certain circumstances. It was highly controversial and politicized — a hybrid Bill that satisfied no one on either side of the abortion debate. In an unprecedented move the Bill was adopted by a majority of the House of Commons, but defeated in the Senate. Since then, no government has tried to legislate on abortion, although there have been private bills in both the House and the Senate.

18. A child cannot sue its mother for damages suffered in the womb as a result of her negligence. For judicial analysis of the cases that allow infants to receive compensation in tort for prenatally inflicted injuries by third parties in Canada, the United Kingdom, and the United States, see Cory J. in *Dobson (Litigation Guardian of)* v. *Dobson*, [1999] S.C.J. no. 41.

19. A bibliography, prepared from BIOETHICSLINE, a National Library of Medicine online bibliography database, and ETHX, the online database of article-length documents at the National Center for Bioethics Literature in the United States, is available at <http://www.guweb.georgetown.edu/nrcbl/biblios/cloning.htm>.

20. Prior to Dolly, the scientific team at the animal breeding station in Roslin, Scotland, cloned identical lambs from differentiated, nine-day-old embryo cells. "Meg" and "Morag" were born in 1995. In July 1996 scientists Ian Wilmut and Keith Campbell cloned "Dolly," using frozen udder cells from an adult ewe, and introduced her to a stunned international audience in February 1997. See I. Wilmut, A.E. Schnieke, J. McWhir, A.J. Kind, and K.H.S. Campbell, "Viable Offspring Derived from Fetal and Adult Mammalian Cells" *Nature* 385 (1997): 810–13. This report was preceded by yet another letter about their attempts the year before. See K.H.S. Campbell, J. McWhir, J. Ritchie, and W. A. Wilmut, "Sheep Cloned by Nuclear Transfer from a Cultured Cell Line," (1996) *Nature* 380 (1996): 64–66. The following year scientists having trouble replicating the experiment in their own laboratories suggested that maybe Dolly was not the product of a mature cell, but of a stem cell, one of the pluripotent, undifferentiated cells that are found in the udder or breast cells in small numbers and help other cells prepare for lactation. The Scottish team was joined by an independent group who compared the DNA of the frozen udder cells that created Dolly and Dolly's own DNA. They were identical. Ian Wilmut et al., *Nature*, 23 July 1998. The team also found that Dolly was aging prematurely and, in effect, had been born at the same age as the ewe from whose udder cells she had been cloned. Ian Wilmut et al., *Nature*, 27 May 1999.

21. For a short chronological history of cloning generally, see Dorothy C. Wertz, "History of Cloning," *The GeneLetter* (August 1998) 3:1, available on the Web at http://www.geneletter.org/0898/historyofcloning.htm>.

22. The announcement about Dolly set off a chain of political and legislative action. Several countries established commissions to look at legislative options to ban or control human embryo and adult cloning and sought advice from existing bioethics committees on the ethical issues that needed to be addressed. In the United States, the president reconfirmed his December 1994 directive to the National Institutes of Health that they were not to fund the creation of human embryos for research purposes; and, in a press statement delivered 4 March 1997, he prohibited federal funding for the cloning of human beings. See <http:///www.pub.whitehouse.gov/uri-res/I2R?urn:pdi//oma.eop.gov.us/1997/3/5/1.text.1>. For a current list of cloning legislation enacted at the

state and federal levels in the United States, see <http://www.pharma.org/genomics/legislation/cloning.legislation/12.14.98.update.html>.

23. The cloning of mice was perhaps the most startling news, as it defied conventional scientific predictions that the mouse would be one of the hardest to clone, and showed how quickly the technology from Dolly was adopted to clones in other animals. In this experiment, which was completed just a few months after the Scottish team published their cloning results, scientists in Hawaii cloned mice and then cloned the clones to show how easily it could be done. Their procedure was a little different from that of Dr. Wilmut, who had put the ewe udder cells into a restive state by basically starving them into hibernation; transferred them into an enucleated sheep's egg, and gave them an electric shock to start the cell development. Drs. Yanagimachi and Wakayama in Hawaii experimented with three cells that were already in a resting state, chose the one they felt would be easiest to clone, and injected it into the enucleated egg. They waited six hours to give the egg a chance to reprogram the cell's DNA (which process no one yet understands) and then chemically induced it to start developing. All the mouse clones were female. Gina Kolata, "In big advance in cloning, biologists create 50 mice," *New York Times*, 23 July 1998, 1; Ryuzo Yanagimachi and Teruhiko Wakayama, "Report on cloning of mice," *Nature*, 23 July 1998.

24. In July 1998 Japanese scientists announced the birth of calves cloned from the cells of adult cattle.

25. The three goats were cloned near Montreal by a Canadian company called Nexia Biotechnology, Inc. for use as producers of spider silk protein in their milk. This substance will be used to make a strong industrial material. Carolyn Abraham, "Cloned animals may age prematurely," *Globe and Mail*, May 27, 1999, A1.

26. See <http://www.geneletter.org/0898/typesofcloning.htm>.

27. For a discussion on umbilical cord blood and stem cells, see Janis Hass, "A little biological insurance: The value of collecting and storing umbilical-cord stem cells for future use in transplants or cancer treatments is a hotly debated issue," *Globe and Mail*, 11 May 1999, A19.

28. According to one author, this type of cloning was first tried in 1979 by a Columbia University researcher who grafted spermatogonium (male germ cells) into enucleated human eggs. See O. Postel-Vinay and A. Millet, "Comment ça va, Dolly?" *La Recherche* 61 (1997) at 297.

29. For an analysis of the ethical and legal aspects of human cloning and a look at legislative and other activity in selected countries, see Sonia LeBris and Marie Hirtle, "Ethical and Legal Aspects of Human Cloning: Comparative Approaches," in *Socio-Ethical Issues in Human Genetics*, Bartha Maria Knoppers, ed. (Montreal: Les editions Yvon Blais, 1998), 283–329.

30. Stem cells are totipotent (cells that give rise to cells of all types) and are found scattered in blood and bone. In late 1996 Canadian researchers used genetically engineered mice that had human genes in them to identify stem cells in blood. But they are most plentiful and concentrated in the early human embryo, where they were first isolated in November 1998, by researcher James Thomson of the University of Wisconsin, who avoided the research ban on human embryos by carrying out his work using private funds. His actions caused a recommendation by the National Bioethics Advisory Commission to change the U.S. government's ban on public funding of this kind of research on stem cells in May 1999. The one proviso is that only research using "extra" embryos from infertility clinics be used and that the funding ban regarding creating embryos for research continue.

When the early embryo is no more than a "mass of undifferentiated cells," it is really a mass of stem cells capable of growing into virtually any kind of cell line and waiting for their unique assignments in the development of the new human the embryo will grow into. Embryonic stem cell researchers are trying to identify how this whole process happens. How are these stem cells told what their job in the body will be and what triggers them to "turn" into the cell that can do that task? If we want them to do something else, can we give them a different set of directions? If so, how? Cloning technology allows us to make endless copies of stem cells and we know that these can be kept alive indefinitely in the laboratory. Once they have answers, scientists can direct stem cells at will to become the specialized cell they need. For instance, a stem cell could be "told" to become a lung cell to be used for repair or even to be used to "build" a larger solid organ like a liver or kidney. These cells could also be injected into people with certain cancers, using gene therapy technologies to target and either block or dominate cells that have gone haywire. Several diseases are targeted as potential beneficiaries of this information, including Parkinson's and Alzheimer's diseases, diabetes, heart disease, strokes, arthritis, certain birth defects, osteoporosis, spinal cord injuries, burns, and most cancers. This research will be worth billions to private companies and governments. Those who manage to get there first will own the patent rights to these processes and technology. But to experiment on the scale required for this research, scientists must have access to lots of stem cells from early embryos. Right now, in the United States, where the race is on to clone human embryos, existing federal law prohibits the destruction of embryos for research. Harold Varmus, director of the National Institutes of Health, has made it clear, though, that this major funding agency distinguishes between this embryonic stem cell research, which it will fund, and other research where the embryo is destroyed as part of the research. In Canada, stem cell research is allowed. It is not covered by the current voluntary moratorium that bans germ-line engineering (a genetic change that would be passed on to the next generation) and the cloning of human embryos. What is cloned are the stem cells, and not the actual embryo. To avoid the abortion issue, some scientists are reported to be looking for alternative ways to make stem cell tissue. One researcher at the University of Massachusetts announced in 1998 that he had made an "embryo-like thing" by merging the DNA from his own cheek cells with cow ova. He found what "looked like a stem cell" in the resulting organism. Predictions are that this research is so valuable that it will continue at any cost. The issues are procedural and philosophical. On the procedural side, how do we regulate embryonic stem cell research and what criteria do we use? How do we ensure that the laws we draft cover *all* research, and not just that carried out using public funds? How do we deal with the trend towards commercialization of human life and its genetically engineered parts, cell lines, and other processes? And, on the philosophical level, "What is the right balance we can draw between respecting embryos and respect for those in need of the therapies stem cell research on early embryos will provide?" See Glenn McGee, "Stem cells: The goo of life, the debate of the century," at <http://www.msnbc.com> 25 May 1999.

31. At the beginning of January 1998, French president Jacques Chirac called for an international ban on human cloning. Nineteen Council of Europe member countries (Germany and the United Kingdom excluded) signed a protocol that would commit their countries to legislation banning "any intervention seeking to create human beings genetically identical to another human being, whether living or dead." He argued that national action alone was futile in preventing this technology in the absence of an international ban on human cloning technology that could result in the cloning of humans. The signing countries were Denmark, Estonia, Finland, France, Greece, Iceland, Italy, Latvia, Luxembourg, Moldova, Norway, Portugal, Romania, San Marino, Slovenia, Spain, Sweden, Macedonia, and Turkey. "Paris wants world ban on cloning of humans," *Globe and Mail*, 13 January 1998, A8.

32. When asked, after the announcement of the successful experiment to clone mice embryos in Hawaii, if human cloning was next, Dr. Lee Silver, mouse geneticist and reproductive biologist at Princeton University and author of *Remaking Eden: Cloning and Beyond in a Brave New World,* answered "absolutely," predicting that "if we follow scientific protocol, it could take 5 to 10 years before in vitro fertilization clinics add human cloning to their repertoires." All that is needed, he noted, was more research. "The method would first have to be perfected in mice [which it almost is] and then monkeys." Gina Kolata, "In big advance in cloning, biologists create 50 mice," *New York Times,* 23 July 1998, 1.

33. Charles Hirshberg, "The Body Shop: Need a nose? A new heart? Someday doctors may be able to grow you one," *Life* (Special issue on medical miracles for the next millennium) (fall 1998) at 51.

34. In 1993 a human embryo-splitting experiment by two American scientists (Jerry Hall and Robert Stillman) caused an international stir as (false) rumours spread that they had cloned a human embryo for reproduction. In fact they had split a human embryo for research. Procedural irregularities (lack of consent from gamete providers and no prior permission from the university's institutional ethics board) meant that both were disciplined, but their claims caused a stir. See J.L. Hall, D. Engels, P.R. Gindoff, et al., "Experimental Cloning in Human Polyploid Embryos Using an Artificial Zona Pellucida," *American Fertility Society,* jointly with the *Canadian Fertility and Andrology Society* (Program Supplement) 1993. S. Newman, "Scientists Clone Human Embryos," *GeneWatch* 93 (1994): 3–4. H.W. Jones, R. Edwards, and G. Seidel, "On Attempts at Cloning in the Human [Editorial]" *Fertility & Sterility* 61, no. 3 (1994): 423–26. However, we know that at least two private companies are now working to be the first to clone human embryos, for which they will seek a patent and then manufacture for sale to institutions needing embryos for research. Rick Weiss, "Private companies race to clone human embryos," *Washington Post,* reprinted in the [Ottawa] *Citizen,* 15 June 1999, A10.

35. For answers that are often given to these concerns, see D.C. Wertz, "Society and the Not-So-New Genetics: What Are We Afraid of? Some Future Predictions from a Social Scientist," *Journal of Contemporary Health Law and Policy* 13 (1997): 299–346; "Twenty-one arguments against human cloning, and their responses," at <http://www.geneletter.org/0898/twentyonearguments.htm>.

36. In the United States a congressional ban, renewable yearly, prohibits the use of federal money for research that creates or destroys human embryos. In spite of this prohibition, embryo research continues in private laboratories. As an example, in the breakthrough on stem cells, the two scientific researchers did not receive National Institutes of Health funds in their research. John Gearhart of Johns Hopkins University obtained stem cells from fetuses aborted legally between five and nine weeks after conception, and James Thomson of the University of Wisconsin used cells from surplus embryos from IVF fertility laboratories. New legislation in Canada must apply to all research funded with both private and public money.

37. Now referred to as the Tri-Council, these three funding agencies are the Medical Research Council of Canada (MRC), the Natural Sciences and Engineering Research Council of Canada (NSERCC), and the Social Sciences and Humanities Research Council of Canada (SSHRCC).

38. See the *Tri-Council Policy Statement, Ethical Conduct for Research Involving Humans* (Ottawa: Public Works and Government Services Canada, 1998), available through the MRC Web site at <http://www.mrc.gc.ca>, which describes standards and procedures for governing research involving human subjects. "As a condition of funding, [the Tri-Councils] require, as a minimum, that researchers and their institutions apply the ethical principles and the articles of this policy" (12). The *Statement* provides that "researchers shall obtain

free and informed consent from the individual whose gametes are to be used for research" (Article 9.1); and states further that "it is not ethical to use in research ova or sperm that have been obtained through commercial transactions, including exchange for service (Article 9.2); "It is not ethically acceptable to create, or intend to create, hybrid individuals by such means as mixing human and animal gametes, or transferring somatic or germ cell nuclei between cells of humans and other species (Article 9.3); "It is not ethically acceptable to create human embryos specifically for research purposes. However, in those cases where human embryos are created for reproductive purposes, and subsequently are no longer required for such purposes, research involving human embryos may be considered to be ethically acceptable, but only if all of the following apply: (a) the ova and sperm from which they were formed are obtained in accordance with Articles 9.1 and 9.2 [above]; (b) The research does not involve the genetic alteration of human gametes or embryos; (c) embryos exposed to manipulations not directed specifically to their ongoing normal development will not be transferred for continuing pregnancy; and (d) research involving human embryos takes place only during the first 14 days after their formation by combination of the gametes" (Article 9.4). Finally, reiterating parts of the voluntary moratorium, the *Statement* provides: "It is not ethically acceptable to undertake research that involves ectogenesis, [the creation of an artificial womb], cloning human beings by any means including somatic cell nuclear transfer, formation of animal/human hybrids, or the transfer of embryos between humans and other species" (Article 9.5).

39. These guidelines expressed the concerns of the Medical Research Council at the time about the (then) future research on embryos. "While issues of consent and autonomy may therefore apply, clear ethical concerns arise from the unarguable fact that embryos and humans are human life forms." Real concern existed that, since IVF-created embryos were available for reproduction and ultimately for research, such research should be limited to prevent abuse and avoid any public concern about the mixing of the two. Under the former rules, embryo research could be performed only up to a maximum of seventeen days after fertilization in vitro where the results could improve infertility management, including the safety and effectiveness of IVF. The purpose of the research was to be assessed on a case-by-case basis. The guidelines that determined access to public medical research funds noted: "In time, with the evolution of social and ethical values and further scientific development, REBs [regional ethics boards] and investigators might contemplate other embryo research, for such purposes, for example as genetic correction." This guideline clearly envisages somatic cell genetic engineering and raises the possibility of germ-line research. See section G.3, "Research on Fetuses and Embryos," in the former *MRC Guidelines on Research on Human Subjects*, at <http://www.mrc.gc.ca>.

40. "The *Councils* trust that other research sponsors, be they in the public, private or not-for-profit sectors, will join in adopting and adhering to this Code as the standard for all Canadian research involving humans." Tri-Council Code of Ethical Conduct for Research Involving Humans. The kinds of research projects that should be reviewed by the regional ethical boards in light of the Tri-Council's Policy Statement are listed at A.1.

41. *Tri-Council Policy Statement*, Articles 9, 9.4, and 9.4(a–d).

42. Explanatory notes to Article 9.4(d) requiring that embryo research take place only during the first fourteen days after their formation by combination of gametes (as opposed to cloning) state: "Research potentially altering the embryo by chemical or physical manipulation should be distinguished from research directed at ensuring normal development" (9.3).

43. *Tri-Council Policy Statement*, Article 9.5.

44. *Ibid.*, Article 9.3. The explanatory notes in the *Tri-Council Policy Statement* state: "Combining human genetic material with that of other species has the potential to create

new life. The creation of hybrid individuals or species which may survive, which are intended to survive violates our basic norm of respect for human life and dignity. Article 9.3 expresses this concern, while acknowledging that other related research may raise fewer ethical objections" (9.2).

45. *Ibid.,* Article 9.4(c).

46. The statement reads: "The broad consensus restricting research on embryos to the first 14 days of development is based on the stages of biological development. Implantation usually begins at approximately the sixth or seventh day of development, and is usually completed at around 14 days, beyond which time the embryo proper starts to develop the primitive streak, or the first indication of neural development." *Ibid.,* the explanatory notes accompanying Article 9.4(d).

47. This term was coined in the *Warnock Report,* which was the United Kingdom's equivalent of our Royal Commission on New Reproductive Technologies. It has been used ever since and now describes a stage of human development from fertilization in vitro to the fourteenth day. See Department of Health and Social Security, *Report of the Committee of Inquiry into Human Fertilisation and Embryology (Warnock Report)* (London: H.M.S.O., 1984) (Chair: Dame Mary Warnock).

48. Recent research activity in private laboratories in the United States makes it clear that the presidential directive that human embryos cannot be created for research, nor can they be cloned, and the congressional ban on the creation and destruction of human embryos, for any purpose, are being violated as they relate to privately funded research. Two companies, Geron Corp. in Menlo Park, California, and Advanced Cell Therapeutics in Worcester, Massachusetts, have started programs to grow human embryos for cloning. In doing this, they will have unlimited access to embryonic stem cells for manufacture and sale for use in new therapies to treat such medical conditions and diseases as diabetes and Parkinson's disease. While banned in publicly funded research laboratories, these rules do not apply to privately funded research, as even heavily pro-life congressmen have been unable to reconcile their religious views with the promise of profit and cure that would come from embryo research, including cloning and stem cell research. Congress has yet to pass any legislation to enlarge the existing ban of public funding for this research to include the private sector, and with the granting of patents for human life forms such as bioengineered cell lines and genes, it is unlikely that it ever will. The prospect of billions of dollars in profit makes any real restrictions unlikely in the private sector.

49. This refers to cells that give rise to cells of all types, as in stem cells.

50. Michael West, president of Advanced Cell Therapeutics, has been quoted as saying: "I don't think people realize that we're talking about cells that have not become anything yet. There's no hands and feet, and I think a lot of this debate is over mental images that words like embryo portray. . . . To prevent science from using cells to cure human diseases would be a horrific step backward." In contrasting *therapeutic cloning* where embryos are cloned for their valuable cells and *reproductive cloning,* where embryos are cloned to be grown into babies, Mr. West argued that the latter may be ethically acceptable (as he insisted the Europeans were finding), even though the former remained both medically unsound and ethically questionable. Rick Weiss, "Private companies race to clone human embryos," *Washington Post,* reprinted in the [Ottawa] *Citizen,* 16 June 1999, A10.

Chapter 5: Knowing Ourselves, Protecting Our Rights

1. Several useful books, written as part of the educational mandate of the Human Genome Project, can be obtained free or at a small charge through the Web at <http://www.ornl.gov/hgmis>. Much of this introduction is based on Catherine Baker, *Your Genes, Your Choices: Exploring the Issues Raised by Genetic Research* (Washington, DC:

American Association for the Advancement of Science, 1987); Department of the Environment (U.S.), *Human Genome Program Reports;* and *Projects in Ethical, Legal and Social Issues,* available through the Department of Energy.

2.   The goals of the Human Genome Project (HGP) are to generate maps for twenty-four different human (and now other microbial) chromosomes, with biochemical landmarks spaced at a minimum of 100,000 bases and, ultimately, to determine the sequence of the 3 billion DNA bases in each chromosome. The U.S. Department of Energy has several publications relating to the HGP. For their quarterly newsletter, *Human Genome News,* see <http://www.ornl.gov/hgmis/publicat/publications.html>. Another interesting publication is the 1996 booklet *To Know Ourselves,* which reviews that department's role in the HGP and introduces its scientific and social aspects; see <http://www.ornl.gov/ hgmis/tko>. See also a report of the Ninth Genome Sequencing and Analysis Conference, held in September 1997, at <http://www.ornl.gov/meetings/hilhead9.html>. Contact the American Society of Law, Medicine and Ethics, at <info@aslme.org> or <http://www.aslme.org>, for an excellent report on CD-ROM of a conference held in April 1998 on the Human Genome Project.

3.   The group includes Australia, Brazil, Canada, China, Denmark, France, Germany, Israel, Italy, Japan, Korea, Mexico, Netherlands, Russia, Sweden, the United Kingdom, and the United States.

4.   Ironically, this huge effort grew out of research in the early 1980s by U.S. scientists studying the impact on genetic mutations of the radiation sickness suffered by the survivors of Hiroshima and Nagasaki. For further reading, see the Human Genome Education Model Project II at <http://www.dml.georgetown.edu/hugem/project.hym>.

5.   It is cheaper and less controversial to use analyses of other organism genomes, such as those of specific bacteria, yeast, roundworms, fruit flies, or mice instead of humans. Other possible benefits from existing genome research could lead to a better understanding of the link between genetic disease and exposure to certain pollutants, pesticides, or radiation. Studying the similarities and differences between human and animal genomes will assist also in animal research. In the future, animals will be genetically engineered to be resistant to disease and to act as living laboratories to produce large quantities of drugs for human use. Biotechnology companies will contribute ever-growing amounts to the economies of the G-7 and other countries. The battleground is being readied for a fight over patents on animal and human life forms and processes (see chapter 7). For additional information, see <http//www.ornl.gov/hgmis/faq/faqs1.html>.

6.   The Medical Research Council (MRC) at present is the major federal agency responsible for funding biomedical health research in Canada, though a radical change has been proposed. In a press release on 18 February 1999, the federal minister of health announced the creation of an interim health research governing council to renew the governance structure for federally sponsored health research in Canada, and replace the existing model with one similar to the U.S. National Institutes of Health by the year 2000. Future federal funding will be channelled through these new "institutes" made up of networks of researchers based in universities, health and resource centres, teaching hospitals and the public, voluntary and private sectors." Legislation to create the proposed Canadian Institutes of Health Research (CIHR) was originally promised for 1999, but was not passed at the time of publication. For a description of the new CIHR, see *A New Approach to Health Research in the 21st Century: The Canadian Institutes of Health Research* at <http://www.hg-sc.ca/english/archives/releases/99_26e.htm>.

7.   Heather Kent, "B.C. to Establish Canada's First Genome-Sequencing Centre," *Canadian Medical Association Journal* 158, no. 3 (1998) at 293. Mark Nicols, "Mapping the Genetic Highways," *Maclean's,* 26 July 1999, 44. Initially, Canada committed $22 million over five

years to the Canadian Genome Analysis and Technology Programs, but it has now virtually eliminated its support.

8. The U.S. Department of Energy and the National Institutes of Health set aside 3 to 5 percent of their respective annual HGP budgets for projects that would look at the ethical, legal, and social issues raised by the HGP. For information on these (nicknamed the ELSI) projects see *ELSI: The New Genetics and You* at <http://www. ornl.gov.hgmis>. The priority areas for study include genetic research, informed consent, privacy, and commercialization, especially the granting of patents and the purchase and sale of human genetic material and information. One of the objectives is to enhance public and professional understanding and acceptance of genetic research and its integration into clinical practice. For additional information, see <http://www.dml.georgetown.edu/ hugem/elsi.htm>. Among its initiatives, the ELSI program has endorsed a *Genetic Privacy Act* (1994) to regulate the collection, analysis, storage, and use of DNA samples and the genetic information obtained from them (see <http://www.ornl.gov/hgmis/resource/ elsi.html>); supported the extension of the Equal Employment Opportunity Commission guidelines to the *American with Disabilities Act* of 1990 (Pub. L. 101-336, 104 Stat. 327 (1990)) to provide employment protection to Americans experiencing discrimination based on genetic information related to illness, disease, or other conditions; joined forces with the National Action Plan on Breast Cancer to recommend state and federal legislation to protect against discrimination by insurance companies; and developed general science courses for judges to help them deal with cases of genetic privacy, use of genetic information in the workplace, insurance, and patents on higher life forms. See *Courts and Science On-Line Magazine (CASOLM)* at <http://www.ornl.gov/courts>.

9. This decision makes sense in cases involving certain cancers, such as breast cancer, where multiple resonance imaging technology can detect even the smallest tumour, and surgical and oncological pre- and post-operative treatments exist. Women with the BRCA-1 and/or BRCA-2 genes, which raise the risk of breast and ovarian cancers dramatically, can then be tested and watched closely from an early age for the development of cancerous tumours. Kristin Leutwyler, "Deciphering the Breast Cancer Gene," *Scientific American* (December 1994), 26.

10. According to a study of thousands of cancer patients at Johns Hopkins University in Baltimore, about 80 percent of women with family histories of breast cancer chose to be tested in its screening program. The study also found that there was no significant difference in the psychological response of children or adults who tested positive from those found to have no genetic risk. Wallace Immen, "Experts Back Genetic Testing for Cancer," *Globe and Mail*, 7 May 1999, A9.

11. Privacy Commissioner of Canada, *Genetic Testing and Privacy* (Ottawa: Minister of Supply and Services Canada, 1992) at 11–15.

12. In order to meet these concerns about individual and group abuse through genetic testing, several national and international organizations, including UNESCO, the Council of Europe, the Human Genome Organization, the Nuffield Council on Bioethics, and the World Health Organization, have published guidelines for scientists, doctors, and researchers.

13. To understand why the commercial frenzy that has overcome the research work surrounding the Human Genome Project is such an aberration of the project's original purpose, it is important to remember some of the key reasons why governments agreed to set aside millions of dollars to participate in the first place. First, it was agreed that this information was essential to help us conquer hereditary diseases and debilitating cancers. Second, everyone around the original Cabinet and research tables knew that the information from this project must never be in the hands of only one government,

country, or company. Third, this was to be a project that alleviated the imbalance between rich and poor, between the developed and developing nations. Because it was conceived as the largest public scientific enterprise of the century, the information was to be shared among citizens the world over. But everything has changed. The U.S. government's decision to seek, and their Patent Office's decision to grant, a patent on the genes that researchers in that country had identified marked an end to the original intent of this great international science project. Other actions since have cemented the change from a public enterprise to a private corporate takeover. There is neither political will nor clout strong enough to change the commercial course that today defines and propels the Human Genome Project. For this reason alone, it is essential that we introduce anti-discrimination and strict privacy laws to protect Canadians from the harm that awaits them within the next decade. See Ainsling Irwin, "The gene genie racing to grab a fast billion: The man who wants to become the Bill Gates of genetic science by patenting the blueprint of life," [London] *Daily Telegraph,* 14 May 1998, 6; Nicholas Wade, "Scientist aims to map entire DNA in 3 years," *International Herald Tribune,* 11 May 1998, 8; Nicholas Wade, "International gene project gets lift: Wellcome Trust doubles commitment to public-sector effort," *New York Times,* 17 May 1998, 20; Aisling Irwin, "Millions at stake as genes war heats up: Goal is to identify and then control the basis of human life," [London] *Telegraph,* reprinted in the *Calgary Herald,* 16 May 1999, D2.

14. This issue moves beyond our borders to include practices of using cells from indigenous peoples around the world to create new cell and tissue lines that are then patented, commercialized, and sold, usually without the knowledge or informed consent of the person whose tissue is "donated." Even when there is consent for samples to be taken, there is no consent for them to be shared with other researchers or commercialized. Few of these "donors" ever receive compensation from the patent royalties of the new "products" their cells gave rise to. See the communiqué on "The Human Tissue Trade," January/February 1997, prepared by the Rural Advancement Foundation International (RAFI) in Ottawa at <http://www.rafi.org/communique/fltxt/19971.html>; Carolyn Abraham, "Cell bank has trillions in assets," *Globe and Mail,* 26 December 1998, A1; "Everyone wants indigenous people's genes," *Globe and Mail,* 7 December 1998, A11; "A world gene hunt targets Canada," *Globe and Mail,* 28 November 1998, A1.

15. For a good analysis of the link between eugenics and genetic research and technologies, see the magazine of the Council for Responsible Genetics, vol. 12, no. 3 (June 1999) at <http:www.gene-watch.org>.

16. Screening tests can be performed for several genetic conditions, including adult polycystic kidney disease, Fragile X syndrome, sickle cell anemia, Duchenne muscular dystrophy, cystic fibrosis, Huntington's disease, hemophilia, phenylketonuria, retinoblastoma, thalassemia, Tay-Sachs disease, familial polyposis, BRC-1 and BRC-2, familial Alzheimer's, and multiple sclerosis. Other tests are being developed as research for the Human Genome Project discovers the genes that cause the mutation.

17. Privacy Commissioner, *Genetic Testing and Privacy,* above note 11 at 16.

18. For a list of publications on bioethics and genetics, see <http://www.cdc.gov/genetics/ethical/htm>. See in particular L. Low et al., "Genetic Discrimination in Life Insurance," *British Medical Journal,* 1998, and a Response by J. Alexander Lowden, 28 December 1998.

19. My questions and the answers from the C.L.H.I.A. were as follows:

QUESTION 1: *"What is the policy of the life and health insurance industry in Canada towards the collection and use of genetic information?*

ANSWER: "It may be helpful to respond to this question in two parts. First, with respect to genetic information in general — research results, etc. — the industry policy is to monitor such information closely, as with any other health-related research, so industry practices and decisions can be based on the most current and complete information possible. Second, and more in line with your question, the industry policy with respect to the collection and use of genetic information about a specific individual is as follows:

(a) The insurer would not require an applicant for insurance to undergo genetic testing, i.e., the insurer would not initiate the testing (as it might with respect to cholesterol or urinalysis, for example).

(b) If genetic testing has been done and the information is available to the applicant for insurance and/or the applicant's physician, the insurer would request access to that information as for other aspects of the health history. This policy is based on the general principle that the insurance contract is a good faith agreement and that both parties have an obligation to disclose any information that may be relevant to the making of the contract. That principle is included in the insurance legislation in each province, and the contract is voidable if any relevant information is withheld or misrepresented. This policy is also based on the general principle that the insurer needs to have as much information about the applicant's risk as the applicant has before the insurer commits the funds of other insurers to share that risk (often referred to as controlling anti-selection).

(c) This and other information would only be collected with the individual's consent. Failure to give consent may lead the insurer to turn down the application, however.

(d) Any genetic information, as with all other personal information, would be used only for the purposes for which it was collected — usually to assess an application for insurance — and would not be used for any other purpose or disclosed to any other party (even a personal physician) except with the individual's consent, or when required by law.

(e) No genetic or other information would be asked for in a risk assessment unless it has been clearly established, e.g., by scientific studies, that the information is relevant to the risk being assessed.

(f) Any genetic information could only be used in conjunction with other health information to establish a full assessment of the individual's risk. The most likely use of such information would be to offset or confirm information available from other sources. Thus, for example, a favourable test result that was available on an individual's file would enable the insurer to ignore some unfavourable information that was available from the family history and proceed to approve the application and issue the insurance contract. At this point and for the foreseeable future, genetic information is not felt to be sufficiently predictive of insurance risk to be of use in isolation from other health information.

(g) Two principles of the industry's Consumer Code of Ethics are especially relevant to the collection and use of genetic information, namely, to use underwriting techniques which are sound and fair, and to respect the privacy of individuals by using personal information only for the purposes authorized and not revealing it to any unauthorized person. The latter principle reflects the industry's long-standing recognition of the need to protect the confidentiality of personal information entrusted to an insurer for risk assessment or claim evaluation purposes. Life and health insurers were the first industry to adopt Right to Privacy guidelines on an industry-wide basis — in 1980 — and have been active participants in the development of the Canadian Standards Association's Model Code for the Protection of Personal Information which forms the basis for the recently introduced federal legislation." [Bill C-54, below note 21, which was withdrawn by the federal government in June 1999].

QUESTION 2: *"The U.S. President has proposed legislation that allows for requirements for the disclosure of genetic traits or information (in an insurance context) if, and only if, that trait has manifested itself as an illness. Is this a policy that the Canadian industry has studied? Would it be acceptable? If so, why? If not, why not?"*

ANSWER: "It is essential to preface any comment on activities in the United States by noting that concerns about the collection and use of genetic information by insurers relate primarily to the role of private health care insurance in funding health care services — indeed in obtaining access to such services in many instances; since the Canadian system of funding health care services is very, very different, it is doubtful that U.S. proposals should be transplanted to Canada, at least not without very thorough analysis. Proposals for limits on the collection and use of such information in the United States are either limited to health care insurance (most frequently) or establish significantly different standards for other types of personal insurance — e.g., life insurance or disability insurance. I believe that is the case with the proposal that is referred to in your question. In general, this proposal as stated represents a serious misunderstanding of the fundamental nature of insurance — namely that insurance deals with contingencies, not certainties or very highly predictable events, i.e., with the risk or probability that an event MIGHT occur, not with the reality that it has occurred. This is probably most evident for types of insurance such as fire insurance; once the event (the fire in that instance) manifests itself, there is no role for assessing whether insurance can be issued. Under certain circumstances, this fundamental aspect can be ignored for some types of insurance — for example, it is common to cover the costs of dental prophylaxis under dental insurance contracts even though the incurral of such costs is highly predictable. For other types of insurance, however, especially where there is wide choice in the amount or other features of the insurance contract or there is high variability in the likelihood of the event, this fundamental aspect cannot be ignored. Those characteristics are found in most forms of life insurance and disability income insurance purchased by individuals, and thus such a proposal would not be acceptable to the industry on the broad basis in the Canadian context."

QUESTION 3: *"Is an insurer's individual medical information ever shared with other companies providing other services to consumers? If so, under what conditions? Is consent required?"*

ANSWER: "No medical or other personal information is shared by insurers with other companies providing other services to consumers unless the individual consents. Even with consent such sharing is rare — most common would be the disclosure of the medical information to a physician designated by the individual if the individual consents."

QUESTION 4: *"What are some of the issues respecting the use of genetic testing and the use of this information in deciding eligibility for both health and life insurance that the industry feels it should address now in light of the huge advances in genetic medicine and science?"*

ANSWER: "Continuing attention to the need for confidentiality is very important with respect to genetic information. Several jurisdictions are developing legislation to protect all personal information in some segments of the private sector (augmenting existing protection in the public sector). For example, Quebec enacted legislation in 1994 to protect all personal information in the private sector; Manitoba has enacted legislation to protect personal health information in the health sector and several other provinces are considering similar legislation; the federal government is acting to protect personal information used in commercial activity. The requirements in the legislation are similar to industry guidelines that life and health insurers have been following since 1980, as noted earlier, but insurers need to assess the particular needs for genetic and other especially sensitive information and ensure that any necessary changes are implemented, regarding the legislated requirements as a minimum and covering any gaps that may exist in and between the various pieces of legislation. The industry also needs to assess emerging information from genetic research on a continuing basis and ensure that its knowledge base is complete and current. Such emerging information must be assessed carefully to ensure that any information used by the industry is sound and relevant to the purposes for which it is used. Close attention to communications is essential to ensure that industry practices are seen to be sound and acceptable, and that any proposals for change (especially for any limitations) are based on realities, not on assumptions. Flowing from the previous two points is the need to reassess industry services and practices periodically to ensure that any collection and use of genetic information is both soundly based and necessary for the provision of insurance services to consumers, as well as acceptable to the public."

QUESTION 5: *"What specific legislative changes to current laws would the industry find helpful/harmful concerning the identification and use of genetic information for qualifying or disqualifying a person from eligibility for health and life insurance?"*

ANSWER: "In general, the industry is not advocating any changes to current laws in this area, though as noted earlier it has been active in the development of sound principles to protect the confidentiality of all personal information. In the harmful category would be legislation — with respect to privacy or other aspects — that varies from one jurisdiction to another (non-harmonious), creating confusion for consumers and insurers alike and requiring non-productive administration that adds to costs but not to consumer protection. The industry also believes that legislation that impedes the development of further knowledge is clearly harmful, and urges that any proposals for legislation be carefully considered and based on wide consultation. Failure to clearly define the scope of any legislation — e.g., what is meant by "genetic information" — would also be harmful. Any restrictions on access to and use of genetic information would materially affect the current basis of insurance, and could reduce the wide range of choice currently available to consumers of insurance services, and could impede the introduction of new insurance products to meet evolving needs. The industry strives to offer insurance to as many Canadians as possible on a sound basis (not to deny services) and views any legislation that hampers these efforts as harmful to consumers."

My personal thanks to Charles Black, senior advisor for policy with the Canadian Life and Health Insurance Association, who answered all my questions and gave me permission to use these answers here. For further information, contact the Canadian Life and Health Insurance Association, Inc., 1 Queen St. E., Suite 1700, Toronto, Ontario M5C 2X9; phone: (416) 777-2221; fax (416) 777-1895; e-mail <http://www.clhia.ca>. Canadians can also call the association's Consumer Assistance Centre at (416) 777-2344 or at 1-800-268-8099.

20. Bill 68, Quebec's *Act Respecting the Protection of Personal Information in the Private Sector,* S.Q. 1993, c. 17, came into effect in 1994.

21. The full title of Bill C-54 was *An Act to support and promote electronic commerce by protecting personal information that is collected, used or disclosed in certain circumstances, by providing for the use of electronic means to communicate or record information or transactions and by amending the Canada Evidence Act, the Statutory Instruments Act and the Statute Revision Act,* 1st Sess., 36th Parl., 1998. It was one of the several parts of the Canadian Electronic Commerce Strategy. Part I was called the "Protection of Personal Information in the Private Sector" and, together with Schedule 1, contained the Canadian Standards Association's Model Code for the protection of personal information in the private sector. At the time of publication, the government had reintroduced Bill C-54 and it is now at Report Stage, where amendments will be made to it again as it goes through the normal legislative process. If it passes, it will be known as the *Personal Information Protection and Electronic Documents Act.* For a legislative summary, see John Craig, "Bill C-54: Personal Information Protection and Electronic Documents Act," *Library of Parliament,* 12 April 1999, revised 20 April 1999.

22. See the presentation of the federal privacy commissioner, Bruce Phillips, before the Senate Committee of the Whole, Ottawa, 18 February 1999, at <http:// www.privcom.gc.ca/WholeCommittee99.htm>.

23. For a discussion of some of the privacy issues involved, see "The End of Privacy: The Surveillance Society," *The Economist,* 1 May 1999, 21–23.

Chapter 6: Biotechnology: Looking to the Future

1. *Genetic engineering* is a process by which one particular piece of genetic material is transferred from one living organism to another. It can be done within species and now across species. For instance, human cells are added to pigs so their parts can be used for human transplant or their milk for substances to be used in drugs. Human genes can also be added to plants. Generally in plants, genetic engineering has concentrated on making them resistant to certain temperatures and pests and enhancing their nutritional value.

2. The *Canadian Environmental Protection Act*, R.S.C. 1985 (4th Supp.), c. 16, subs. 3(1), defines biotechnology as the use of living organisms or their parts for the production of goods and services.

3. Although Ontario and Quebec share most of the action in the biotechnology health care sectors, Saskatchewan is a world leader in agbiotech. A coordinated provincial strategy has meant excellent partnerships among universities, government, and the private sector. They focus on developing disease-resistant crops to lower the cost of food production and the use of pesticides, and on using such crops as canola to make such diverse products as plastic, nylon, and cosmetics. See Marian Stinson, "Biotech industry raises $1-billion," *Globe and Mail,* 12 March 1997, B9.

4. The term *eugenics* comes from the Greek word meaning "well born" or "good birth." "Negative eugenics" in the early part of this century was a policy that discouraged or prevented the birth of children whose parents suffered from "undesirable" characteristics, defined often as mentally and even socially unfit. Provincial sterilization laws in Canada were an example of how the state carried out this eugenics policy. Today, through genetic technologies like pre-implantation and prenatal diagnosis, embryos and fetuses that suffer from a physical or genetic anomaly are identified and are either not implanted or (usually) aborted. "Positive eugenics" at its most basic included programs to encourage "healthy" women and men to breed big families. Now, with genetic engineering technologies, genetically "enhanced" children will be a possibility in the future. It is a real criticism of genetic technologies that they started as tools to prevent the birth of "handicapped" children and can now be used to "enhance" people. This fact alone challenges all of us to carry on regular, open, and vigorous debate about how we discipline science to protect our human rights. For an excellent look at the link between genetics and eugenics, see the special edition of *GeneWatch* 12, no. 3 (June 1999). This publication of the Council for Responsible Genetics can be found at <http://www.gene-watch.org>.

5. This process is achieved at the molecular level and alters the organism's production of protein by adding, deleting, or reorganizing its DNA or genetic make-up. For a list of the genetically engineered agricultural products coming to market, refer to the U.S. Food and Drug Administration Center for Food Safety at <http://vm.cfsan.fda.gov/~lrd/ biotechm.html> and the USDA Animal and Plant Health Inspection Service at <http:// www.aphis.usda.gov/bbep/bp/index.html>.

6. Since 1988 there have been over 4,000 field trials involving genetically altered plants (referred to as "plants with novel traits") in Canada. Food safety approval has been granted by Health Canada to thirty-six such plants, including canola, corn, tomatoes, potatoes, soybeans, cottonseed, and squash. General environmental releases have been

granted for thirty-one of these plants, including canola, corn, potatoes, soybean, wheat, and flax. Of these, nine have been registered as crop varieties. Corn is not subject to variety registration in Canada. In the category of "novel feeds," thirty-one approvals have been granted to plants with novel traits to be used as livestock feed, including canola, corn, potatoes, soybeans, and cotton. For further sources and other information, see Health Canada at <http://www.hc-sc.gc.ca/datafood/english/pub/ofb/decis96e.htm> and the Canadian Food Inspection Agency at <http://www.cfia-acia.agr.ca/english/ppc/biotech/statute.html>.

7. Two new tomato strains have been approved for sale in Canada, but are not yet available in our stores. On another front the genetically modified "New Leaf potato" (approved in 1995) resists the Colorado potato beetle and is in our stores.

8. Calgene's "Flavr Savr" tomato was approved by the Food and Drug Administration in the United States in 1994. It cost Calgene $95 million in research and development to bring its new tomato to market. Sold under the brand name "MacGregor's," the tomato's ripening process was altered by blocking the expression of the newly identified enzyme responsible for that process.

9. Examples of current research in the agricultural biotechnology sector include attempts to increase the unsaturated fat content of corn, soybean, and canola plants; to remove lactose from milk products; to increase the lysine content in rice; and to increase the tolerance of plants to both dry and cold climates. Health Canada at <http://www.hc-sc.gc.ca/datafood/english/pub/ofb/decis96e/statute.html>. See also Martin Mittelstaedt, "Genetic experiments on Canadian crops top 4,200 in decades," *Globe and Mail*, 19 March 1999, A6.

10. Tobacco plants were chosen because they are not human food, have no close relatives, and die each year when winter comes. Nonetheless, strict rules have been put on the growth of these plants. They must not be closer than 10 metres to other tobacco plants in the AgCanada plots, must be harvested before they flower, and both harvested and stored in a secure manner. See CP story "Unique experiment plants human genes in field tobacco," *Globe and Mail*, 14 June 1999, A6.

11. Chromos Molecular Systems, Burnaby, B.C. See "Designer gene can be passed to future generations," [Ottawa] *Citizen*, 21 October 1999, A1.

12. For the full report of the research findings, see the article by Dr. Carol Tacket, of the University of Maryland's Center for Development in Baltimore, which appeared in the journal *Nature Medicine*, May 1998. The researchers are also working on a potato vaccine against cholera and hepatitis B.

13. Although it takes years longer to grow the genetically engineered banana plants into fruit-producing trees, most children prefer bananas to raw potatoes and eat them as a regular part of their daily diet. In many developing countries banana crops are widely grown, making this an efficient and cost effective vaccination method in an otherwise cash-strapped public health care system. The vaccine-bearing bananas can also become a valuable cash crop, giving added vibrancy to poor rural and local economies.

14. Rick Weiss, "Eating your way to immunity," *International Herald Tribune*, 11 May 1998.

15. Belgium underwent a crisis when it was announced on 26 May 1999, in the middle of an election campaign, that several foods, including pork, beef, eggs, poultry, and dairy products, may contain cancer-causing dioxin, a contaminant traced to a fats-processing plant there. Adding to the crisis was the revelation that the dioxin in the animal feed was discovered in April and that two other countries — France and Holland — had not enforced the European rules or informed authorities in Brussels of breaches or health risks. With two-thirds of Belgians polled saying they were very worried about their health, and one-third insisting that the fiasco would cause them to change their vote, the crisis again raised the need for a European body, rather than separate national organizations, to enforce the regulations. The model most often cited is the Medicines

Evaluation Agency, which oversees pharmaceutical products for all members of the European Community. In addition to the "mad cow" disease scare, other incidents of non-enforcement have raised questions about the safety of the European food supply: antifreeze found in Austrian wine; benzene in Perrier water; and listeria contamination in unpasteurized French milk and cheese. In many European countries, large lobby groups oppose genetically modified foods and hormone-treated beef from the United States and Canada. French advocates called for a ban on the production and sale of feeds for poultry, pig, and fish that contain animal parts. If the European Union refuses to act, the French agricultural minister has threatened to call for a European-wide ban on these products and their importation and use on French farms. *Globe and Mail*, 10 June 1999, A12. Peter Cook, "What's behind Europe's food fights," *ibid.*, 9 June 1999, B2.

16. When the giant multinational biotech company Monsanto spent $1.68 million on advertising its genetically engineered foodstuffs in the United Kingdom, it had the undesired effect of alerting the British to the fact that bioengineering was everywhere in their stores. In response, Prince Charles and other leaders organized a campaign against bioengineered foods. *The Economist*, "The selling of science," 2 January 1999, 67.

17. The most common example is the human growth hormone, which makes rats larger, but pigs smaller, leaner, and subject to arthritis.

18. A study by researchers at Cornell University, published in the journal *Nature* on 20 May 1999, found that Monarch butterfly larvae that fed on milkweed growing near genetically modified corn were more likely to die than butterflies that fed on milkweed, their sole diet, near traditional cornfields. It was the first scientific (as opposed to anecdotal) evidence that pollen from a transgenic plant can harm non-pest species and have unforeseen negative effects on the environment. The pest-resistant corn, known as Bt corn, was introduced by seed companies three years ago, and now is planted on an estimated 10 to 20 million acres in the U.S. cornbelt, where the Monarch butterfly mainly breeds. The three giants that sell Bt corn — Novartis Agribusiness Biotechnology, Monsanto, and Pioneer Hi-Bred International Inc. — challenged the significance of the findings for Monarch caterpillars or larvae, insisting that the impact would be extremely small, if any, and relied on their successful completion of the U.S. Environmental Protection Agency approval process, which had shown that predatory insects and honeybees were found not to be harmed by Bt corn. *New York Times,* 20 May 1999, A1 and A20. In an immediate response the same day, the European Union advised that it would suspend the approval process for a genetically modified corn from Pioneer Hi-Bred International, the world's largest seed company. Regulators announced they would also review earlier European approvals of genetically altered corn produced by the Monsanto and Novartis companies in light of the scientific findings. *Ibid.,* 21 May 1999, C4.

19. For further research on this question see, for instance, D. Blumenthal, E.G. Campbell, N. Causino, and K.S. Louis, "Participation of Life-Science Faculty in Research Relationships with Industry," *New England Journal of Medicine* 335 (1996): 1734–39.

20. I. Rabino, "A Study of Attitudes and Concerns of Genetic Engineering Scientists in Western Europe," *Biotech Forum Europe* 9 (1992): 636–40; and I. Rabino, "What U.S. Researchers Think of Regulations and Regulators," *Nature Biotechnology* 14 (1996): 147–50.

21. The *1998 Biotechnology Strategy* lays out the importance of biotechnology to Canada's future world leadership in the agricultural and transgenic food industries.

22. See W. Halman, "Public Perceptions of Biotechnology: Another Look," *Nature Biotechnology* 14 (1996): 35–38; and I. Rabino, "The Impact of Activist Pressures on Recombinant DNA Research," *Science, Technology and Human Values* 16 (1991): 70–87.

23. The delay leaves unresolved the issue of whether countries have the right under GATT or other trading rules to reject genetically engineered crops that they believe might harm ecological diversity. At present, World Trade Organization rules allow such a ban only if

the country wanting to prevent entry of any agricultural commodity onto its soil can show that it would likely harm people or wildlife. The United States has not signed the Convention on Biodiversity, and remains the world leader in the biotechnology sector. The main genetically engineered crops in Canada are potatoes, corn, soybeans, and canola. About 30–50 percent of our $3 billion canola crop is genetically modified, mainly for resistance to herbicides and pesticides, and about a quarter of our soy and corn crops are genetically altered. See Christopher Shulgan, "Canada blocks move to regulate trade of 'Frankenfood,'" [Ottawa] *Citizen,* 26 February 1999, A2.

24. For a critique of the present American approach, see <http://www.essential.org.crg/consumeralert.html> and the special edition on genetically modified foods in *GeneWatch* 11, nos. 1–2 (April 1998).

25. This policy is supported by the important U.N. committee, the Codex Alimentarius Committee, which was established by the Food and Agriculture Organization and the World Health Organization in 1962 and is the rule-making body under GATT for international trade issues relating to food. Not surprisingly, its membership is heavily weighted towards industry (104:7 in 1998). See Diane McCrea, "Codex Food Labelling Committee Debates International Guidelines," *GeneWatch* 11, nos. 1–2 (April 1998) at 5.

26. The battle over the labelling of genetically modified foods even affected the organic food industry. Proposed rules for the U.S. Department of Agriculture's new organic program were attacked as undermining the strict national standards mandated by the Organic Foods Production Act in 1990. For more on the status of organic foods in the United States, see the home page for the National Organic Program at <http://www.ams.usda.gov/nop> and both the Canadian and the U.S. Web sites for their respective federal departments of agriculture.

27. Several groups have joined together to sue the American Food and Drug Administration to force it to change its current practice and require labelling. See *Center for Food Safety et al.* v. *Jane Henney (FDA)* and *Alliance for Bio-Integrity et al.* v. *Shalala (FDA).* For an update on the lawsuit, see <http://www.purefood.org/ge/gelablawsuit.cfm>. For further information, see the U.S. Campaign for Food Safety Web site at <http//www.purefood.org>.

28. The European Community has set out a fourth criterion for the approval of genetically modified foods. In addition to the standard ones of safety to the public and the environment, and efficacy and quality of the final product, a manufacturer has to show that it will not have any adverse socioeconomic impacts. It is unlikely that a place will be found in the U.S. model for this larger societal interest.

29. See the *Food and Drugs Act,* R.S.C. 1985, c. F-27. There is evidence of infection and bacteria in the milk of cows treated with rBGH, including milk "known to be contaminated with pus from udder infections, with antibiotics administered to stem those infections, with foreign growth hormones, and with high levels of insulin-like growth factor (IGF-I) which has been linked to human breast and gastrointestinal cancers." *GeneWatch* 12, no. 1 (February 1999) at 8. The United States is the only developed country permitting the use of BST, of which there are four manufacturers.

30. For further information about this report, see <http://www.hc-sc.gc.ca/english/archives/rbst>.

31. See the *Journals of the Senate,* 14 May 1998.

32. For a copy of the Senate *Interim Report,* contact the Senate Committee's Directorate at (613) 990-0088 or consult the Web site at <http://www.parl.gc.ca/sencom.ca>.

33. For a list of the participants and their backgrounds, see <http://www.ucalgary.ca>. Among the groups presenting was an Ottawa-based not-for-profit group, nicknamed RAFI (Rural Advancement Foundation International), which has played a leading role in defending the rights and interests of native communities in the developing world. See <http://www.rafi.ca/> and for the United States, <http:/www.rafiusa.org/>.

34. A copy of the eleven-page report is available through the University of Calgary. See the Web site for the conference, entitled "Designer Genes at the Dinner Table," at <http://www.ucalgary.ca/~pubconf/>.

35. Serious debate continues worldwide on the use of antibiotics in animal feed to promote growth and productivity, since they have been shown to contribute to the growing resistance to a number of drugs. Reports indicate that at least one form of tuberculosis in the United States is resistant to all drugs. Health Canada has introduced a policy to restrict the availability of new antibiotics, which may be used only by prescription to treat sick animals and not to promote growth. See "Warning given on animal-feed antibiotics," *Globe and Mail*, 8 April 1997, A2.

Chapter 7: The Commercialization of Life

1. Commercialization raises other issues for science. In a 1995 study fully one-third of the academics polled were involved in university-industry collaborations to make up for decreased public funding; 96 percent of them approved, even though 65 percent had serious reservations about the commercialization of recombinant DNA research. Their reasons for this reservation included the fact that industrial sponsorship of research leads to secrecy rather than scientific openness and that it shifts the focus away from scientific research (especially basic research) towards research where there is greatest financial gain. See Issac Rabino, "The Biotech Future," *American Scientist* 86 (1998): 110–12 at 111.

2. The Canadian *Patent Act*, R.S.C. 1985, c. P-4, does not explicitly exclude life forms from patentability. Until 1982 the Canadian Patent Office (now the Canadian Intellectual Property Office, or CIPO) refused patents for life forms. See, for instance, *Re Application of Pallos* (1978), 1 C.P.R. (3d) 334, and *Re Application No. 079,973* (now Patent No. 1,069,071) (1979), 54 C.P.R. (2d) 124 (Pat. App. Bd.). Generally speaking, parts of living organisms were patentable, while the living organisms themselves were not. The development of commercial biotechnology revolutionized the field of patent practice and brought the issue of patents on both lower (i.e., micro-organisms, unicellular life forms, and viruses) and higher (i.e., multicellular life forms including plants, animals, and humans) life forms to a head. Currently the CIPO grants patents for single cell organisms, but not for higher life forms like plants and animals. The first case to break with this tradition was *Re Application of Abitibi Co.* (1982), 62 C.P.R. 81 (Pat. App. Bd.). The *Plant Breeders Rights Act*, S.C. 1990, c. 20, covers issues of ownership and control over seeds and plants. The CIPO continues to receive patent applications for higher life forms, including plants and animals — for instance, genetically engineered plants resistant to disease and genetically altered mice (the oncomouse) for pharmaceutical and cancer research. The CIPO does grant patents for *processes* for producing higher life forms, but not for the higher life forms themselves. Under s. 2 of the *Patent Act*, "invention" is defined as "any new and useful art, process, machine, manufacture or composition of matter, or any new and useful improvement in any art, process, machine, manufacture or composition of matter."

3. *Williams* v. *Williams,* 20 Ch. D. 659 (1882).

4. *Sinai Temple* v. *Kaplan,* 54 Cal. App. 3d 1103, 127 Cal. Rptr. 80 (1976).

5. For example, s. 10 of the *Human Tissue Gift Act*, R.S.B.C. 1996, c. 211, reads: "A person must not buy, sell or otherwise deal in, directly or indirectly, for a valuable consideration, any tissue for a transplant, or any body parts or parts other than blood or a blood constituent, for therapeutic purposes, medical education or scientific research." Section 11 of the same Act reads: "Any dealing prohibited by s. 10 is invalid as contrary to public policy."

6. The exceptions are blood and sperm, although we agree that the money received is for expenses and not to be considered as a payment. This distinction is important and leaves

intact our firm public policy that the human body, its parts, and processes, are not to be treated in any way as objects of commerce.

7. One of the main purposes for seeking a patent is to achieve a commercial monopoly during the lifespan of the patent. The argument in this case is that patents are essential to the ordered and continued development of biotechnology, whose start-up costs are very high. Several issues need to be addressed, if we consider patents to be the most suitable legal/commercial tool to protect an interest and reward research innovation in this exploding field. Some of these issues include whether human life, its parts, and processes should ever be considered as patentable subject matter; how "discoveries" of human genes as part of the Human Genome Project and in later research should be considered within the meaning of the word *discovery* in the *Patent Act*; the public's interests and rights as the raw material of the research; and, finally, the impact of this change on the field of science and its traditions. In Canada, unlike in the United States, medical treatment is not considered to be an "invention." See *Tennessee Eastman Co.* v. *Canada (Commissioner of Patents)* (1970), 62 C.P.R. 117 (Ex. Ct.), aff'd [1974] S.C.R. 111, 33 D.L.R. (3d) 459 (involving a method of bonding tissue following an operation), and *Imperial Chemical Industries Ltd.* v. *Canada (Commissioner of Patents)* (1986), 3 F.C. 40, 9 C.P.R. (3d) 289 (C.A.) (where the Court reaffirmed the decision in *Tennessee Eastman* in this case, which involved a cleaning method for the removal of plaque and stains). In both countries, repeatable non-therapeutic and prophylactic processes, including those for "producing or preserving or manipulating antibodies of cells or parts thereof, recombinant DNA techniques, fused cell techniques and assay methods," will be considered as patentable matter. See *Patents for Lifeforms,* Canadian Intellectual Property Office, 5 January 1994.

8. The first Canadian decision to accept a patent on living organisms was *Re Application of Abitibi Co.* (1982), 62 C.P.R. 81 (Pat. App. Bd.), where a patent was sought on a mixed fungal yeast culture created to degrade pulp and paper waste. The patent examiner found that it was not patentable, but his decision was overturned on appeal. The Patent Board held that in the light of the leading U.S. case of *Diamond* v. *Chakrabarty*, 447 U.S. 303 (1980), a patent could be granted for the fungal yeast culture itself. Since then, lower life forms have been patentable subject matter. Now new life forms, including all micro-organisms, yeasts, moulds, fungi, bacteria, actinomycetes, unicellular algae, cell lines, viruses or protozoa, which are produced en masse and possess uniform properties and characteristics, are patentable. The board reserved judgment on higher life forms such as plants and animals.

In *Re Application for Patent of Connaught Laboratories* (1982), 82 C.P.R. (2d) 32 at 33 (Pat. App. Bd.), the board applied and followed its decision in *Re Abitibi* stating that "the results of our own investigation of the development of patent law throughout the world, have brought us to the conclusion that we can no longer be satisfied that at law a patent for a micro-organism or other new life forms would not be held allowable by our own courts." On 4 March 1986, the Patent Appeal Board extended the scope of the term "invention" in s. 2 of the *Patent Act* in the case of *Re Application for Patent of Pioneer Hi-Bred Ltd.* (1986), 11 C.P.R. (3d) 311 (Pat. App. Bd.). A strain of soybean had been developed from artificial cross-breeding of three known bean varieties and was then cultivated naturally. Noting that Canadian courts, unlike their American counterparts, had limited the definition of invention to exclude "some subject-matter areas and human activities from patentability" (at 315), the board distinguished this case from *Re Abitibi*, saying that it was only relevant to lower life forms (at 319).

In its decision in *Re Pioneer Hi-Bred*, the Patent Board found that there was "no direction from the Canadian courts that a plant growing according to the laws of nature" should be considered a manufacture that may be acceptable under s. 2 (at 319). All previous proposals to that point to enact plant breeders' rights by Parliament had failed. On appeal to the Federal Court in 1987, the scope of the definition of the terms "manufacture" and "composition of matter" as accepted in the leading U.S. case of *Chakrabarty* was examined. See *Pioneer Hi-Bred Ltd.* v. *Canada (Commissioner of Patents)* (1987), 3 F.C. 8, 14 C.P.R. (3d) 491 (F.C.A.) [hereinafter *Pioneer Hi-Bred* cited to F.C.], where Marceau J. (with Pratte J. generally agreeing) wrote: "It seems to me that the common ordinary meaning of the words "manufacture" and "composition" of matter would be distorted if a unique but simple variety of soybean were to be included within their scope" (at 13–14). He argued that had Parliament wanted plant varieties to be included, members would have done so. The absence of terms like *strain, variety,* and *hybrid* was fatal to the inclusion of plants within the scope of the s. 2 definition of *invention.* He added that Canadian case law does not reject the notion that life forms are patentable subject matter, and limited the authority of the commissioner of patents to determining what is or is not patentable subject matter under the Act. Both description and deposit of the seed were required under the Act, and the board had erred in holding in *Re Abitibi* that mere deposit of the seed would suffice.

On appeal to the Supreme Court of Canada, [1989] 1 S.C.R. 1623, 60 D.L.R. (4th) 223 [cited to S.C.R.] only one of the two issues was addressed. The first issue, whether the new soybean could be considered as an *invention,* was not resolved. Two distinct processes were recognized: hybridization and genetic engineering. Lamer C.J. recognized that "[t]he real issue in this appeal is the patentability of a form of life" (at 1632). He noted that "[t]he courts have regarded creations following the laws of nature as being mere discoveries the existence of which man [*sic*] has simply uncovered without thereby being able to claim he invented them" (at 1634). Although the Court did not pronounce on whether higher life forms are patentable subject matter, the Chief Justice did provide guidance on what would be required in order for a patent application to succeed. Mere hybridization would not pass the test, because it is evolutionary and based strictly on heredity and Mendelian principles. But a genetically engineered life form that requires a change in genetic material at the molecular level would probably succeed. The question remains whether the Court will grant a patent for the technological process or whether the new life form will also qualify.

9.   The United States allows patents for non-human multicellular organisms, such as the Harvard mouse. The patent in that case is for the mouse itself and not just the actual DNA sequence. This change is significant, as it is a break with the previous practice that granted patents for DNA, but in conjunction with a specific process or product. It began with the U.S. decision to seek patents on all the genetic fragments its government researchers had sequenced from human brain tissues in 1994 as part of the work of the National Institutes of Health in the Human Genome Project.

10. Patents protect the *invention* of a new and useful product, process, composition, or apparatus. They were developed as a form of protection for inventors to ensure that their work was recognized and that they shared in the returns earned from the use of their inventions by others. "A patent is a grant from the Canadian government, which gives the inventor the exclusive right to make, use and sell his invention [for] 20 years from the filing date, once the patent is issued. It is only good in Canada, so [the inventor] will have to apply separately in any other country where it wants similar protection." Law Society of Upper Canada information sheet. For general information on patents, copyright, and trademarks as they apply in Ontario, see the Law Society of Upper Canada Web page at <http://www.lsuc.on.ca/public/other_patents_en.shtml>.

11. In this section on patents I thank Scott Forsyth, a student in my classes at the University of Calgary, whose insight and research were most helpful to me. For additional reading, see

"Patenting Life-Forms and Owning Human Tissue," a paper by Judge Michele Rivet presented to the Canadian Institute for the Administration of Justice, Vancouver, August 1989.

12. Above note 8.

13. Chief Justice Warren Burger wrote: "[T]he patentee has produced a new bacterium with markedly different characteristics from any found in nature and one having the potential for significant utility. His discovery is not nature's handiwork but his own; accordingly, it is patentable subject matter" (at 310).

14. *In Re Allen*, 2 U.S.P.Q. 2d, 1425, and P.T.O. Bd. App. & Int. (1987).

15. See (1987), 1077 Official Gazette of the U.S. Patent and Trademark Office.

16. When the patent commissioner refused the patent request, he found a two-step process, one of which was patentable and the other not. The patentable part involved the man-made creation of plasmids, and the non-patentable step was the production of the mouse through natural reproduction according to the laws of nature. He stated: "In my view, different considerations apply between claims to the lower life forms of the *Abitibi* decision and the higher life forms claimed in the instant application." He found that he could not extend the s. 2 definitions of *manufacture* or *composition of matter* to include a non-human mammal, since a mouse could not fall within the definition of an invention. "The inventors do not have full control over all the characteristics of the resulting mouse since the intervention of man [*sic*] ensures that the reproducibility extends only as far as the cancer forming gene." The decision was appealed to the Federal Court, which upheld the commissioner's finding: see *Harvard College* v. *Canada (Commissioner of Patents)* (1998), 79 C.P.R. (3d) 98, 146 F.T.R. 279 (F.C.T.D.) [hereinafter *Harvard College*]. Leave to appeal to the Supreme Court of Canada is sought.

17. *Moore* v. *The Regents of the University of California*, 51 Cal.3d 120, 793 P.2d 479 (S.C. 1990) [hereinafter *Moore* cited to Cal.3d].

18. *Ibid.* at 142.

19. *Ibid.* at 143.

20. U.S. patent 5,397,696.

21. See R.S. Eisenberg and R.P. Merges, "Opinion Letter as to the Patentability of Certain Inventions Associated with the Identification of Partial cDNA Sequences" *AIPLA Quarterly Journal* 23 (1995) at 1.

22. Under Canada's *Patent Act*, s. 2, a patentable invention is any new and commercially useful art, process, machine, manufacture, composition or matter; or any new and useful improvement on any of these items. It must also be unobvious and described completely and in enough detail to enable anyone skilled in the particular technology to make or use the invention from that description. The simple deposit (here of a seed) or other biological material alone will not suffice as such a description. A patent provides the right in the patent holder to exclude others from making, using, or selling the invention within Canada for twenty years from the date the application is filed here (s. 44). All the terms and conditions of a patent are set out by statute.

23. Several news stories appeared following the Federal Court's decision on the Harvard oncomouse. See, for example, Tom Spears, "Patent denied: Harvard did not 'invent the mouse,'" [Ottawa] *Citizen*, 23 April 1998, A1.

24. In *Harvard College*, above note 16, the issue was whether higher life forms including mammals such as mice were patentable subject matter under the current law on patents. It was found that, at best, the mouse in question was created by both human intervention and nature and was not an invention under s. 2 of the *Patent Act*, R.S.C. 1985, c. P-4. The mouse was treated as a complex life form and not merely as a bit of raw material to which new qualities are given by a scientist. For further discussion, see <http://www.fja-cmf.gc.ca/en/cf/1998/vol3/html/1998fca22348.p.en.html>.

25. Rural Advancement Foundation International (RAFI) continues to make the case against patents on any life form. See Stephen Strauss, "Manitoban leads strong drive on ethics of gene ownership," *Globe and Mail*, 6 July 1996, A1. For concerns this group has expressed on the patenting of indigenous cells, see the RAFI Web site at <http://www.rafi.org/communique/fltxt/19962.html>.

Chapter 8: Keeping Control

1. For further references on issues covered in Part Three, see *Martin's Annual Criminal Code* (Toronto: Canada Law Book, 1999), under some of the following section headings: *assault, sexual assault, mental disorder, psychiatric assessment, death, attempt murder, manslaughter, homicide, infanticide, parties to offence, search and seizure, breach of trust, Charter of Rights, child, child-birth, evidence, common law, competence and compellability, concealment, consent, corroboration, counselling, aiding suicide, counselling offences, credibility, criminal negligence, criminal responsibility, dangerous acts, defences, duty of persons undertaking surgical or medical treatment, endangering life, judges, medical treatment, necessity defence, saving life.*

2. See, for example, *Malette* v. *Shulman* (1987), 63 O.R. (2d) 243 (Ont. H.C.J.), where a doctor ignored a card on the plaintiff (a Jehovah's Witness) at the time of her accident which indicated that she refused all blood transfusions in any circumstance. In finding the physician guilty of battery and in awarding the plaintiff damages, the judge (Donnelly J.) wrote that a "conscious, rational patient is entitled to refuse any medical treatment and the doctor must comply, no matter how ill advised he may believe that instruction to be" (at 269). See also the Supreme Court decision in *Ciarlariello* v. *Schacter* (1993), 100 D.L.R. (4th) 609 at 618 (S.C.C.), which reconfirms the individual right to bodily integrity; and *Van Wijngaarden* v. *Tzalalis* (1992), *(sub nom. Wijngaarden* v. *Tzalalis)* 11 O.R. (3d) 779, 60 O.A.C. 236 (C.A.).

3. In an emergency, where a person cannot express a preference and there is no advance directive indicating otherwise, he or she is deemed to choose life over death. The legal presumption is that, barring any evidence to the contrary and given the choice, a person would choose medical treatment. Consent to treatment is *implied*, and doctors who treat in a competent manner are protected from legal action.

4. The Senate Report offered a good definition for the term *free and informed consent*: "the voluntary agreement by a person who, in the possession and exercise of sufficient mental capacity, as defined by an appropriate medical professional, makes an intelligent choice as to treatment options. It supposes knowledge about the consequences of having or not having the treatment and about possible alternatives. The consent must be free from coercion, duress and mistake." *Of Life and Death: The Report of the Special Senate Committee on Euthanasia and Assisted Suicide* (Ottawa, June 1995) at 15.

5. Part VIII of the *Criminal Code*, R.S.C. 1985, c. C-46, covers crimes against the person. See in particular ss. 265 and 266.

6. Some key cases dealing with informed consent are *Reibl* v. *Hughes* (1980), 114 D.L.R. (3d) 1 (S.C.C.); *Hopp* v. *Lepp*, [1980] 2 S.C.R. 192; *Stamos* v. *Davies* (1985), 52 O.R. (2d) 10 (Ont. H.C.); *Reynard* v. *Carr* (1986), 38 C.C.L.T. 217 (B.C.C.A.); *Ciarlariello* v. *Schacter*, [1993] 2 S.C.R. 119, 15 C.C.L.T. (2d) 209.

7. See Lorne E. Rozovsky and Fay A. Rozovsky, *The Canadian Law of Consent to Treatment* (Toronto: Butterworths, 1990) at 53.

8. Brian F. Hoffman, *The Law of Consent to Treatment in Ontario* (Toronto: Butterworths, 1997) at 15. This means a translator will be required to ensure a valid consent when people are unfamiliar with the language their doctor is speaking.

9. See *Criminal Code*, above note 5, defences subs. 150.1(2) *child*, s. 14 *consent to death*, subs. 265(4) *accused's belief as to consent*, s. 8.3 *necessity, common law defences preserved.*

10. Section 215 of the *Criminal Code* imposes a legal duty on parents and guardians to provide the necessaries of life for their children or other persons under their charge. Medical and surgical treatment is included in the term *necessaries of life*. See *R.* v. *Cyrenne* (1981), 62 C.C.C. (2d) 238 (Ont. Dist. Ct.), which held that medical treatment tending to preserve life is a necessary of life. If it is established that the parent of a minor denied treatment with a reckless disregard for the minor's life and safety, and in so doing accelerated that minor's death, he or she could be convicted of criminal negligence causing death. See also *R.* v. *Senior*, [1899] 1 Q.B. 283, 68 L.J.Q.B. 175 (C.C.R.); *R.* v. *Brooks* (1902), 9 B.C.R. 13, 5 C.C.C. 372 (B.C.C.A.), for a definition of the words *necessaries of life*, which mean those that tend to preserve life and not merely those in the common meaning of the phrase.

11. See *Gillick* v. *West Norfolk and Wisbech Area Health Authority*, [1986] A.C. 112, [1985] 3 All E.R. 402 (H.L.). Although a case dealing with providing minors with contraception, the case addressed the issue of when a minor becomes competent to consent to treatment. The court restated the norm (requirement of parental consent to medical and related health treatment) and then outlined what would happen when the decision of parent and child conflicted. It decided that the norm of the parental right to decide would be vacated when a child achieved sufficient intelligence and understanding to fully understand the medical treatment proposed. Age would be an important factor, but not a sole criterion. The public policy goal is clear — to encourage family cohesion and promote parental control and responsibility for their minor children.

12. In *B. (R.)* v. *Children's Aid Society of Metropolitan Toronto*, [1995] 1 S.C.R. 315, the Supreme Court found that the challenged sections of the Ontario *Child Welfare Act* dealing with the definition of a *child in need of protection* did not deny parents a right to choose appropriate medical treatment for their children, contrary to s. 7 of the *Charter*, or violate their s. 2 *Charter* right to freedom of religion. In its finding the Court noted that "the protection of a child's right to life and to health is a basic tenet of our legal system [and that] [a]n exercise of parental liberty which seriously endangers the survival of the child should be viewed as falling outside of s. 7 of the *Charter*" (at 319).

13. In *Re Y. (A.)* (1993), 111 Nfld. & P.E.I.R. 91, 348 A.P.R. 91 (Nfld. U.F.C.), a fifteen-year-old Jehovah's Witness who refused chemotherapy that might eventually require him to undergo blood transfusions was declared on the evidence to be a mature minor and found not to be in need of protection. Note, however, that on medical evidence it was argued that blood transfusions as a follow-up to the chemotherapy were not essential. Note also the finding that forcing the teenager against his will to undergo a treatment would seriously compromise the success of the treatment. In *Ney* v. *Canada (Attorney General)* (1993), 79 B.C.L.R. (2d) 47, [1993] 6 W.W.R. 135, 102 D.L.R. (4th) 136 (S.C.), the question of capacity of children to consent to or refuse treatment was discussed. At common law a child is capable of consenting to medical treatment if he or she has sufficient intelligence and maturity to fully appreciate the nature and consequences of a medical procedure to be performed for his or her benefit. The doctor decides. If the child does not meet this test, then the parents' consent will be required for treatment. In the controversial Saskatchewan case involving Tyrell Dueck, a thirteen-year-old whose parents refused chemotherapy in favour of an alternative cancer treatment in Mexico, the court held on the evidence before it that he was not a mature minor and required that he resume medical treatment. This judgment was later suspended when the doctors discovered that the cancer had spread from his leg to his lungs. The story galvanized

public opinion on the role of the courts in these health care decisions and the reasonable limits of the authority of parents over their children in health care decision-making: *Re Dueck* (1999), 171 D.L.R. (4th) 761 (Sask Q.B.).

14. In *Walker (Litigation Guardian of)* v. *Region 2 Hospital Corp.* (1994), 4 R.F.L. (4th) 327, 116 D.L.R. (4th) 477 (*sub nom. Region 2 Hospital Corp.* v. *Walker*), 150 N.B.R. (2d) 366, 385 A.P.R. 366 (C.A.), the issue of a minor was also raised. In this case, a fifteen-year-old member of the Jehovah's Witnesses suffering from leukemia refused all blood transfusions. His parents and two of his doctors believed he was mature enough to understand the consequences of his decision to refuse all blood-related therapies. On this basis, the hospital and doctor applied unsuccessfully for a declaration that the boy was a mature minor capable of refusing consent to this and to all treatment. The trial judge disagreed and awarded Crown guardianship, instructing that blood transfusions were to be given if necessary to save the boy's life. On appeal, this decision was vacated and the boy declared a mature minor with full capacity to give or withhold his consent to treatment. In such a situation, there was no further jurisdiction for the Court's *parens patriae* jurisdiction. See also the *Medical Consent of Minors Act*, S.N.B. 1976, c. M-6.1.

15. Barney Sneiderman et al., *Canadian Medical Law: An Introduction for Physicians and Other Health Care Professionals* (Toronto: Carswell, 1989), chap. 3.

16. Generally, the term *child in need of protection* when used in the context of medical and health decision-making describes a child whose legal guardian neglects or refuses to provide or obtain proper medical, surgical or other recognized remedial care or treatment necessary for the child's health and well-being.

17. For an outline of the practice and procedure to determine the jurisdiction of the court to exercise its *parens patriae* jurisdiction in cases of mental incompetence, see *Re S. (A.M.) (Guardian ad litem of)* (1993), 49 E.T.R. 307, (*sub nom. Re S. (A.M.)*) 107 Nfld. & P.E.I.R. 350, 336 A.P.R. 350 (Nfld. T.D.).

18. Most provinces now have a Consent to Treatment Act that codifies criteria for substituted decision-making for people in institutional settings such as hospitals and publicly funded seniors' residences. These laws generally make provision for assessing a patient's capacity to consent, the content of advance directives and living wills, the setting up of consent and capacity review boards, psychiatric care and treatment, and appeal provisions from the decisions of persons acting within the framework of the statute.

19. New life enhancing and prolonging technologies and procedures are adding a new cost to the health care system. American statistics show that about half the growth in real per capita health costs is associated with medical technology. While many can actually reduce costs, the demand for everything from laser surgery to respirators and stents has grown tremendously, thereby increasing the costs. See Milt Freudenheim, "A new strain on the cost of health care: Latest medical devices bring bigger bills," *New York Times*, 9 April 1999, C1.

20. *Nancy B.* v. *Hôtel-Dieu de Québec* (1992), 86 D.L.R. (4th) 385 (Que. Sup. Ct.) [hereinafter *Nancy B.*]. Nancy B. died on 13 February 1992, shortly after being disconnected from the respirator.

21. The *Quebec Civil Code* states that "no person may be made to undergo care of any nature . . . except with [his or her] consent."

22. The *Criminal Code*, above note 5, makes counselling or aiding suicide an indictable offence punishable by up to fourteen years in prison (s. 241).

23. "No person is entitled to consent to have death inflicted on him, and such consent does not affect the criminal responsibility of any person by whom death may be inflicted on the person by whom consent is given." (*Ibid.*, s. 14) Notwithstanding this section, in the case of a genuine suicide pact, the surviving party should have a defence to murder in

certain circumstances. See *R. v. Gagnon* (1993), 84 C.C.C. (3d) 143, 24 C.R. (4th) 369, [1993] R.J.Q. 1716 (C.A.).

24. The *Criminal Code, ibid.*, provides: "Every one who undertakes to administer surgical or medical treatment to another person or to do any other lawful act that may endanger the life of another person is, except in cases of necessity, under a legal duty to have and to use reasonable knowledge, skill and care in so doing (s. 216). A legal duty is imposed under s. 217 of the *Code* on persons undertaking acts. The offences of criminal negligence causing death (s. 220) and bodily harm (s. 221) apply. Section 45 defines the duty to use reasonable knowledge, skill, and care in administering surgical care.

25. A doctor stopping respiratory support treatment of a patient at the freely made and informed request of the patient so that nature may take its course will be considered reasonable within the meaning of s. 45 of the *Criminal Code*, which states that "everyone is protected from criminal responsibility for performing a surgical operation on any person for the benefit of that person if (a) the operation is performed with reasonable care and skill; and (b) it is reasonable to perform the operation, having regard to the state of health of the person at the time the operation is performed and to all the circumstances of the case." In the case of *Nancy B.*, above note 20, the doctor who stopped the respiratory support treatment and the hospital where he worked were held free of any criminal liability.

26. Charles P. Sabatino, "The Legal and Functional Status of the Medical Proxy: Suggestions for Statutory Reform," *The Journal of Law, Medicine and Ethics* 27, no. 1 (1999) at 46. See also Ann Alpers and Bernard Lo, "Avoiding Family Feuds: Responding to Surrogate Demands for Life-Sustaining Interventions," *ibid.* at 69.

27. An advance directive is a power of attorney for personal care in which we can direct what treatment we would accept or refuse were we to become incapacitated due to a very serious accident or illness. For instance, we might cherish our physical independence and never want to be kept alive in a vegetative state in a hospital. In this situation, we might ask for palliative care and no resuscitation in case of an emergency. The purpose of a living will is to help us direct our care if we were to become unable through disease or disability to do so. In effect, this is an extension of our right to refuse treatment. Preparing a living will allows us to exercise our autonomy over our personal care, just as we have always done for our financial affairs through wills.

28. See *Health Care Consent Act*, 1996, S.O. 1996, c. 2, Schedule A, and *Substitute Decisions Act*, 1992, S.O. 1992, c. 30, as am. by S.O. 1996, c. 2. In Ontario, the Public Guardian and Trustee (PGT) has several new responsibilities following all the legislative activity in this area since 1992. The legislation combines in one place the two former offices of Official Guardian (where treatment decisions for children in need of care or protection and persons under the *Mental Health Act*, R.S.O. 1990, c. M.7, were made) and the previous Public Trustee (decisions mainly about people's estates in cases of incompetency and/or intestacy). The *Health Care Consent Act*, 1996, which replaced the *Consent to Treatment Act* (S.O. 1992, c. 31), combined the various functions and administration under the 1992 Act and the *Substitute Decisions Act* into the new office of the PGT. For a full analysis of these changes in Ontario, see Brian F. Hoffman, *The Law of Consent to Treatment in Ontario*, above note 8, chap. 5.

29. Substituted decision-makers for personal care (SDMs) are people who will speak on our behalf if, for reasons of age, illness, or disability, we cannot do so for ourselves. Ontario really has a cluster of three laws which deal with several aspects of health care decision-making. For a listing of these, see Hoffman, *The Law of Consent to Treatment in Ontario*, above note 8 at 104–5.

Chapter 9: Organ and Tissue Donation: An Urgent Need

1. See the April 1999 Report of the Standing Committee on Health, *Organ and Tissue Donation and Transplantation: A Canadian Approach*, available on the Internet at <http://www.parl.gc.ca/InfoComDoc/36/1/HEAL/Studies/Reports/healrp05-e.htm>.

2. The first successful limb transplant was performed on 23 September 1998, at the Edouard Herriot hospital in Lyon, France. A hand from a brain-dead man was transplanted onto the arm of Australian businessman Clint Hallam, who three months later was experiencing sensation in the fingertips. *Globe and Mail*, 11 December 1998, A12. A similar operation was performed on an American in Louisville, Kentucky. Surgeons have also successfully performed knee, larynx, trachea, femur, nerve, and muscle transplants. The costs remain high, and the recipients face a lifetime on anti-rejection drugs, with side effects that include risk of infection, diabetes, and cancer. See Lawrence Altman, "Rebuilding the body: A special report," *New York Times*, 2 May 1999, 1.

3. See <http://www.transplantawareness.org> for a quick factual and historical overview of organ and tissue transplantation.

4. According to estimates from Organ Donation Ontario (formerly M.O.R.E.), about one hundred out of every million people need a transplant, and only twenty to thirty out of every million may become potential donors. Even if one donates, there is no guarantee that the organs will be used for transplant. For instance, organs may not be healthy at the relevant time or a suitable match may be impossible. In the Report of the Parliamentary Committee on Health, the following organs were transplanted in 1998: kidneys (991 of which 665 were cadaveric and 336 living donors), liver (342), heart (154), lung (75 lung and 7 heart/lung), pancreas (9 pancreas and 33 pancreas/kidney), bowel (2).

5. The first successful heart transplant was performed in 1967 by South Africa's Dr. Christiaan Barnard, but until advances in effective immunosuppressant drugs were achieved in the 1990s, many patients died when their bodies rejected the new organ. There have been great advances in heart research, from artificial hearts to lifesaving devices such as the artificial heart device system, called HeartSaver, developed by Canada's World Heart Corp., which can now be remotely monitored and altered across great distances. This system will have profound health care impacts in countries like ours, where distance and the distribution of hospitals and specialized cardiac units make it difficult for many people to have care. Karyn Standen, "World heart picks up the pace," [Ottawa] *Citizen*, 21 November 1998, D1. See also <http://www.transplantawareness.org> for further information on transplant technology.

6. Scientists at the University of Pittsburgh's McGowan Center for Artificial Organ Development have almost completed a temporary artificial lung, called an intravenous membrane oxygenator (IMO), which can be inserted through the femoral vein in the leg and snaked through to the chest cavity to pump oxygen into red blood cells and remove carbon dioxide from the blood circulating towards the heart and lungs, giving diseased or damaged lungs a chance to heal. "Medical technology," *Globe and Mail*, 23 March 1999, A20.

7. In 1999 scientists are planning the world's first tongue transplant to restore the ability of oral cancer victims to speak and eat. The network of nerve fibres, blood vessels, and muscle tissue within the tongue make the procedure very difficult, although it has been shown to be technically possible with dogs. Other transplant surgery advances include the first voice box transplant in 1998, the transplantation of a scalp onto a cancer victim, the transplantation of a penis, and a new hand. According to Dr. John Barker, head of the American hand transplant team at the University of Louisville, "the key to breaking the final frontier in transplantation is working with composite tissue, including skin,

bone, muscle, nerves and blood vessels. Once the hand transplant is mastered, then transplanting other extremities (including faces) from cadavers to people should be possible. John Barber, *Globe and Mail*, 5 November 1998, A8.

8. Transplants can reduce the cost to Canada's health care system. A kidney transplant, for instance, costs about $20,000, plus an annual anti-rejection drug bill of $6,000. This cost compares with about $60,000 annually for dialysis treatment.

9. *Human Tissue Gift Act*, R.S.A. 1980, c. H-12; *Human Tissue Gift Act*, R.S.B.C. 1996, c. 211; *The Human Tissue Act*, R.S.M. 1987, c. H180; *Human Tissue Gift Act*, R.S.N.B. 1973, c. H-12; *Human Tissue Act*, R.S.N. 1990, c. H-15; *Human Tissue Act*, R.S.N.W.T. 1988, c. H-6; *Human Tissue Gift Act*, R.S.N.S. 1989, c. 215; *Human Tissue Gift Act*, R.S.O. 1990, c. H.20; *Human Tissue Donation Act*, S.P.E.I. 1992, c. 34; *Civil Code of Quebec*, arts. 19, 42–45; *Human Tissue Gift Act*, R.S.S. 1978, c. H-15; *Human Tissue Gift Act*, R.S.Y.T. 1986, c. 89.

10. In March 1998 the Canadian Medical Association announced that British Columbia had developed the first computerized organ donor registry. Funded by the private sector and the provincial government, the registry is part of British Columbia's efforts to meet the growing need for organs for transplant, especially kidneys and eyes. The goal is to increase donors by half a million people by the year 2000; to reduce waiting lists, estimated at an average of 809 days for a kidney transplant; and to meet the current annual need for at least 350 organs and 900 corneas. Donors will only need to register once, through a participating drugstore chain or through their BC Care Card or driver's licence. They can consent to donate all or only specified organs for use in transplant or for other therapeutic purposes, medical education, or scientific research. All intensive care units in B.C. hospitals will have confidential phone and fax number links to the new registry. See *Canadian Medical Association Journal* 158 (1998) at 579.

11. In Ontario, for instance, a provincewide centralized list of people in need of a transplant is kept to ensure the fair allocation of organs throughout the province. Once a hospital advises that it has an organ donor, the provincial program will begin searching the computerized waiting list for people in need of the organs in question. The most urgent cases are given priority. Thanks to modern computer, medical, and transportation technology, this effort can be carried out on a national (and international) basis. The final decision as to who receives the organs is always made by the medical team based on the computer recommendations for a match between organ donor and recipient. According to Organ Donation Ontario, since 1990 such advanced computer technology has helped in the selection of more than 4,800 patients for transplants.

12. There are only three uses recognized by the various Human Tissue Gift Acts — human transplant, medical education, and scientific research.

13. While most of the provincial laws specify that tissue includes an organ, they specifically exclude skin, blood, any blood constituent, bone, or other tissue that is regenerative. This may not be a perfect definition, because some organs (such as the liver, for instance) can regenerate. A court would rely on the common medical understanding of the term at the time to clarify any question on a case-by-case basis. This is important because only the tissue covered by the Acts, which is defined to include organs but to exclude regenerative tissue, must be harvested and handled in accordance with the legislation.

14. Because genetic testing will allow for the identification of an individual's genetic traits and, in cases of inheritable genetic diseases, of their families' through the analysis of tissue like blood, the Acts should be amended to require *specific consent* to the retrieval and use of regenerative tissue.

15. The Law Reform Commission of Canada outlined the objectives it sought to achieve in redefining death. These were as follows: "(1) The proposed legislation must avoid arbitrariness and give greater guidance to doctors, lawyers and the public, while

remaining flexible enough to adapt to medical changes. (2) The proposed legislation must not attempt to solve all the problems created by death, but only the problem of establishing criteria for its determination. (3) The one proposed piece of legislation must apply equally in all circumstances where a determination of death is at issue. (4) The proposed legislation must recognize only the standards and criteria of death; it must not define the medical procedure to be used, nor the instruments or procedures by which death is to be determined. (5) The proposed legislation must recognize standards and criteria generally accepted by the Canadian public. (6) To remain faithful to the popular concept, the proposed legislation must recognize that death is the death of an individual person, not of an organ or cells. (7) The proposed legislation must not in practice lead to wrong or unacceptable situations. (8) The proposed legislation must not determine the criteria of death by reference only or mainly to the practice of organ transplantation." Law Reform Commission of Canada, *Criteria for the Determination of Death*, Report 15 (Ottawa: Supply and Services Canada, 1981) at 12.

16. The process began in 1968 with the publication of the Harvard criteria for the diagnosis of brain death. See "Ad Hoc Committee of the Harvard Medical School to Examine the Definition of Brain Death, A Definition of Irreversible Coma," *Journal of the American Medical Association* 205, no. 6 (1968) at 337. Manitoba was the first province to adopt the new definition. See *The Vital Statistics Act*, R.S.M. 1987, c. V60. The Canadian Medical Association published guidelines that have been revised on several occasions since then. For further legal analysis of issues, see Law Reform Commission of Canada, *Criteria for the Determination of Death*, Working Paper 23 (Ottawa: Supply and Services Canada, 1979) and Report 15 (Ottawa: Supply and Services Canada, 1981).

17. The CMA's *Guidelines for the Diagnosis of Death* at <http://www.cma.ca/inside/policybase/1987/1-15.htm> at 1 reads: " Although irreversible cessation of circulatory and respiratory functions acceptably defines death, irreversible cessation of brain function is also equivalent to death even though the heart continues to beat while the patient is on a respirator." The Parliamentary Report (April 1999) defines brain death as "[t]otal cessation of brain function as manifested by the absence of consciousness, spontaneous movement, absence of spontaneous respiration, and absence of all brainstem function" (see the Report's Glossary of Terms at <http://www.parl.gc.ca/InfoComDoc/36/1/HEAL/Studies/Reports/healrp05/09-gloss-e.htm>.

18. In its 1992 report, *Procurement and Transfer of Human Tissues and Organs*, Working Paper 66 (Ottawa: Supply and Services Canada, 1992), the Law Reform Commission of Canada (LRCC) noted that "[t]here is evidence that the public is reluctant to participate in the organ donation process, in part, because of fear about premature determination of death. While the standard of death may work to facilitate organ transplantation, undue bias in the standard setting may itself erode public confidence in both the law and the organ donation process. Thus, concern about the relationship between medical practice, the legal definition of death and the public's confidence and willingness to participate in the organ donation process is legitimate. The delicacy of that relationship itself would seem to suggest prudence and caution" (at 102). This statement highlights the many societal factors that complicate and colour public policy decisions affecting legal regulation (including prohibitions) of organs and tissue transplants in Canada.

19. Generally, the wording of the section dealing with the donation of human eyes specifically excludes the otherwise legal requirement that the doctors determining death are different from those associated with either the donor or a potential cornea transplant recipient. The wording in every province is generally similar to subs. 7(4) of the Ontario Act, which states: "Nothing in this section [s.7] in any way affects a physician in the removal of eyes for cornea transplants."

20. According to the Eye Bank of Canada, although each hospital has its own policy and procedures for eye donations, there is a general process that is followed. A signed consent form is obtained from the next of kin by a physician, nurse, social worker, or chaplain. When the families request a donation, the hospital's consent form is used. A hospital's consent form is acceptable in all the centres. Most hospitals, especially in the Metropolitan Toronto region, use the Organ Donation Ontario consent form, which includes consent for both organs and tissue. An oral consent can also be obtained over the telephone. However, there must be two witnesses who hear the consent, and each witness must be introduced to the next of kin. Written reply to author's questions from the Eye Bank of Canada (Ontario), 30 April 1998.

21. In 1997 the Eye Bank of Canada (Ontario) received 2,954 eyes (1,477 donors) from over 130 hospitals in Ontario and currently receives on the average 200 to 250 eyes per month. Despite being ranked as the fourth most successful eye bank in North America and the top eye bank in Canada, it had to cancel fifty-nine corneal transplant surgeries in 1996 due to lack of availability of suitable tissue. *Ibid.*

22. At the time of writing, the Eye Bank of Canada (Ontario) listed the following facilities in Canada as part of its provincial network: Eye Bank of B.C., Vancouver, B.C.; Lions Eye Bank, Calgary, Alta.; Eye Bank, Edmonton, Alta.; Lions Eye Bank of Saskatchewan, Inc., Saskatoon, Sask.; Lions Eye Bank of Manitoba and NW Ontario, Inc., Winnipeg, Man.; Eye Bank of Canada (Ontario) Toronto, Ont.; Banque d'Yeux Nationale, Ste Foy, Que.; New Brunswick Eye Bank, St. John, N.B.; and Halifax Tissue Bank, Halifax, N.S. The Ontario Division of the Eye Bank of Canada was the first in Canada and began in 1955.

23. This prohibition is generally contained in s. 10 of the various provincial Human Tissue Gift Acts. The Act of the Northwest Territories (s. 3) does not include such a prohibition, containing rather a clause that states: "Nothing in this Act makes unlawful any dealing with the body of a deceased person or any part or parts of the body that would be lawful if this Act had not been enacted." Section 3 of the New Brunswick Act contains a similar provision.

24. According to Organ Donation Ontario, the family of the donor will be advised by phone, and later in writing, of what organs were retrieved for transplant. The Acts in every province prohibit the release of information that could identify the donor or the recipient, unless the parties agree. Anonymous letters can be passed between the family of the donor and the recipient(s) should they all agree. See s. 11 or 12 of most of the Acts.

25. *In the matter of Karen Quinlan,* 70 N.J. 10, 355 A.2d 647 (S.C. 1976).

26. Anencephalic infants are born without most of the brain, skull, and scalp. Those born with this condition exhibit brain stem activity that allows them initially to breathe on their own and to respond to external stimuli. Death normally occurs within a matter of hours or days, although some infants survive longer. Under the existing definition of brain death as whole brain death, organ donation from such infants could only be carried out when all brain stem activity had stopped. This is usually too late for donation purposes as the organs have deteriorated. See the Medical Task Force on Anencephaly, "The Infant with Anencephaly," *New England Journal of Medicine* 322, no. 10 (1990) at 669.

27. In its report on these issues in the early 1990s, the Law Reform Commission of Canada recommended against redefining brain death, arguing that to do so would lead to abuse and too broadly enlarge the category of people who would be used as donors, including anencephalic newborns and the thousands of Canadian patients presently in hospitals in a persistent vegetative state with no hope of ever regaining consciousness. It also recommended specifically excluding the harvesting of organs or tissue from fetal and embryonic human life and from gametes (ova and sperm). See *Procurement and Transfer of Human Tissues and Organs,* above note 18.

28. "The Committee agrees that the involvement of families in the donation process is essential and recommends that the new national body oversee that any national public awareness campaign on donation provide reassurance that consent of next-of-kin will be acquired regardless of the patient's intent status." Report of the Standing Committee on Health, *Organ and Tissue Donation and Transplantation: A Canadian Approach*, April 1999, recommendations 9 and 9.1 The committee was advised that in all but 5 percent of cases, a family would respect a donor's legally binding wishes at the time of death. They felt that it was better to meet the public's concern about premature organ harvesting with increased education on the value and purpose of organ and tissue donation, sacrificing individual autonomy to achieve a potentially larger trust in the process and system of donation among the public. The report is available free at <http://www.parl.gc.ca/InfoComDoc/36/1/HEAL/Studies/Reports/healrp05-e.htm>.

29. According to the 1998 Quarterly Report of the Canadian Organ Replacement Registry (CORR), the organ donor rate in Canada is 13.7 per million (down from 14.4 in 1997).

30. In its April 1999 report, above note 28, the federal Standing Committee on Health recommended the creation of the Canadian Transplant Network, which would have four permanent program areas using expert advisory groups to address respective areas, including donor intent and consent; management and procurement; waiting, sharing, and allocation; and transplantation outcomes. In the first, it recommended that the expert committee "assist in the design and implementation of ongoing national public awareness and education campaigns" (rec. 3.2) and of "ongoing national professional education and training campaigns" (rec. 3.3).

31. Research team leader Dr. John Dick of Toronto's Hospital for Sick Children was joined by researchers André LaRochelle and Josef Vormoor in identifying stem cells in the blood. A correction made to a deficient or deadly gene in a stem cell only would be passed on to all future generations of cells and would overcome the present problem of inadvertently reinjecting cancerous cells as part of cancer treatments. People with inherited blood diseases like leukemia, thalassemia, and sickle cell anemia could be helped in this way. See John Dick, André LaRochelle, and Josef Vormoor, *Nature Medicine*, 3 December 1996.

32. For further reference, see Janis Hass, "A little biological insurance," *Globe and Mail*, 11 May 1999, A19.

33. See Report of the Standing Committee on Health, above note 28, recommendation 4.3.

34. The term *mandated donation* is used rather than the current term *mandated choice* as the reality is that, in the system as it exists in some countries and is proposed for Canada, there is no choice, except to try and opt out of a system that would require donation even where a person was unaware of the law or unable to act in time to revoke the legally imposed "consent" to donate. In addition to the suspicion of abuse that such a legal system would create, countries with mandated donation laws now have not found that it has solved the shortage of organs and other human tissue for transplant. This is because doctors will only honour the legal requirement if the family agrees, in order to maintain confidence in the system.

35. On 9 October 1997, a Private Member's Bill was introduced by Reform Member of Parliament Dr. Keith Martin to address the shortage of available donated organs for transplant in Canada. The Bill proposed the creation of a full-time national database of donors; use of the federal income tax process to make "donation" mandatory; payment to hospitals to cover the cost of retrieval and transplant; and the passage of a federal law to prevent families from vetoing an otherwise valid advance directive concerning post-mortem organ donations.

36. *Xenotransplantation* is cross-species transplantation. In this book it will be used to refer to animal-to-human transplants.

37. See David J. Mooney and Antonios G. Mikos, "Growing New Organs," *Scientific American,* April 1999, at 60. See also Robert S. Langer and Joseph P. Vacanti, "Tissue Engineering: The Challenges Ahead," *ibid.* at 86. Available at the magazine's Web site at <http://www.sciam.com>.

38. For a brief and understandable presentation of the process of rejection of tissue and organs in transplantation between humans and between animals and humans, see the *U.K. Report of the Advisory Group on the Ethics of Xenotransplantation,* Ian Kennedy, Chair, Department of Health (London: H.M.S.O., 1997) [hereinafter the *Kennedy Report*] at 20–28.

39. "In the UK, Imutran plc is developing genetically modified pigs for use as a source of organs and tissue for xenotransplantation. Their interest is primarily with the transplant of solid organs. In September 1995, they announced the result of research involving the heterotopic transplant of pigs' hearts into cynomologous monkeys and their intention to move to xenotransplants involving humans over the next twelve months." The *Kennedy Report,* above note 38 at 15.

40. Diacrin Inc. of Charlestown, Mass., in the United States received FDA approval for its phase 1 open-label trial using xenografts in combination with depth-electrode investigations to help with epileptic seizures. It uses depth electrodes to pinpoint the site of a seizure; and where surgery is not possible, fetal pig brain cells are injected through the electrode to produce an acid that inhibits the nerve cells in the host brain from responding too quickly and causing seizures.

41. For a brief summary of the major concerns, see Paul Taylor, "Medical miracle has potential dark side," *Globe and Mail,* 3 January 1998, A4.

42. The *Kennedy Report,* above note 38, summed up the public health and safety issues as follows: "As regards the three main concerns associated with xenotransplantation, we conclude as follows: *Physiology:* although it would appear that hearts and lungs may be capable of functioning as intended in the recipient, questions remain about kidneys, livers and islet cells, in view of the more complex biochemical functions which they perform. *Immunology:* research is proceeding into the neutralisation of hyper-acute rejection and there are indications that such research is having some significant success. However, the operation and control of other rejection processes are not well known, particularly as neither human nor primate recipients of foreign tissue have survived for long enough for these processes to be studied. *Infection:* SPF [Specific-Pathogen-Free — where animals are bred to exclude any infections or disease-causing agents] or similar conditions could reduce many of the risks associated with fungi, parasites and bacteria but are thought to be of more limited use in reducing the risk from viruses, which would have the greatest potential for onward transmission" (at 37).

43. The first heart xenotransplant occurred in 1964 when a chimpanzee's heart was transplanted to a human but failed within a couple of hours. See J.D. Hardy, C.M. Chavez, et al., "Heart Transplantation in Man: Developmental Studies and a Report of a Case." *Journal of the American Medical Association* 188, 1132–40. Four years later, two other xenotransplants — a sheep's heart in the United States and a pig's heart in the United Kingdom were tried and failed immediately. This was before the recent discovery of genetic engineering techniques through which animals can be "humanized" through the injection into their embryos of certain human genes. At the time of the xenotransplant attempts noted above, hyper-acute rejection made successful xenotransplantation impossible. Since then several xenotransplants involving solid organs and tissue have been performed. For a listing of the cases of xenotransplants to 1997, see the *Kennedy Report,* above note 38 at 10–15.

44. Work in xenotransplantation slowed following the finding that pig genes harbour retroviruses called porcine endogenous retroviruses that may be able to infect human cells. Calls on various governments for a moratorium on all xenotransplant clinical trials ensued, but have been largely ignored; one of the bell-wether agencies, the FDA in the United States, issued a mere cautionary statement for researchers and the public. Since then the FDA has refused to prevent xenotransplantation clinical trials, even approving clinical trials in American companies provided they agree to proceed with caution and supply extensive data showing the balances of harm to benefit. Media coverage reported two shipments of genetically modified pigs that were imported from the United Kingdom to Canada in April, 1998, but not inspected by Health Canada. The transgenic pigs contained a human gene to make them more compatible donors for human transplant. Their progeny will be used for experimental purposes. This highlights the need for systems to be in place *prior* to research. Transparency and accurate, timely information are essential to ensure public trust. Carolyn Abraham, "Donor-organ pigs not inspected by Health Canada," *Globe and Mail*, 13 February 1999, A2.

45. There are several ways this is being done now. As well as "humanizing" animals through the insertion of human genes into animal embryo cells, some companies are proposing that we "animalize" humans by giving them a pig's immune system. The idea is that the future human recipient will have a combined immune system (say human and pig) and therefore be less likely to reject the animal organ. *Ibid.*

46. "The observation that pigs have passed only a few pathogens to humans despite centuries of close contact assures many people that transplanting organs from these animals would not give rise to any new and dangerous diseases. Still, there are reasons to be cautious. Certain retroviruses — viruses that incorporate their genetic blueprint directly into the host's DNA — pose a possible threat. Pigs, as well as other mammals, contain within their genetic stores so-called proviruses — sequences of genetic code that can potentially direct the production of infectious viral particles. (As much as 1 percent of the DNA people carry is made up of such viral genes.) These sequences owe their presence in modern animals to past episodes of retroviral infection in their ancestors, when the viruses inserted their genetic code into sperm or egg cells. The offspring of the infected animals retained these viral genes, which were then passed on from generation to generation. Robert P. Lanza, David K.C. Cooper, and William L. Chick, "Xenotransplantation," *Scientific American* (July 1997): 54–59 at 59.

47. The *Kennedy Report*, above note 38, addressed the difficulty of balancing the role of government in protecting individual rights and community interests with that of the private sector to earn a profit on their investment: "Quite apart from questions concerning the ethics of scientific research which this changed environment poses, there are significant issues of public policy. Government requires the best and most reliable information on which to base its policy decisions. When knowledge becomes a commodity in the market place, the Government's task is made more difficult and the public interest harder to determine" (at 87).

48. Viruses and other disease-causing pathogens can be transferred from animals to humans and the closer the species is to the human species on the evolutionary chain, the greater the risk. For an outline of the infections possible in xenotransplants, strategies for their control, and animal pathogens, see the *Kennedy Report*, above note 38 at 29–38.

49. Held in Ottawa, 7–9 November 1997, the forum's purpose was "to present information and initiate discussion on the risks, benefits and ethics of xenotransplantation; to identify key regulatory issues; and to define areas where research and new information is required." The public report is available free from Health Canada at <http://www.hc-sc.gc.ca>.

50. Health Canada's January 1997 proposal paper sought public and drug industry input on a regulatory model that Health Canada was proposing. Parliament, the provincial and

territorial legislatures, corporate and community stakeholders, and the public at large were asked to comment on the proposed regulatory model to establish health safety standards to eliminate the risk of any transmission of disease from animals to humans and among humans from transplantation of organs and tissue. Free copies are available from Health Canada. See its Web site at <http://www.hc-sc.gc.ca>.

51. Entitled *Report of WHO Consultation on Xenotransplantation,* released in Geneva on 30 October 1997, this document is merely the re-articulation of the advantages and disadvantages of cross-species organ, tissue, and cell transplantation from animals into humans. It assumes that xenotransplantation will proceed regardless, and merely recommends international cooperation and coordination to establish a uniform set of rules to guide its use and development.

52. *The Nuffield Council on Bioethics, Animal-to-Human Transplants: The Ethics of Xenotransplantation,* United Kingdom, Report of the Council's Working Party, Albert Weale, Chair (London: The Council, March 1996). The principal conclusions and recommendations of the report were as follows: (1) Xenotransplantation may meet the future need for human organs, but ethical and safety issues must be resolved. (2) The special breeding of pigs for organ transplants into humans is ethically justified. (3) A special Advisory Committee on xenotransplantation should be struck to assess the public health risks such transplants raise. (4) Once the safeguards are in place, xenotransplantation should be offered to suitable patients who have provided a freely given and informed consent. (5) Xenotransplantation should be introduced into clinical practice. Once this is done, its impact on individual patients should be the subject of research.

53. For a thorough analysis of the ethical arguments against xenotransplantation, including the use of animals, the religious argument, and the issue of animal rights generally, see the *Kennedy Report,* above note 38, chap. 4, 59–88.

54. See *Report of the Inquiry on Xenotransplantation.* The Nuffield Council on Bioethics, Rt. Hon. Sir Patrick Nairne, Chairman, March 1996.

55. The Standing Committee on Health adopted the following terms of reference for their work: (1) to consult, analyze, and make recommendations regarding the state of organ and tissue donation in Canada; (2) to consult broadly with stakeholders; (3) to consider the appropriate role for the federal government in the development of national safety, outcome, and process standards for organ and tissue donations, [and promoting public awareness]; (4) to consider the legislative and regulatory regimes governing organ and tissue donations in other countries.

56. Dr. Keith Martin, MP for Esquimalt-Juan de Fuca, B.C., presented Motion 222 on 9 October 1997, which proposed four steps to address the Canadian shortage of organs for donation. It received unanimous consent. In a letter on 24 November 1998, Health Minister Allan Rock asked the members of the Standing Committee on Health (through his officials) to provide him with advice on the appropriate role for the federal government in addressing this issue.

57. Canada's human organ donor rate is low at 13.7 persons per million [see above note 29], behind Austria (25.2), Spain (21.7), Belgium (19.0), the United States (17.7), France (17.0), and the United Kingdom (15.5). See Anne McIlroy, *Globe and Mail,* 10 February 1999, A14.

58. For a copy of the Standing Committee on Health's Report, *Organ and Tissue Donation and Transplantation: A Canadian Approach,* see <http://www.parl.gc.ca/InfoComDoc/36/1/HEAL/Studies/Reports/healrp05-e.htm>.

59. *Ibid.,* recommendations 2–11.

60. Provincial regulations came into effect in April 1999 in British Columbia.

Chapter 10: A Right to Die? Assisted Suicide

1. At common law, suicide was treated as murder. In 1972 Parliament abolished the criminal offences of suicide and assisted suicide, deciding that suicide was better handled as a medical-social issue than a crime. See *Criminal Law Amendment Act, 1972,* S.C. 1972, c. 13, s. 16. See also *London Life Insurance Co.* v. *Lang Shirt Co's Trustee,* [1929] S.C.R. 117, [1929] 1 D.L.R. 328, where it was held that a successful suicide was not a "homicide" within the meaning of now s. 222. In such cases, the accused has an election as to mode of trial under the present subs. 536(2).

2. Section 241 of the *Criminal Code* provides: "Every one who (a) counsels a person to commit suicide, or (b) aids or abets a person to commit suicide, whether suicide ensues or not, is guilty of an indictable offence and liable to imprisonment for a term not exceeding fourteen years." *Criminal Code,* R.S.C., 1985, c. C-46.

3. *Rodriguez* v. *British Columbia (Attorney General),* [1993] 3 S.C.R. 519, 107 D.L.R. (4th) 342, 24 C.R. (4th) 281 [hereinafter *Rodriguez* cited to S.C.R.].

4. *R.* v. *Latimer* (1998), 172 Sask. R. 161, 131 C.C.C. (3d) 191 (C.A.).

5. *R.* v. *Morrison* (1998), 174 N.S.R. (2d) 201 (S.C.).

6. Section 7 provides: "Everyone has the right to life, liberty and security of the person and the right not to be deprived thereof except in accordance with the principles of fundamental justice."

7. Section 15 provides Canadians with the right to equality. Subsection 15(1) provides: "Every individual is equal before and under the law and has the right to the equal protection and equal benefit of the law without discrimination and, in particular, without discrimination based on race, national or ethnic origin, colour, religion, sex, age or mental or physical disability." Subsection 15(2) provides for affirmative action to ensure the equality promised in subs. 15(1). It promises substantive as well as procedural equality and reads: "Subsection (1) does not preclude any law, program or activity that has as its object the amelioration of conditions of disadvantaged individuals or groups including those that are disadvantaged because of race, national or ethnic origin, colour, religion, sex, age or mental or physical disability."

8. Section 12 provides: "Everyone has the right not to be subjected to any cruel and unusual treatment or punishment."

9. *Rodriguez* v. *British Columbia (Attorney General)* (1992), 18 W.C.B. (2d) 279, [1993] B.C.W.L.D. 347 (B.C.S.C.).

10. *Rodriguez* v. *British Columbia (Attorney General)* (1993), 76 B.C.L.R. (2d) 145, 79 C.C.C. (3d) 1, [1993] 3 W.W.R. 553 (B.C.C.A.) [hereinafter *Rodriguez* cited to B.C.L.R.].

11. See *Rodriguez,* above note 3. The appeal was heard on 20 May 1993, and judgment rendered on 30 September of the same year. Reasons for judgment for the majority were rendered by Mr. Justice Sopinka.

12. The majority consisted of Mr. Justices La Forest, Sopinka, Gonthier, Iacobucci, and Major.

13. In her opinion, Madam Justice McLachlin added the following statement: "Certain of the interveners raise the concern that the striking down of s. 241(b) might demean the value of life. But what value is there in life without the choice to do what one wants with one's life, one might counter. One's life includes one's death. Different people hold different views on life and on what devalues it. For some, the choice to end one's life with dignity is infinitely preferable to the inevitable pain and diminishment of a long, slow decline. Section 7 protects that choice against arbitrary state action which would remove it" (at 624).

14. While suicide and attempted suicide may not be illegal, s. 14 of the *Criminal Code,* above note 2, makes it illegal to consent to death. It reads: "No person is entitled to consent to have death inflicted on him, and such consent does not affect the criminal responsibility of any person by whom death may be inflicted on the person by whom consent is given."

15. *Rodriguez*, above note 3 at 585 (S.C.R.).

16. Sopinka wrote: "In this case, it is not disputed that in general s. 241(b) is valid and desirable legislation which fulfils the government's objectives of preserving life and protecting the vulnerable. The complaint is that the legislation is over-inclusive because it does not exclude from the reach of the prohibition those in the situation of the appellant who are terminally ill, mentally competent, but cannot commit suicide on their own. It is also argued that the extension of the prohibition to the appellant is arbitrary and unfair as suicide itself is not unlawful, and the common law allows a physician to withhold or withdraw life-saving or life-maintaining treatment on the patient's instructions and to administer palliative care which has the effect of hastening death. The issue is whether, given this legal context, the existence of a criminal prohibition on assisting suicide for one in the appellant's situation is contrary to the principles of fundamental justice" (at 590). In finding that no principle of fundamental justice was violated in this case, Sopinka J. wrote: "The principles of fundamental justice cannot be created for the occasion to reflect the court's dislike or distaste of a particular statute. While the principles of fundamental justice are concerned with more than process, reference must be made to principles which are 'fundamental' in the sense that they would have general acceptance among reasonable people. From the review I have conducted above, I am unable to discern anything approaching unanimity with respect to the issue before us. Regardless of one's personal views as to whether the distinctions drawn between withdrawal of treatment and palliative care, on the one hand, and assisted suicide on the other are practically compelling, the fact remains that these distinctions are maintained and can be persuasively defended. To the extent that there is a consensus, it is that human life must be respected and we must be careful not to undermine the institutions that protect it. . . . In upholding the respect for life, it [the prohibition on assisted suicide] may discourage those who consider that life is unbearable at a particular moment, or who perceive themselves to be a burden upon others, from committing suicide. To permit a physician to lawfully participate in taking life would send a signal that there are circumstances in which the state approves of suicide. . . . Given the concerns about abuse that have been expressed and the great difficulty in creating appropriate safeguards to prevent these, it can not be said that the blanket prohibition on assisted suicide is arbitrary or unfair, or that it is not reflective of fundamental values at play in our society. I am thus unable to find any principle of fundamental justice is violated by s. 241(b)" (at 607–8).

17. Sopinka wrote: "That respect for human dignity is one of the underlying principles upon which our society is based is unquestioned. I have difficulty, however, in characterizing this in itself as a principle of fundamental justice within the meaning of s. 7. While respect for human dignity is the genesis for many principles of fundamental justice, not every law that fails to accord such respect runs afoul of these principles" (at 592). In contrast, see the judgment of McEachern J. in this case in the B.C. Court of Appeal, above note 10 at 164 (B.C.L.R.), where he argued that "s. 7 was enacted for the purpose of ensuring human dignity and individual control, so long as it harms no one else."

18. Sopinka wrote: "There must be some more active state process in operation, involving an exercise of state control over the individual, in order for the state action in question, whether it be positive action, inaction or prohibition, to constitute 'treatment' under s. 12. In my view, to hold that the criminal prohibition in s. 241(b), without the appellant being in any way subject to the state administrative or justice system, falls within the bounds of s. 12 stretches the ordinary meaning of being 'subjected to . . . treatment' by the state. For these reasons, in my view, s. 241(b) does not violate s. 12" (at 612).

19. Sopinka wrote: "These issues would require the Court to make fundamental findings concerning the scope of s. 15. Since I am of the opinion that any infringement is clearly

saved under s. 1 of the *Charter*, I prefer not to decide these issues in this case. . . . I will assume that s. 15 is infringed and consider the application of s. 1" (at 612–13).

20. Section 1 provides: "The *Canadian Charter of Rights and Freedoms* guarantees the rights and freedoms set out in it subject only to such reasonable limits prescribed by law as can be demonstrably justified in a free and democratic society."

21. In his dissent, the Chief Justice noted: "I accept that s. 241(b) was never intended to create such an inequality, and that that provision, which contains no distinction based on personal characteristics, does at first sight treat all individuals in the same way. . . . saying this does not dispose of the argument that the provision creates inequality. Even if this was not the legislature's intent, and although s. 241(b) does not contain any provision specifically applicable to persons with disabilities, the fact remains that such persons, those who are or will become incapable of committing suicide unassisted, are on account of their disability affected by s. 241(b) of the *Criminal Code* differently from others . . . since by the *effect* of that provision persons unable to commit suicide without assistance are deprived of any ability to commit suicide in a way which is not unlawful, whereas s. 241(b) does not have that effect on those able to end their lives without assistance" (at 550–51). [Emphasis in original.]

22. The Chief Justice held that the appeal should be allowed with costs; that s. 241(b) should be declared of no force or effect; and that a year be allowed to pass before the declaration could be acted upon, to allow Parliament and the medical profession time to establish the suggested criteria for those seeking physician-assisted suicide. He held that during that year an application seeking a constitutional exemption to s. 241(b) would have to be made to a superior court in all cases requesting assisted suicide. Sue Rodriguez was exempted from this application requirement. In an addendum three weeks after his opinion, following the receipt of a letter from her doctor, the Chief Justice amended his order to reduce to twenty-four hours the three-day notice period proposed in his judgment.

23. The Chief Justice wrote: "While I share a deep concern over the subtle and overt pressures that may be brought to bear on such persons if assisted suicide is decriminalized, even in limited circumstances, I do not think legislation that deprives a disadvantaged group of the right to equality can be justified solely on such speculative grounds, no matter how well intentioned" (at 566). "The fear of a "slippery slope" cannot, in my view, justify the over inclusive reach of the *Criminal Code* to encompass not only people who may be vulnerable to the pressure of others but also persons with no evidence of vulnerability, and, in the case of the appellant, persons where there is positive evidence of freely determined consent."

24. The Chief Justice wrote: "I remain unpersuaded by the government's apparent contention that it is not possible to design legislation that is somewhere in between complete decriminalization and absolute prohibition. In my view, there is a range of options from which Parliament may choose in seeking to safeguard the interests of the vulnerable and still ensure the equal right of self-determination of persons with physical disabilities" (at 569).

25. In refusing to treat this case as one of equality, McLachlin wrote (at 616): "I have read the reasons of the Chief Justice. Persuasive as they are, I am of the view that this is not at base a case about discrimination under s. 15 of the *Canadian Charter of Rights and Freedoms*, and that to treat it as such may deflect the equality jurisprudence from the true focus of s. 15 — 'to remedy or prevent discrimination against groups subject to stereotyping, historical disadvantage and political and social prejudice in Canadian society.': *R.* v. *Swain*, [1991] 1 S.C.R. 933 at 992, per Lamer C.J."

26. *Rodriguez*, above note 3 at 616 (S.C.R.).

27. See *Re B.C. Motor Vehicle Act*, [1985] 2 S.C.R. 486.

28. In addressing this issue, she said: "Were the task before me that of taking the pulse of the nation, I too should quail, although as a matter of constitutional obligation, a court faced with a *Charter* breach may not enjoy the luxury of choosing what it will and will not decide. I do not, however, see this as the task which faces the Court in this case. We were not asked to second guess Parliament's objective of criminalizing the assistance of suicide. Our task was the much more modest one of determining whether, given the legislative scheme regulating suicide which Parliament has put in place, the denial to Sue Rodriguez of the ability to end her life is arbitrary and hence amounts to a limit on her security of the person which does not comport with the principles of fundamental justice. Parliament in fact has chosen to legislate on suicide. It has set up a scheme which makes suicide lawful, but which makes assisted suicide criminal. The only question is whether Parliament, having chosen to act in this sensitive area touching the autonomy of people over their bodies, has done so in a way which is fundamentally fair to all. The focus is not on why Parliament has acted, but on the way in which it has acted" (at 628–29).

29. McLachlin wrote: "These provisions may be supplemented, by way of a remedy on this appeal, by a further stipulation requiring court orders to permit the assistance of suicide in a particular case. The judge must be satisfied that the consent is freely given with a full appreciation of all the circumstances. This will ensure that only those who truly desire to bring their lives to an end obtain assistance. While this may be to ask more of Ms. Rodriguez than is asked of the physically able person who seeks to commit suicide, the additional precautions are arguably justified by the peculiar vulnerability of the person who is physically unable to take her own life" (at 627–28).

30. The *Sue Rodriguez* case and her death in 1994 fuelled a public debate that resulted in publication of the report, *Of Life and Death: The Report of the Special Senate Committee on Euthanasia and Assisted-Suicide* (Ottawa, June 1995), the following year. The committee's broad mandate was to "examine and report upon the legal, social and ethical issues relating to euthanasia and assisted-suicide." Copies are available through the Senate. The toll-free Senate telephone number is 1-800-267-7362.

31. *Ibid.* at 173.

32. The minority of the committee members who would allow an exemption would do so only under clearly defined safeguards. They wrote: "The members were asked to ponder many aspects of life and death, including life as a fundamental value in any society, autonomy as an individual value, and suffering as a reality generally associated with the end of life" (at 69). "The Committee members hold differing views as to how society can deal with the suffering of these individuals. While they recognize the different ethical arguments and points of view, all of them have deep concerns about the implications of permitting assisted suicide. They also recognize that the values of individual autonomy and the interests of society can at times be in conflict, and that, in some circumstances, individual autonomy must be restricted in the interests of society. Some members feel that aid should be provided to the dying in ways other than assisted suicide because they believe that the societal interest in upholding the respect for life must prevail. Other members think that intolerable suffering justifies providing assistance in committing suicide. The Committee agreed, however, about the need for tolerance and respect for opposing points of view" (at 70).

33. See, for instance, the following private members' bills. Bill C-351, *An Act to amend the Criminal Code (terminally ill persons)*, 2d Sess., 34th Parl., 1991, was introduced on 27 March 1991, and was read for the first time but died on the Order Paper when that parliamentary session ended. Bill C-203, *An Act to amend the Criminal Code (terminally ill persons)*, 3d Sess., 34th Parl., 1991, was introduced on 16 May 1991, and suffered a

similar fate. Bill C-261, *An Act to legalize the administration of euthanasia under certain conditions*, 3d Sess., 34th Parl., 1991, was introduced on 19 June 1991, read for the first time, and later dropped from the Order Paper. Bill C-385, *An Act to amend the Criminal Code (aiding suicide)*, 3d Sess., 34th Parl., 1992, was introduced on 9 December 1992, read for the first time, and died on the Order Paper with the call of the election in 1993. Bill C-215, *An Act to amend the Criminal Code (aiding suicide)*, 1st Sess., 35th Parl., 1994, was introduced on 16 February 1994, read for the first time, and not passed.

34. McEachern in the B.C. Court of Appeal, above note 10 at 168–70 (B.C.L.R.).

35. For a copy of *A Model State Act to Authorize and Regulate Physician-Assisted Suicide*, see <http://www.finalexit.org/mdlact.shtml>.

36. In 1906 Ohio considered one of the first bills on euthanasia in any English-speaking country; it concerned the administration of drugs to mortally injured and diseased persons. In 1937 a similar bill was introduced in Nebraska. In 1938 the Euthanasia Society of America was founded, but, after the Second World War, legislative attempts at amendment waned, as did public interest in the subject. In the 1960s, thanks to modern medical technology, euthanasia reappeared as a public issue. In 1970 Florida introduced the first proposals dealing with the "right to death with dignity" to amend its constitution; they passed the House, but were defeated in the Senate. Between 1969 and 1976 some thirty-five bills were introduced on euthanasia and assisted suicide in twenty-two states. Generally, they permitted passive, but not active, euthanasia and required a patient's consent or request. Throughout, the common thread was the requirement to request the "painless administration of death"; the requirement for an advance directive (as in the Karen Quinlan case) showing clearly what the permanently comatose patient's wishes would have been as she had expressed them in life; and the clarification of rights dealing with accepting and refusing treatment. The charge of homicide or murder remained, and motive (such as compassion for a disabled child or responding to the plea of a dying person in pain) was not recognized as a defence. The states had the right to legislate, under their right to legislate privacy. The U.S. Supreme Court held in *Griswold* v. *Connecticut* in 1965 that the individual states had the right to limit privacy rights where their specific interests were compelling, but required such limiting to be narrowly drawn. This case added further to the debate about euthanasia and assisted suicide, reconfirming that such personal privacy rights are "fundamental and implicit in the concept of ordered liberty." In 1976 the *California Natural Death Act* was introduced and passed the following year, recognizing the right of a competent person to decline life-prolonging treatment and providing for living wills: see Cal. Health and Safety Code preceding § 7185 (Deering, LEXIS through 1999). In 1973 the American Medical Association declared that euthanasia was against its policies; the decision to end treatment and other extraordinary means to prolong life, where there was irrefutable evidence that death was imminent, was left to the family, with the doctor merely providing medical counsel.

37. Oregon's *Death with Dignity Act*, O.R.S. § 127.800 (LEXIS through 1997 Supp.), can be found at <http://www.islandnet.com/deathnet/ergo_orlaw.html>.

38. *Ibid.*, s. 2.01.

39. *Ibid.*

40. Section 3.13 reads: "The sale, procurement, or issuance of any life, health, or accident insurance or annuity policy or the rate charged for any policy shall not be conditioned upon or affected by the making or rescinding of a request, by a person, for medication to end his or her life in a humane and dignified manner. Neither shall a qualified patient's act of ingesting medication to end his or her life in a humane and dignified manner have an effect upon a life, health, or accident insurance or annuity policy."

41. Section 3.12 reads: "(1) No provision in a contract, will or other agreement, whether written or oral, to the extent the provision would affect whether a person may make or rescind a request for medication to end his or her life in a humane and dignified manner, shall be valid. (2) No obligation owing under any currently existing contract shall be conditioned or affected by the making or rescinding of a request, by a person, for medication to end his or her life in a humane and dignified manner."

42. Section 3.14.

43. The first legislative attempt in Oregon was in 1991, when a bill sponsored by Senator Frank Roberts (D-Portland) was introduced to allow physician-assisted suicide for the terminally ill. It was rejected, but its defeat gave rise to a political action committee in 1993 called the Oregon Right to Die, which was dedicated exclusively to introducing and having passed a citizens' ballot initiative. On 4 November 1994, 57 percent of the eligible voters in Oregon voted 51–49 percent in favour of physician-assisted suicide, but, owing to court challenges, the *Death with Dignity Act* was not implemented until 27 October 1997. In the meantime, the legislature refused either to amend or to repeal the Act, choosing instead to return it to the electorate for a second vote. On 4 November 1997, 60 percent of the eligible voters turned out to vote on the question of whether they wanted the Act to be repealed. In a 60–40 split they voted to keep the law. On 18 August 1998, Oregon's Health Division released its first report on the new law. Ten Oregonians (an equal number of women and men, nine suffering from cancer and one from heart disease, and whose average age was seventy-one) had used their prescriptions. Nine doctors were involved. On 18 February 1999, the Health Division released its second report on the Act and found that there had been no reported abuses or problems, and that all physicians were in full compliance with the Act. Regardless, several new bills have been proposed whose effect would be to deny state funds for the assistance of suicides under the Act (HB 2374), to require the Oregon Health Division to share all its data under the Act with the Attorney General (HB 5547), and to require mandatory psychiatric evaluation and limiting access to the law in other ways (SB 491). See *Chronology of Events* at <http://www.dwd.orf/chron.htm>.

44. Assistance to die, performed in accordance with the wishes of a competent person who has expressed these views directly or in a legally valid advance directive.

45. In her judgment, McLachlin made it clear that this case was similar in intent to *R.* v. *Morgentaler*, [1988] 1 S.C.R. 30. She wrote (at 617): "In the present case, Parliament has put into force a legislative scheme which does not bar suicide but criminalizes the act of assisting suicide. The effect of this is to deny some people the choice of ending their lives solely because they are physically unable to do so. This deprives Sue Rodriguez of her security of the person (the right to make decisions concerning her own body, which affect only her own body) in a way that offends the principles of fundamental justice, thereby violating s. 7 of the *Charter*. The violation cannot be saved under s. 1. This is precisely the logic which led the majority of this Court to strike down the abortion provisions of the *Criminal Code* in *Morgentaler*."

46. In the one case where this issue was argued, the court held that suicide was not a constitutional right. The court found that s. 7 protected a right to life, not death. See *Burke* v. *Prince Edward Island* (1991), 93 Nfld. & P.E.I.R. 356 (P.E.I.S.C.).

Chapter 11: Euthanasia

1. *R.* v. *Latimer* (1997), 121 C.C.C. (3d) 326, 12 C.R. (5th) 112 (Sask. Q.B.) [hereinafter *Latimer* cited to C.C.C.].

2. *R.* v. *Morrison* (1998), 174 N.S.R. (2d) 201 (S.C.).

3.   All definitions in this chapter are those used in the document: *Of Life and Death: The Report of the Special Senate Committee on Euthanasia and Assisted-Suicide* (Ottawa: June 1995) at 13–15.

4.   For a historical description of cases and legislative attempts to deal with euthanasia and assisted suicide in Canada, see *ibid.*, the section entitled "Major Chronology of Canadian Developments and Events" at A-27 to A-34.

5.   Several sections of the *Criminal Code*, R.S.C. 1985, c. C-46 [hereinafter *Code*], touch on euthanasia. Section 14 provides that no one can consent to have death inflicted upon him or her, and makes the person carrying out the killing criminally responsible. Section 241 makes counselling, aiding, and abetting suicide a criminal offence. Section 245 makes administering or directing the administration of a noxious substance a criminal offence, with a maximum prison term of fourteen years for endangering that person's life or two years if the intent was merely to "aggrieve or annoy." Sections 265–69 cover acts of assault, including aggravated assault and unlawfully causing bodily harm. Section 222 deals with homicide. Section 742 deals with sentencing and parole.

6.   *Ibid.*, s. 205.

7.   See the Senate Report, above note 3, at note 7, appendix F, for a listing of the relevant provisions of both the *Criminal Code* and the *Quebec Civil Code* at A-35 to A-42.

8.   Above note 5.

9.   The minimum punishment for murder is life imprisonment. For first degree-murder, this means life imprisonment with no chance of parole (generally) for twenty-five years. For second-degree murder, the term is reduced to ten years. As was seen in the *Latimer* case, above note 1, this inflexibility leads to extraordinary action, including the granting of a constitutional exemption to the mandatory provision on "compassionate" grounds. See s. 742 of the *Code*.

10. *R.* v. *Latimer*, [1999] S.C.C.A. No. 40 (QL), and see above note 1. Tracy Latimer suffered from cerebral palsy caused by brain damage at birth and was a quadriplegic, unable to feed herself, move, or speak. She had to undergo surgery on several occasions for chronic and current problems caused by her condition.

11. Mr. Justice Ted Noble of the Saskatchewan Court of Queen's Bench responded to the jury's request that Latimer be imprisoned for only one year by granting him a constitutional exemption from the mandatory sentence. He termed Latimer's actions as "a rare act of homicide that was committed for caring and altruistic reasons" (at 343) and agreed with his lawyer that to adhere to the mandatory minimum sentence would amount to a violation of his constitutional right to be free from cruel and unusual punishment.

12. Alanna Mitchell, "Supreme Court to hear Latimer appeal," *Globe and Mail*, 7 May 1999, A6.

13. All these cases are tragic and desperate. See, for instance, *R.* v. *Brush*, [1995], O.J. No. 656 (Prov. Div.), and the Nova Scotia case (1993) of *R.* v. *Myers*, [1994] N.S.J. No. 688 (S.C.) (QL).

14. The Canadian and American Medical Associations (the CMA and the AMA), and their provincial and state counterparts, debate euthanasia regularly and seek legislative guidance to protect their members from criminal charges. In 1993 the CMA published a series of five papers dealing with the dying process, with the stated goal of providing the physicians' perspective to help educate doctors about the legal, social, and ethical aspects of euthanasia and assisted suicide. See Frederick H. Lowy, Douglas Sawyer, and John R. Williams, *Canadian Physicians and Euthanasia* (Ottawa: Canadian Medical Association, 1993).

15. For a discussion of these issues of palliative care and medical training, see the Senate Report, above note 3, chapters 3 and 4.

16. For a complete story on this case, see Nancy Robb, "Death in a Halifax Hospital: A Murder Case Highlights a Profession's Divisions," *Canadian Medical Association Journal* 157 (1997): 757–62.

17. "Physician-Assisted Death," *Canadian Medical Association Journal* 152 (1995): 248A–248B at <http://www.cma.ca/inside/policybase/1995/1%2D15.htm>.

18. *Ibid.*

19. Section 226.

20. According to the Senate Report, above note 3, "total sedation" (also referred to as artificial sleep) is the "practice of rendering a person totally unconscious through the administration of drugs without potentially shortening that person's life." It is a practice used both for temporary treatment of patients in acute circumstances and for terminal patients for whom regular pain regimes have failed. No formal and consistent guidelines to regulate this practice exist.

21. As part of its report, *ibid.*, the Senate Committee recommended that "the *Criminal Code* be amended to clarify the practice of providing treatment for the purpose of alleviating suffering that may shorten life [and recommended] education and training with respect to pain control be expanded and improved for all health care professionals" (at 32).

22. In Quebec, health care professionals could be held civilly liable in such situations pursuant to Articles 1457–1481 of the *Quebec Civil Code.*

23. Above note 3 at 31.

24. Bill S-13, *An Act to Amend the Criminal Code (protection of Health Care Providers)*, 2d Sess., 35th Parl., 1996, Sen. Sharon Carstairs, seconded by Dr. Wilbert Keon, received first reading on 27 November 1996.

25. The Preamble makes it clear that the Bill sought to address two major issues. First, the uncertainty both within the medical profession and among the larger public about the legal consequences of withholding and withdrawing life-sustaining treatment and certain drug treatments for pain prevention or control which shorten life; second, how to protect health care providers as they carried out their professional duties.

26. *Ibid.*, sections 3, 4, and 7.

27. For further information, see the submission of the Canadian Bar Association to the Senate Committee on Euthanasia and Assisted-Suicide, submitted in March 1995 and referred to in the final report at 26.

28. "The administration of drugs designed for pain control in dosages which the physician knows will hasten death constitutes active contribution to death by any standard. However, the distinction drawn here is one based upon intention — in the case of palliative care the intention is to ease pain, which has the effect of hastening death; while in the case of assisted suicide, the intention is undeniably to cause death. . . . In my view, distinctions based upon intent are important, and in fact form the basis of our criminal law. While factually the distinction may, at times, be difficult to draw, legally it is clear." *R.* v. *Rodriguez*, [1993] 3 S.C.R. 519 at 607.

29. See the Senate Report, above note 3 at 26.

30. For more information on euthanasia in the Netherlands, see <http://www.netlink.co.uk/users/vess/dutch.html>. In Germany, Italy, Switzerland, Denmark, Norway, and Poland, euthanasia is called "homicide on request," not murder. Motivation is a mitigating factor. For more details, see Lynn Tracy Nerland, "A Cry for Help: A Comparison of Voluntary, Active Euthanasia Law," *Hastings International and Comparative Law Review* 13 (1989) at 115. For a review of the cases concerning euthanasia and assisted suicide that have been judicially considered by the U.S. Supreme Court, see Karen Capen's article on the subject in *Canadian Medical Association Journal* 157 (1997): 169–71. See also a review of the 1997 U.S. Supreme Court decisions in *Washington* v. *Glucksberg*, 521 U.S. 702, 117 S. Ct. 2258; and *Vacco* v. *Quill et al.*, 521 U.S. 793, 117 S. Ct. 2293. In both these cases from Washington and from Florida, decided on 26 June 1997, in two unanimous judgments, the Supreme Court ruled that terminally ill Americans have no constitutional

right to assisted suicide, and upheld both existing bans in these two states and the right of the states to legislate in this area. As a result, the debate will continue, for no change was imposed to existing practices of providing pain relief medication in doses that both control pain and could result in the patient's death. This decision follows almost seven years after the same Court recognized a constitutional right to die in *Cruzan* v. *Director, Missouri Dept. Of Health,* 497 U.S. 261 (1990), when it ruled that terminally ill people could refuse life-sustaining medical treatment. The Chief Justice, (Rehnquist) who wrote that decision for the Court added that there was a clear difference between doctors respecting a patient's right to refuse treatment for a terminal disease and their actually helping in the death. See James V. Lavery and Peter Singer, "The 'Supremes' Decide on Assisted Suicide: What Should a Doctor Do?" *Canadian Medical Association Journal* 157 (1997): 405–6; David J. Garrow, "Letting the public decide about assisted suicide," *New York Times,* 29 June 1997, 4; Associated Press, "U.S. Supreme Court rules against assisted suicide," *Globe and Mail,* 27 June 1997, A7; Sheryl Gay Stolberg, "The good death: Embracing a right to die well," *New York Times,* 29 June 1997, section 4, 1. See also a full coverage of the issue in *The Economist,* 21 June 1997, 15 and 21–24.

31. At the time of publication, euthanasia is illegal everywhere. Australia's Northern Territory was the only place in the world that passed a right-to-die law. Before it was overturned in March 1997, four cancer patients were helped by a doctor to end their lives legally. Physician-assisted suicide is now legal in Oregon, and Colombia passed a law making it legal in 1997. The Dutch Parliament has introduced a Bill to legally recognize the practice codes and rules on assisted suicide and euthanasia now followed in that country.

32. In 1995 there were 3,200 registered cases of euthanasia in the Netherlands, compared with 2,300 cases in 1993. In 1990 Dutch doctors received 8,900 requests for help in dying, with some 1.7 percent of all deaths from active voluntary euthanasia. In 1995 that number rose to 9,700. In both years, 0.2 percent of the deaths were from physician-assisted suicides; about 19 percent of all deaths were from administering pain killers in large dosages; and 20 percent were from decisions to forgo treatment – up 2 percent from 1990. Only 5 percent of requests for euthanasia and assisted-suicide were from people describing themselves as being in unbearable pain; the largest number of those seeking help were cancer victims between fifty-five and seventy-five years of age. In 1995, 0.7 percent of deaths were active euthanasia without the patient's consent. See *New England Journal of Medicine* , November 1996, for a report of interviews with 500 Dutch doctors and questionnaires mailed to another 6,000 doctors. Euthanasia and assisted suicide may have different legal consequences in the Netherlands, but physicians must comply with the same procedural and substantive requirement for both. See Leonard Stern, "Holland's mercy killers," [Ottawa] *Citizen,* 23 November 1997, A1.

33. In the Netherlands, euthanasia and assisted suicide are both criminal acts under the *Penal Code,* but are not prosecuted provided that certain conditions are met and safeguards ensured to protect the vulnerable. Their extensive reporting scheme is meant to ensure a full review of each euthanasia death that is registered. Where there are irregularities or the rules are not followed, both a formal prosecution and a review by the Dutch medical system can ensue. Doctors must first fill in the required questionnaire and forward it to the local coroner, who then provides a copy to the local prosecutor. It is then reviewed by the five courts of appeal, and the decision *not* to charge is left to the justice minister. Dutch doctors practise both voluntary and involuntary euthanasia, which are covered by the guidelines that set out the legal conditions and safeguards that must be followed whenever there is an *unnatural death.* The only concern is the failure of donors to report such cases. Legislative changes to make euthanasia legal have just been introduced.

34. There are some 300 nursing homes in Holland supported by doctors specially trained in the nursing home specialty, which requires three years after receipt of the basic medical qualification. Two to three doctors serve between 100 and 300 beds, with 50 to 150 nurses and additional nursing assistants. In these circumstances, it would be "almost impossible for nursing home doctors to terminate the lives of patients who did not request it." Senate Report, above note 3 at A-120.

35. Article 293 of the Dutch *Criminal Code* states: "Anyone who takes the life of another person at the other's express and serious request will be punished with a prison sentence of a maximum of twelve years, or a category five fine." Article 294 makes assistance in committing suicide a criminal offence. "Anyone who deliberately incites another to commit suicide, assists him in so doing or provides the means for him to do so will, if suicide follows, be punished with a prison sentence of a maximum of three years, or a category four fine."

36. The Department of Public Prosecutions is made up of the advocate general, who is an independent counsel appointed by the government for life, the advocates general and solicitors general at the courts of appeal, and the public prosecutors and traffic magistrates attached to all the district and cantonal courts, for a total of about 250 people. The advocate general is a most senior and respected person, consulted by the Dutch Supreme Court in all the cases brought before it, who has the power to initiate an appeal "in the interests of the law" on his or her own initiative.

37. The Senate Report, above note 3 at A-124, pointed out that the division of powers under the Canadian Constitution means that, with a few specific exceptions, criminal prosecutions are initiated by provincial Crown prosecutors, and that this process would complicate the creation of a national system similar to the Dutch one.

38. Article 40.

39. See Barney Sneiderman, "Euthanasia in the Netherlands: A Model for Canada," *Humane Medicine* 8 (April 1992): 104–15. Medical disciplinary bodies act as courts of law in the Netherlands. A physician performing an act of euthanasia can be open to investigation and prosecution under both the Dutch *Penal Code* and the medical disciplinary court.

40. See the testimony of Dr. Gerrit van der Wal, Senate Report, above note 3 at A-116.

41. One witness summed up the acceptance of cases of psychological or mental suffering as follows: "In Holland, we finally agreed that suffering is always mental, even if it has a somatic [physical] source. Suffering is a mental process. . . . The Supreme Court found itself caught in the principle of equality. . . . It was clear that suffering can be as exhaustive and unbearable when it has psychiatric roots as when it is caused by terminal cancer. There was no reason to exclude those categories of sufferers requesting death. . . . Our Supreme Court agreed that there should be no distinction made between suffering from a psychiatric disease or a somatological condition." Mr. Eugene Sutorius, a witness and defence counsel specializing in the Dutch law on euthanasia, a deputy judge in the Court of Appeal in Amsterdam, and a member of the Ethics Committee of the Royal Dutch Medical Association. *Ibid.* at A-130.

42. The "mercy killing" cases vary. In *Latimer,* above notes 1 and 10, a man admitted killing his severely mentally and physically handicapped young daughter, arguing that he was a loving father who did not want to see her suffer. He was found guilty by a jury of second-degree murder, with no chance of parole for ten years. In an unusual turn of events, the judge agreed with his argument that this was cruel and unusual punishment and granted his request for a constitutional exemption to the mandatory provision. This was the first time in Saskatchewan that the mandatory minimum had been successfully challenged in a murder conviction. The judge held that the murder was a "compassionate homicide" (at 345) and sentenced Latimer to one year in prison and one year of house

arrest to be served on his farm. The case is on appeal to the Supreme Court of Canada. In *R. c. Blais,* [1997] A.Q. No. 2157 (QL) a severely depressed woman drowned her six-year-old autistic son in the bathtub. The trial judge found her to be sick and guilty of manslaughter, and imposed no minimum sentence. He refused the Crown's call for a three-year prison term in favour of a twenty-three-month suspended sentence. In *R.v. Doerksen,* (1998) [not yet reported], a seventy-eight-year-old man had not intervened while his wife had killed herself through carbon monoxide poisoning in her car in the family's garage. The garage door and car window were sealed with duct tape. She suffered from chronic illness, none of which was terminal. He defended his actions by relying on a copy of her advance directive in which she asked not to be resuscitated. He was charged with aiding a suicide, the first such charge in Manitoba.

Further Readings
and Resources

The Web site and e-mail addresses in this book were current at the time of publication.

Chapter 1: Reproductive Technologies: Challenges for Regulation

Basen, Gwynne, Margrit Eichler, & Abby Lippman, eds., *Misconceptions: The Social Construction of Choice and the New Reproductive and Genetic Technologies* (Hull, QC: Voyageur Publishing, 1993)

Canadian Research Institute for the Advancement of Women, *Reproductive Technologies and Women: A Research Tool* (Ottawa: CRIAW/ICREF, 1989)

Ontario Law Reform Commission, *Report on Human Artificial Reproduction and Related Matters* (Toronto: Ministry of the Attorney General, 1995), vols. 1 and 2

Law Reform Commission of Canada, *Crimes against the Fetus*, Working Paper 58 (Ottawa: The Commission, 1989)

Law Reform Commission of Canada, *Medically Assisted Procreation*, Working Paper 65 (Ottawa: The Commission, 1990)

Stotland, Nada L., *Psychiatric Aspects of Reproductive Technology* (Washington, DC: American Psychiatric Press, 1990)

Chapter 2: Issues of Legitimacy and Inheritance

Glover, Jonathan, et al., *Ethics of New Reproductive Technologies: The Glover Report to the European Commission* (DeKalb: Northern Illinois University Press, 1989)

Kennedy, Ian, *Treat Me Right: Essays in Medical Law and Ethics* (Oxford; New York: Clarendon Press, 1991)

Knoppers, Bartha Maria, ed., *Socio-Ethical Issues in Human Genetics* (Cowansville: Les Editions Yvon Blais, 1998)

Law Reform Commission of Canada, *Human Dignity and Genetic Heritage,* Study Paper (Ottawa: The Commission, 1991)

Law Reform Commission of Canada, *Sanctity of Life or Quality of Life in the Context of Ethics, Medicine and Law,* Study Paper by Edward W. Keyserlingk (Ottawa: Supply and Services Canada, 1981)

Law Reform Commission of Canada, *Towards a Canadian Advisory Council on Biomedical Ethics,* Study Paper (Ottawa: The Commission, 1990)

Resources

For further information contact the International Council on Infertility Information Dissemination, Inc. (INCIID), P.O. Box 6836, Arlington, Virginia, 22206, U.S.A. Phone (703) 379-9178; fax (703) 379-1593; e-mail <INCIIDinfo@inciid.org>.

For information and updates on the latest infertility and pregnancy loss research and treatment programs, see their Web site at <http://www.inciid.org>. There is no fee, and the Web site includes more than 150 referrals and links to non-profit organizations that provide other medical information on infertility — for example, the American Society of Reproductive Medicine and the International Federation of Fertility Societies.

The Human Fertilisation and Embryology Authority (HFEA) is the licensing and accreditation authority for infertility centres in the United Kingdom. It publishes an annual report and has gathered extensive policy and research information over the past decade. It can be reached at Paxton House, 30 Artillery Lane, London, E1 7LS, England. Phone 011.44.171.377-5077; fax 011.44.171.377-1871; Web site <http://www.hfea.gov.uk>.

For a Canadian directory of mini sites for physicians, therapists, and lawyers, see <http://www.inciid.org/canada.html>.

The International Federation of Fertility Societies, which helps standardize terminology and evaluate diagnostic and therapeutic procedures for medically assisted reproduction, can be accessed either through the INCIID site (above) or at <http://www.mnet.fr/iffs/a_artbis.htm>.

For a glossary of infertility terms and acronyms, see:

<http://www.inciid.org/glossary.html> and
<http://www.hfea.gov.uk/glossary/index.htm>.

Chapter 4: Embryos: The New Frontier of Human Research

Abraham, Carolyn, "Cloned animals may age prematurely," *Globe and Mail,* 27 May 1999

"British scientists create headless frog," [Ottawa] *Citizen,* 19 October 1997, A12

Caplan, Arthur L., "Why the rush to ban cloning?" *New York Times,* 28 January 1998, A27

Cohen, Susan, "What is a baby: Inside America's unresolved debate about the ethics of cloning," *The Washington Post Magazine,* 12 October 1997,12

Kass, Leon, "The Wisdom of Repugnance," *The New Republic,* 2 June 1997, 17–26

Kass, Leon R., & James Q. Wilson, *The Ethics of Human Cloning* (Washington, DC: AEI Press, 1998)

Kimbrell, Andrew, *The Human Body Shop: The Engineering and Marketing of Life* (San Francisco: HarperCollins, 1993)

Kolata, Gina, *Clone: The Road to Dolly and the Path Ahead* (New York: William Morrow, 1998)

Maranto, Gina, *Quest for Perfection: The Drive to Breed Better Human Beings* (New York: Scribner, 1996)

Nussbaum, Martha C., & Cass R. Sunstein, *Clones and Clones* (New York: W.W. Norton & Company, 1998)

Silver, Lee M., *Remaking Eden: Cloning and Beyond in a Brave New World* (New York: Avon Books, 1997)

Tudge, Colin, "Cloning: Get used to it," *Sunday Independent,* 25 January 1998, section 2

Verkey, A.D., "Cloning: Revisiting an Old Debate" *Kennedy Institute of Ethics Journal* 4, no. 3 (1994): 227–34

Wilson, Edward O., *The Diversity of Life* (New York: W.W. Norton & Company, 1992)

Wilmut, Ian, et al., [article on premature aging in cloned sheep] *Nature,* 27 May 1999

Resources

Standing Committee on Health (federal), House of Commons, Wellington Street, Ottawa, Canada, K1A 0A6. Phone (613) 947-6729; fax (613) 992-9069; <http://www.parl.gc.ca>

National Bioethics Advisory Commission report on human cloning <http://www.bioethics.gov/pubs.htm>.

"Cloning: In Our Own Image," Special report from the *L.A. Times* with links to bioethics sites <http://www.latimes.com/HOME/NEWS/SCIENCE/ REPORTS/CLONING>

Chapter 5: Knowing Ourselves, Protecting Our Rights

Bodner, Walter, and Robin McKie, *The Book of Man: The Human Genome Project and the Quest to Discover Our Genetic Heritage* (New York: Scribner, 1994)

British Medical Association, *Our Genetic Future: The Science and Ethics of Genetic Technology* (New York: Oxford University Press, 1992)

Coughlan, Michael J., *The Vatican, the Law and the Human Embryo* (Iowa City: University of Iowa Press, 1990)

Gustafson, James M., and W. French Anderson, *Genetic Engineering and Humanness: A Revolutionary Prospect* (Washington, DC: Washington National Cathedral, 1992)

Harper, Peter, "The Human Genome Project and Medical Genetics," *Journal of Medical Genetics* 29 (1992): 1

Hubbard, Ruth, and Elijah Wald, *Exploding the Gene Myth* (Boston: Beacon Press, 1993)

Jacob, Francois, *The Logic of Life: A History of Heredity* (Princeton, NJ: Princeton University Press, 1973) (translation)

Jordan, Elk, "The Human Genome Project: Where Did It Come From, Where Is It Going?" *American Journal of Human Genetics* 51 (1992): 1

Kaye, Howard L., "Are We the Sum of Our Genes?" *Wilson Quarterly* (spring 1992): 77

Kevles, Daniel J., *In the Name of Eugenics: Genetics and the Uses of Heredity* (New York: Alfred A. Knopf, 1985)

Lawson, Ian B., *Privacy and Free Enterprise*, 2d edition revised by Bill Jeffery (Ottawa: Public Interest Advocacy Centre, 1997). This book has an excellent bibliography for any reader wanting to do further research in the field of privacy in the private sector.

Lenoir, Noelle, and Bertrand Mathieu, *Le droit international de la bioéthique: textes* (Paris: Presses universitaires de France, 1998)

Lewontin, Richard, Steven Rose, and Leon J. Kamin, *Not in Our Genes: Biology, Ideology, and Human Nature* (New York: Pantheon Books, 1984)

Low, L., et al., "Genetic Discrimination in Life Insurance: Empirical Evidence from a Cross Sectional Survey of Genetic Support Groups in the U.K." *British Medical Journal* (1998) and a Response by J. Alexander Lowden, Lab One Canada, *British Medical Journal* (28 December 1998). Both are available at <http://www.cdc.gov/genetics/Ethical.htm>.

Privacy Commissioner, *Genetic Testing and Privacy* (Ottawa: Minister of Supply and Services Canada, 1992)

Rifkin, Jeremy, *The Biotech Century: Harnessing the Gene and Remaking the World* (New York: Putnam, 1998)

Suzuki, David, and Peter Knudtson, *Genethics: The Ethics of Engineering Life* (Toronto: Stoddart, 1988)

Wingerson, Lois, *Mapping Our Genes: The Genome Project and the Future of Medicine* (New York: Dutton, 1990)

Wingerson, Lois, *Unnatural Selection: The Promise and the Power of Human Gene Research* (New York: Bantam Books, 1998)

Resources

Science teachers can find a wealth of information on the Human Genome Project (HGP) to interest and inform their students. Two publications I found useful are *Your Genes, Your Choices: Exploring the Issues Raised by Genetic Research* by Catherine Baker (Washington, DC: American Association for the Advancement of Science, 1987), which describes in plain language the science behind the HGP, and many of the social, legal, and ethical dilemmas it raises. It was a project of the American Association for the Advancement of Science and funded by the U.S. Department of Energy. The second publication specifically written for students is *Your World/Our World: Biotechnology and You,* which highlights biotechnology applications in health care, agriculture, the environment, and industry. Each issue presents recent scientific advances in biotechnology and their impact on society. For more information on this industry-government sponsored publication for young people, see: <http://www.bio.com/pha>.

For information on the HGP, teachers can visit the following education Web sites, which were current at the time of publication:

- <http://www.ornl.gov/hgmis/resource/education.html>
- <http://whyfiles.news.wisc.edu> (for illustrated explanations of the science behind the news)
- <http://phoenix.mcet.edu/humangenome/index.html> (for a presentation for high school students of the ethical, legal, and social issues of HGP)

- <http://outcast.gene.com/ae/index.html> (for the Access Excellence site, and an extensive list of genetic and biotechnology resources for teachers, students, and non-scientists)

- <http://www.netspace.org/MendelWeb> (explores the origins of classical genetics, introductory data analysis, elementary plant science, and the history of science)

- <http:www-shgc.stanford.edu/bio-ed> (includes genome curricula from the Stanford University Human Genome Center and numerous resources, especially for elementary and high school teachers)

- <http://www.carosci.com/Tips.htm> (lists teaching materials for all levels and mini-lessons on selected scientific topics, on-line magazines, software, catalogues, and publications)

- <http://raven.umnh.utah.edu> (natural history of genes; provides genetic science activities and hands-on experiments for teachers and students)

- <http://www-sci.lib.uci.edu> (science and mathematics resources: more than 200 Web references, including Frank Potter's Science Gems and Martindale's Health Science Guide for teachers at all levels)

- <http://www.cellsalive.com> (for static and moving images of different types of cells)

- <http://www.ornl.gov/hgmis/publicat/glossary.html> (a glossary of terms related to genetics)

- <http://lenti.med.umn.edu/~mwd/courses.html> (for virtual courses on the Web and links to Web tutorials in biology, genetics, and other areas)

- <http://www.dml.georgetown.edu/hugen/project.htm>

- <http://policyresearch.schoolnet.ca/main-e.htm>

- Internet magazine HMS Beagle at <http://www.hmsbeagle.com>

- <http://www.embryo.mc.duke.edu> (allows for the viewing of MRM images)

If you want to be put on the American Department of Energy mailing list, free of charge, contact <http://www.er.doe.gov/production/oher/hug_top.html>.

The material on the U.S. government Web site is not copyrighted and can be used freely without permission or request to do so.

For families suffering from a genetic condition or facing a disease that runs in families, several sources are available online:

- Online Mendelian Inheritance in Man (OMIM) provides a comprehensive and current catalogue on human gene and genetic disorders. See <http://www.ncbi.nlm.nih.gov/Omim>.

- For a directory of voluntary support organizations and related resources, see <http://medhlp.netusa.net/agsg/agsgup/htm>.

Chapter 6: Biotechnology: Looking to the Future

Designer Genes at the Table. Report of the Canadian Citizens' Conference on Food Biotechnology, 5–7 March 1999. Available at <http://www.ucalgary.ca/~pubconf/>.

Genetic Engineering: Unresolved Issues — A Biotechnology Reader. Collection of articles on current topics in genetic technologies reproduced from *GeneWatch.*

Goudey, John, and Deepika Nath, *Canadian Biotechnology: Coming of Age,* 4th Report (Canada: Ernst & Young, 1997)

Krimsky, Sheldon, and Roger Wrubel, *Agricultural Biotechnology and the Environment: Science, Policy and Social Issues* (Urbana: University of Illinois Press, 1996.)

Lappe, Marc, and Britt Bailey, *Against the Grain: Biotechnology and the Corporate Takeover of Your Food* (Common Courage Press, 1998)

National Biotechnology Advisory Committee, 6th Report (Ottawa: Industry Canada, 1998). Available at <http://www.strategis.ic.gc.ca/bio>.

Federal Departments: Biotechnology Regulation

Agriculture
Canadian Food Inspection Agency (Agriculture and Agri-Food), Biotechnologies Strategies (Office). Phone (613) 225-2342; Web site: <http://www.cfia-acia.agr.ca>

Environment
Canadian Environmental Protection Act. Available at <cepa@ec.gc.ca>
The Biosafety Protocol. Available at (819) 953-0142 and <BCO@ec.gc.ca>

Fisheries and Oceans
Aquaculture. Available at (613) 990-0219 or 990-0275 and <http://www.ncr.dfo.ca>

Foreign Affairs and International Trade
Phone (613) 995-9259
Human Genome Declaration. Available at <http://www.dfait-maeci.gc.ca>

Health
Phone (613) 952-7322
Office of Food Biotechnology. Available at <http://www.hc-sc.gc.ca/datahpb/datafood>

Industry

Phone (819) 952-2527

Intellectual Property Policy Directorate. Phone 1-800-328-6189

Office of Consumer Affairs. Available at <http://strategis.ic.gc.ca>

Resources

Agriculture and Agri-Food Canada
<http://www.agr.gc.ca>

Ag-West Biotech
Phone: (306) 975–1939
<http://www.agwest.sk.ca>

Campaign for Food Safety
<http://www.purefood.org/>

The Canadian Food Inspection Agency's Office of Biotechnology
Phone: (613) 225–2342; 1-800-442-2342; or <http://www.cfia-acia.agr.ca>

The Codex Committee on Food Labelling <http://www.fao.org/waicent/
faoinfo/economic/esn/codex/Default.htm>

Council for Responsible Genetics
<http://essential.org/crg>

The European Campaign to Ban Genetically Engineered Foods
<http://www.netlink.de/gen/home.html>

Food Biotechnology Communications Network
<http://www.foodbiotech.org>

Greenpeace Biodiversity Campaign
<http://www.greenpeace.org/cbio.html>

Institute for Agriculture and Trade Policy
<http://www.iatp.org/iatp/>

Rural Advancement Foundation International (Canada)
<http://www.rafi.ca/>

Rural Advancement Foundation International (U.S.A.)
<http://www.rafiusa.org/>

Third World Network
<http://www.twnside.org.sg/souths/twn/bio.htm>

Union of Concerned Scientists (U.S.A.)
<http://www.uscusa.org>

Chapter 7: The Commercialization of Life

Canadian Intellectual Property Office, *Manual of Patent Office Practice* (Hull: CIPO, 1 October 1996), available at <http://info.ic.gc.ca/ic-data/marketplace/cipo/prod_ser/download/mopop/mopop-e.html>

Canadian Intellectual Property Office, *Patent Application and Information.* Available at <http://www.cipo.gc.ca/patents> and <http://www.strategis.ic.gc.ca/patents>

Crucible Group, *People, Plants and Patents: The Impact of Intellectual Property on Biodiversity, Conservation, Trade, and Rural Society* (Ottawa: International Development Research Centre, 1994)

Reid, W.V.C., *Biodiversity Prospecting: Using Genetic Resources for Sustainable Development* (Washington, DC: World Resources for Sustainable Development Institute, 1993)

Shiva, Vandana, *Biopiracy: The Plunder of Nature and Knowledge* (Boston: South End Press, 1997)

Vaver, David, *Intellectual Property Law: Copyright, Patents, Trade-marks* (Toronto: Irwin Law, 1997), chap. 3

Chapter 8: Keeping Control

The Law Society of Upper Canada publishes general legal information on wills, advance directives, and medical situations which is available also on the Internet. Articles of interest include the following:

- "Making a Will" at <http://www.lsuc.on.ca/public/other_makingwill_en.shtml>
- "Power of Attorney — Personal Care" at <http://www.lsuc.on.ca/public/other_papersonalcare_en.shtml>
- "Power of Attorney — Property" at <http://www.lsuc.on.ca/public/other_paproperty_en.shtml>
- "Medical Practice" at <http://www.lsuc.on.ca/public/other_medicalmalpractice_en.shtml>

Resources

For more information on advance directives, contact the University of Toronto Joint Centre for Bioethics, phone (416) 978-1906 or fax (416) 978-1911. Video and workbook on drafting an advance directive available for cost: about $25.00

The Consent and Capacity Board in Ontario is an independent body appointed by the provincial government that conducts hearings under three Acts: the *Mental Health Act*, the *Health Care Consent Act*, and the *Substitute Decisions Act*. For copies of the Fact Sheets describing their role and rules, contact the Chair's Office, 151 Bloor St. West, Toronto, Ontario M5S 2T5, phone (416) 327-0542.

Chapter 9: Organ and Tissue Donation: An Urgent Need

Board of Directors of Multiple Organ Retrieval and Exchange (MORE) Program of Ontario, "Organ Procurement Strategies: A Review of Ethical Issues and Challenges" (Report of the Task Force on Presumed Consent) (Toronto, 1994). Call 1-800-263-2833 for availability.

Caplan, Arthur L., and Daniel H. Coelho, eds., *The Ethics of Organ Transplants* (Amherst, N.Y.: Prometheus Books, 1998)

Dickens, B.M., "Legal Aspects of Transplantation — Judicial Issues," *Transplantation Proceedings* 24, no. 5 (October 1992): 2118–19

"Guidelines for the Diagnosis of Brain Death," *Canadian Medical Association Journal* 136 (1987): 200A

Kluge, Eike-Henner, "Decisions about Organ Donation Should Rest with Potential Donors, Not Next of Kin," *Canadian Medical Association Journal* 157 (1987): 160–61

Lanza, Robert P., David K.C. Cooper, and William L. Chick, "Xenotransplantation," *Scientific American* (July 1997): 54–59

Law Reform Commission of Canada, *Criteria for the Determination of Death*, Report 15 (Ottawa: Supply and Services Canada, 1981)

Law Reform Commission of Canada, *The Procurement and Transfer of Human Tissues and Organs*, Working Paper 66 (Ottawa: Supply and Services Canada, 1992)

Moutarah, Fady, "Organ Procurement: Let's Presume Consent," *Canadian Medical Association Journal* 158 (1988): 231–34

Nuffield Council on Bioethics, *Animal-to-Human Transplants: The Ethics of Xenotransplantation*, Report of the Council's Working Party, Albert Weale, Chair (London: The Council, March 1996)

"Organ Donation," *Canadian Medical Association Journal* 136 (1987): 752A

Report of the Advisory Group on the Ethics of Xenotransplantation, *Animal Tissue into Humans*, Ian Kennedy, Chair, Department of Health (London: H.M.S.O., 1997)

Report of the National Consensus Conference on Safety of Organs and Tissues for Transplantation (Ottawa: Minister of Supply and Services, 1995) (Health Canada Cat H49-102/1995E; ISBN 0-662-24153-3)

Report of the Standing Committee on Health, "Organ and Donation Tissue Donation and Transplantation: A Canadian Approach," Joseph Volpe, MP, Chair (April 1999). Available on the Internet at <http://www.parl.gc.ca/InfoComDoc/36/1/HEAL/Studies/Reports/healrp05-e.htm>

Schwartz, Howard S., "Bioethical and Legal Considerations in Increasing the Supply of Transplantable Organs: From UAGA to 'Baby Fae,'" *American Journal of Law and Medicine* 10, no. 4 (winter 1985): 397–437

Resources

Copies of most reports (including the *National Forum on Xenotransplantation*) and additional information on xenotransplantation can be found on Health Canada's Therapeutic Products Programme Web site at <http://www/hc-sc.gc.ca/hpb-dgps/therapeut/htmleng>.

For further information on standards for organ and tissue transplants, contact:

Health Canada, Therapeutic Products Directorate (setting standards for organ and tissue transplants)

The Canadian Medical Association (CMA), phone (613) 731-9331, ext. 2289; fax (613) 731-1779; <www.cma.ca>

Chapter 10: A Right to Die

Berger, Arthur, and Joyce Berger, eds., *To Die or Not to Die: Cross-Disciplinary, Cultural and Legal Perspectives on the Right to Choose Death* (New York: Praeger, 1990)

Bachman, Jerald G., et al., "Attitudes of Michigan Physicians and the Public toward Legalizing Physician Assisted Suicide and Voluntary Euthanasia," *New England Journal of Medicine* 334, no. 5 (February 1996): 303–9

Battin, Margaret P., *Ethical Issues in Suicide* (New Jersey: Prentice Hall, 1995)

Battin, Margaret P., *Least Worst Death: Essays in Bioethics on the End of Life* (New York: Oxford University Press, 1994)

Dworkin, Ronald, *Life's Dominion: An Argument about Abortion, Euthanasia, and Individual Freedom* (New York: Knopf, 1993)

Law Reform Commission of Canada, *Report on Euthanasia, Assisting Suicide and Cessation of Treatment* (Ottawa: The Commission, July 1983)

Lee, Melinda, et al., "Legalizing Assisted-Suicide: Views of Physicians in Oregon," *New England Journal of Medicine* 334, no. 5 (February 1996): 310–15

Meir, Diane, et al., "A National Survey of Physician-Assisted Suicide and Euthanasia in the United States" *New England Journal of Medicine* 338, no. 17 (April 1998): 1193–1201

Orentlicher, David, "Sounding Board: The Legalization of Physician-Assisted Suicide," *New England Journal of Medicine* 335, no. 9 (August 1996): 663–67. See for a defence of the Second Circuit Court's ruling in *Quill* v. *State of New York*.

Quill, Timothy, *Death and Dignity: Making Choices and Taking Charge* (New York: W.W. Norton, 1993)

Werth Jr., James L., *Rational Suicide: Implications for Mental Health Professionals* (Bristol, Penn.: Taylor & Francis, 1996)

Chapter 11: Euthanasia

Canadian Medical Association, *Canadian Physicians and Euthanasia* (Ottawa: 1993)

Kubler-Ross, Elisabeth, *The Wheel of Life: A Memoir of Living and Dying* (New York: Scribner, 1997)

Law Reform Commission of Canada, *Sanctity of Life or Quality of Life in the Context of Ethics, Medicine and Law,* Study Paper by Edward W. Keyserlingk (Ottawa: Supply and Services, 1981)

Leary, Timothy, with R.U. Sirius, *Design for Dying* (San Francisco: Harper, 1997)

Silver, Lee, *Remaking Eden: Cloning and Beyond in a Brave New World* (New York: Avon Books, 1997)

Singer, Peter, *Rethinking Life and Death: The Collapse of Our Traditional Ethics* (Oxford: Oxford University Press, 1995)

Special Senate Committee on Euthanasia and Assisted-Suicide, *Of Life and Death: The Report of the Special Senate Committee on Euthanasia and Assisted Suicide* (Ottawa: The Senate, 1995)

Selected Bibliography

Andrews, Lori B., *The Clone Age: Twenty Years at the Forefront of Reproductive Technology* (New York: Henry Holt, 1999)

Arditti, Rita, Renate Duelli Klein, and Shelley Minden, eds., *Test-Tube Women: What Future for Motherhood?* (Winchester Mass.: Pandora Press, 1989)

Battin, Margaret Pabst, Anita Silvers, and Rosamond Rhodes, eds., *Physician Assisted Suicide: Expanding the Debate* (New York: Routledge, 1998)

Boyens, Ingeborg, *Unnatural Harvest: How Corporate Science Is Secretly Altering Our Food* (Toronto: Doubleday Canada, 1999)

Cohen, Sherrill, and Nadine Taub, eds., *Reproductive Laws for the 1990s* (Clifton, NJ: Humana Press, 1989)

Davis, Bernard D., *The Genetic Revolution: Scientific Prospects and Public Perceptions* (Baltimore: Johns Hopkins University Press, 1991)

Duster, Troy, *Backdoor to Eugenics* (New York: Routledge, 1990)

Engelhardt, H. Tristram, *The Foundations of Bioethics* (New York: Oxford University Press, 1986)

Fenwick, Lynda Beck, *Private Choices, Public Consequences: Reproductive Technology and the New Ethics of Conception, Pregnancy, and Family* (New York: Dutton, 1998)

Harris, John, *The Value of Life* (London: Routledge and Kegan Paul, 1985)

Harris, John, and Holm Soren, eds., *The Future of Human Reproduction: Ethics, Choice, and Regulation* (Oxford; New York: Clarendon Press, 1998)

Heinberg, Richard, *Cloning the Buddha* (Wheaton, Ill.: Quest Books, 1999)

Humphrey, *Lawful Exit: The Limits of Freedom for Help in Dying* (Junction City: Oreg.: Norris Lane Press, 1993)

Kevles, Daniel J., and Leroy Hood, eds., *The Code of Codes: Scientific and Social Issues in the Human Genome Project* (Cambridge: Harvard University Press, 1992)

Kimbrell, Andrew, *The Human Body Shop* (San Francisco: Harper Collins, 1993)

Kneen, Brewster, *Farmageddon: Food and the Culture of Biotechnology* (Gabriola Island, B.C.: New Society, 1999)

Kuhn, Helga, *The Sanctity of Life Doctrine in Medicine: A Critique* (Oxford: Oxford University Press, 1987)

Lyon, Jeff, *Playing God in the Nursery* (New York: Norton, 1985)

McGee, Glenn, ed., *The Human Cloning Debate* (Berkeley, Cal.: Berkeley Hills Books, 1998)

McMahan, Jeff, *Killing at the Margins of Life* (New York: Oxford University Press, 1995)

Rothman, David, *Strangers at the Bedside* (New York: Basic Books, 1991)

Rowland, Robyn, *Living Laboratories: Women and Reproductive Technologies* (Great Britain: Lime Tree Press, 1992)

Shipman, Pat, *The Evolution of Racism: Human Differences and the Uses and Abuses of Science* (New York: Simon & Schuster, 1994)

Strathern, Marilyn, *Reproducing in the Future: Anthropology, Kinship, and the New Reproductive Technologies* (New York: Routledge, 1992)

Weir, Robert F., ed., *Physician-Assisted Suicide* (Bloomington: Indiana University Press, 1997)

Wisot, Arthur L., and David R. Meldrum, *Conceptions and Misconceptions: A Guide through the Maze of In Vitro Fertilization and Other Assisted Reproduction Techniques* (Point Roberts, Wash.: Hartley & Marks, 1997)

Wymelenberg, Suzanne, *Science and Babies: Private Decisions, Public Dilemmas* (Washington, DC: National Academy Press, 1990)

Yoxen, Edward, *The Gene Business: Who Should Control Biotechnology?* (New York: Harper and Row, 1983)

Selected Table of Statutes

Adoption Legislation

Convention on Protection of Children and Co-operation in Respect of Intercountry Adoption, 29 May 1993, 32 I.L.M. 1134, Can. T.S., 1997/12

British Columbia, *Adoption Act*, R.S.B.C. 1996, c. 5
Manitoba, *Adoption and Consequential Amendments Act*, S.M. 1997, c. 47
Newfoundland, *Adoption of Children Act*, R.S.N. 1990, c. A-3
Nova Scotia, *Adoption Information Act*, S.N.S. 1996, c. 3
Saskatchewan, *Adoption Act*, S.S. 1989–90, c. A-5.1

Child Welfare Legislation

Alberta, *Child Welfare Act*, S.A. 1984, c. 8.1
British Columbia, *Child, Family and Community Service Act*, R.S.B.C. 1996, c. 46
Manitoba, *Child and Family Services Act*, S.M. 1985–86, c. 8
New Brunswick, *Family Services Act*, S.N.B. 1980, c. F-2.2
Newfoundland, *Child Welfare Act*, R.S.N. 1990, c. C-12

Northwest Territories, *Child Welfare Act*, R.S.N.W.T. 1998, c. C-6
Nova Scotia, *Child and Family Services Act*, S.N.S. 1990, c. 5
Ontario, *Child and Family Services Act*, R.S.O. 1990, c. C.11
Quebec, *Loi sur la protection de la jeunesse*, L.R.Q. 1979, c. P-34.1
Saskatchewan, *Child and Family Services Act*, S.S. 1989–90, c. 7.2
Yukon Territory, *Children's Act*, R.S.Y.T. 1986, c. 22

Health Insurance Legislation

Alberta Health Care Insurance Act, R.S.A. 1980, c. A-24
British Columbia, *Hospital Insurance Act*, R.S.B.C. 1996, c. 204, and
    Medicare Protection Act, R.S.B.C. 1996, c. 286
Manitoba, *Health Services Insurance Act*, R.S.M. 1987, c. H35
New Brunswick, *Health Services Act*, R.S.N.B. 1973, c. H-3, and *Medical
    Services Payment Act*, R.S.N.B. 1973, c. M-7
Newfoundland, *Medical Care Insurance Act*, R.S.N. 1990, c. M-5
Northwest Territories, *Medical Care Act*, R.S.N.W.T. 1988, c. M-8
Nova Scotia, *Health Services and Insurance Act*, R.S.N.S. 1989,
    c. 197
Ontario, *Health Insurance Act*, R.S.O. 1990, c. H.6
Prince Edward Island, *Hospital and Diagnostic Services Insurance Act*,
    R.S.P.E.I. 1988, c. H-8, and *Health Services Payment Act*, R.S.P.E.I.
    1988, c. H-2
Quebec, *Health Insurance Act*, R.S.Q. 1977, c. A-29
Saskatchewan Medical Care Insurance Act, R.S.S. 1978, c. S-29
Yukon Territory, *Health Care Insurance Plan Act*, R.S.Y. 1986, c. 81

Human Rights Legislation

Canadian Bill of Rights, S.C. 1960, c. 44, reprinted in R.S.C. 1985, App. III
Canadian Charter of Rights and Freedoms, Part I of the *Constitution Act,
    1982*, being Schedule B to the *Canada Act 1982* (U.K.) 1982, c. 11
Canadian Human Rights Act, R.S.C. 1985, c. H-6
Alberta, *Human Rights, Citizenship and Multiculturalism Act*, R.S.A.
    1980, c. H-11
British Columbia, *Human Rights Code*, R.S.B.C. 1996, c. 210
Manitoba, *Human Rights Code*, S.M. 1987–88, c. 45
New Brunswick, *Human Rights Code*, S.N.B. 1973, c. H-11
Newfoundland, *Human Rights Code*, R.S.N. 1990, c. H-14
Northwest Territories, *Fair Practices Act*, R.S.N.W.T. 1988, c. F-2
Nova Scotia, *Human Rights Act*, R.S.N.S. 1989, c. 214

Ontario, *Human Rights Code*, R.S.O. 1990, c. H.19
Prince Edward Island, *Human Rights Act*, R.S.P.E.I. 1988, c. H-12
Quebec, *Charter of Human Rights and Freedoms*, R.S.Q. 1977, c. C-12
Saskatchewan Human Rights Code, S.S. 1979, c. S-24.1
Yukon Territory, *Human Rights Act*, S.Y. 1987, c. 3

Human Tissue Gift Acts

Alberta, *Human Tissue Gift Act*, R.S.A. 1980, c. H-12
British Columbia, *Human Tissue Gift Act*, R.S.B.C. 1996, c. 211
Manitoba, *The Human Tissue Act*, R.S.M. 1987, c. H180
New Brunswick, *Human Tissue Gift Act*, R.S.N.B. 1973, c. H-12
Newfoundland, *Human Tissue Act*, R.S.N. 1990, c. H-15
Northwest Territories, *Human Tissue Act*, R.S.N.W.T. 1988, c. H-6
Nova Scotia, *Human Tissue Gift Act*, R.S.N.S. 1989, c. 215
Ontario, *Human Tissue Gift Act*, R.S.O. 1990, c. H.20
Prince Edward Island, *Human Tissue Donation Act*, S.P.E.I. 1992, c. 34
Quebec, *Civil Code of Quebec*, arts. 19, 42–45
Saskatchewan, *Human Tissue Gift Act*, R.S.S. 1978, c. H-15
Yukon Territory, *Human Tissue Gift Act*, R.S.Y.T. 1986, c. 89

Privacy Acts and Freedom of Information Acts

Canada, *Privacy Act*, R.S.C. 1985, c. P-21
Alberta, *Freedom of Information and Protection of Privacy Act*, S.A. 1994, c. F-18.5
British Columbia, *Privacy Act*, R.S.B.C. 1996, c. 373
British Columbia, *Freedom of Information and Protection of Privacy Act*, R.S.B.C. 1996, c. 165
Manitoba, *Privacy Act*, R.S.M. 1987, c. P125
Manitoba, *Freedom of Information Act*, S.M. 1985–86, c. 6
New Brunswick, *Right to Information Act*, S.N.B. 1978, c. R-103
Newfoundland, *Privacy Act*, R.S.N. 1990, c. P-22
Newfoundland, *Freedom of Information Act*, R.S.N. 1990, c. F-25
Northwest Territories, *Access to Information and Protection of Privacy Act*, S.N.W.T. 1994, c. 20
Nova Scotia, *Freedom of Information and Protection of Privacy Act*, S.N.S. 1993, c. 5
Ontario, *Freedom of Information and Protection of Privacy Act*, R.S.O. 1990, c. F.31

Quebec, *Access to Documents Held by Public Bodies and the Protection of Personal Information (Act Respecting)*, R.S.Q. 1977, c. A-2.1

Quebec, *Protection of Personal Information in the Private Sector (Act Respecting)*, S.Q. 1993, c. 17

Saskatchewan, *Privacy Act*, R.S.S. 1978, C. P-24

Saskatchewan, *Freedom of Information and Protection of Privacy Act*, S.S. 1990–91, c. F-22.01

Yukon Territory, *Access to Information and Protection of Privacy Act*, S.Y. 1995, c. 1

Miscellaneous Legislation

Canada, *Constitution Act, 1867* (U.K.), 30 &31 Vict., c. 3

Canada, *Criminal Code*, R.S.C. 1985, c. C-46

Canada, *Divorce Act*, R.S.C. 1970, c. D-8, s. 2 and R.S.C. 1985, c. 3 (2d Supp.) as amended

Canada, *Food and Drugs Act*, R.S.C. 1985, c. F-27

Canada Health Act, R.S.C. 1985, c. C-6

Canada, *Patent Act*, R.S.C. 1985, c. P-4

Canadian Environmental Protection Act, R.S.C. 1985 (4th Supp.), c. 16

Ontario, *Health Care Consent Act* (S.O. 1996, c. 2)

Ontario, *Mental Health Act*, R.S.O. 1990, c. M.7

Quebec, *Civil Code of Québec*, S.Q. 1991, c. 64

Index